A Place in the

Places, Cultures and Globalization

The Shape of the World Course Team

The Open University

John Allen	Senior Lecturer in Economic Geography and Course Team Chair
James Anderson	Senior Lecturer in Geography
Robin Arkle	Graphic Designer, BBC
Melanie Bayley	Editor
Brian Beeley	Senior Lecturer in Geography
Pam Berry	Compositor, TPS
Gail Block	Assistant Producer, BBC
John Blunden	Reader in Geography
Chris Brook	Lecturer in Geography
Margaret Charters	Course Secretary
Allan Cochrane	Senior Lecturer in Urban Studies
Lene Connolly	Print Buying Co-ordinator
Debbie Crouch	Graphic Designer
Stuart Hall	Professor of Sociology
Chris Hamnett	Professor of Urban Geography
Fiona Harris	Editor
Tom Hunter	Editor
Christina Janoszka	Course Manager
Pat Jess	Lecturer in Geography
Jack Leathem	Producer, BBC
Michèle Marsh	Secretary
Doreen Massey	Professor of Geography
Anthony McGrew	Senior Lecturer in Politics
Diane Mole	Graphic Designer
Eleanor Morris	Series Producer, BBC
Ray Munns	Graphic Artist
Judith Rolph	Series Production Assistant, BBC
Philip Sarre	Senior Lecturer in Geography
Paul Smith	Media Librarian
Doreen Warwick	Discipline Secretary
Kathy Wilson	Production Assistant, BBC
Chris Wooldridge	Editor

External Assessor

Nigel Thrift	Professor of Geography, University of Bristol

Consultants

Rick Ball	Tutor Panel
Erlet Cater	Lecturer in Geography, University of Reading
Ray Hall	Senior Lecturer in Geography, University of London
Russell King	Professor of Geography, University of Sussex
Andrew Leyshon	Lecturer in Geography, University of Hull
Matthew Lockwood	Lecturer in Sociology, University of Sussex
Jenny Meegan	Tutor Panel
Richard Meegan	Senior Lecturer in Geography, University of Liverpool
Phil Pinch	Tutor Panel
Gillian Rose	Lecturer in Geography, University of Edinburgh
Steven Yearley	Professor of Sociology, University of Ulster

The Shape of the World: Explorations in Human Geography

Volume 1: Geographical Worlds

Edited by John Allen and Doreen Massey

Volume 2: A Shrinking World? Global Unevenness and Inequality

Edited by John Allen and Chris Hamnett

Volume 3: An Overcrowded World? Population, Resources and the Environment

Edited by Philip Sarre and John Blunden

Volume 4: A Place in the World? Places, Cultures and Globalization

Edited by Doreen Massey and Pat Jess

Volume 5: A Global World? Re-ordering Political Space

Edited by James Anderson, Chris Brook and Allan Cochrane

A Place in the World ?

Places, Cultures and Globalization

edited by
Doreen Massey and Pat Jess

The Open University

OXFORD
UNIVERSITY PRESS

The five volumes of the series form part of the second-level Open University
course D215 *The Shape of the World*. If you wish to study this or any other
Open University course, details can be obtained from the Central
Enquiry Service, PO Box 200, The Open University,
Milton Keynes, MK7 6YZ.

For availability of the video- and audiocassette materials, contact Open University
Educational Enterprises Ltd (OUEE), 12 Cofferidge Close, Stony Stratford,
Milton Keynes, MK11 1BY.

Oxford University Press, Walton Street, Oxford OX2 6DP

Oxford   New York

Athens   Auckland   Bangkok   Bombay
Calcutta   Cape Town   Dar es Salaam   Delhi
Florence   Hong Kong   Istanbul   Karachi
Kuala Lumpur   Madras   Madrid   Melbourne
Mexico City   Nairobi   Paris   Singapore
Taipei   Tokyo   Toronto
and associated companies in
Berlin   Ibadan

Oxford is a trade mark of Oxford University Press

Published in the United States
by Oxford University Press Inc., New York

Published in association with The Open University

First published 1995, Reprinted 2000.

Edited, designed and typeset by The Open University

Printed in the United Kingdom by
The Alden Press Limited

A catalogue record for this book is available from the British Library

Library of Congress Cataloguing in Publication Data applied for

ISBN 0 19 874191 X (paper)

ISBN 0 19 874190 1 (cloth)

A Place in the World?
Places, Cultures and Globalization

Contents

Preface

A Place in the World? Places, Cultures and Globalization is the fourth of five volumes in a new series of human geography teaching texts. The series, entitled *The Shape of the World: Explorations in Human Geography* is designed as an introduction to the principal themes of geographical thought: namely, those of space, place and the environment. The five volumes form the central part of an Open University course, with the same title as that of the series. Each volume, however, is free-standing and can be studied on its own or as part of a wide range of social science courses in universities and colleges.

The series is built around an exploration of many of the key issues which are shaping our world as we move into the twenty-first century and which, above all else, are geographical in character. Each volume in various ways engages with taken-for-granted notions such as those of nature, distance, movement, sustainability, the identity of places and local cultures to put together what may be referred to as the building blocks of our geographical imagination.

In fact, our understanding of the nature of the geographical imagination is one of three shared features which distinguish the five volumes as a series. In developing the contribution that geography can make to our understanding of a changing world and our place within it, each volume has something distinct to offer. A second feature of the volumes is that the majority of chapters include a number of selected readings – extracts drawn from books and articles – which relate closely to the line of argument and which are integral to the discussion as it develops. The relevant readings can be found at the end of the chapter to which they relate and are printed in two columns to distinguish them from the main teaching text. The third shared feature of the volumes is the student-orientated nature of the teaching materials. Each volume is intended as part of an interactive form of study, with activities and summaries built into the flow of the text. These features are intended to help readers to grasp, consider and retain the main ideas and arguments of each chapter. The wide margins – in which you will find highlighted the concepts that are key to the teaching – are also intended for student use, such as making notes and points for reflection.

While each book is self-contained, there are a number of references back (and a small number of references forward) to the other books in the series. For those readers who wish to use the books as an exploration in human geography, you will find the references to chapters in the other volumes printed in bold type. This is particularly relevant to the final chapters of Volumes 2–5 as they form a sequence of chapters designed to highlight the uneven character of global development today. On a related teaching point, we have sometimes referred to the group of less developed and developing countries by the term 'third world' in inverted commas to convey the difficulty of continuing to include the diverse range of countries – which embraces some rapidly industrializing nations – under this conventional category. The 'disappearance' of a second world with the demise of the Communist bloc, also questions the usefulness of the category and, in one way, simply reaffirms the significance of the world's changing geography.

Finally, it remains only to thank those who have helped to shape this Open University course. The names of those responsible for the production of this course are given in the list of Course Team members on page *ii*. Of those, we would like to extend our thanks to a number in particular. It is fair to say that the course would not have had the shape that it does were it not for the breadth of intellectual scholarship provided by our external assessor, Professor Nigel Thrift. Over a two-year period, Nigel, among other activities, commented and offered constructive advice on every draft chapter discussed by the Course Team – in all, some eighty-plus drafts! The Course Team owe him a major debt. We also owe a special debt to our Tutor Panel – Rick Ball, Jenny Meegan and Phil Pinch – for their ceaseless concern that the teaching materials were precisely that: materials which actually do teach. Our editors at the Open University, Melanie Bayley and Fiona Harris, not only raised the professional standard of the series as a whole with their meticulous editing, they also became involved at an early stage in the Course's life and thus were able to smooth the path of its development. Thanks also to Ray Munns for his cartographic zeal and to Paul Smith, our media librarian, who, as ever, translated our vague descriptions of this or that image into an impressive array of illustrations. The typographic design and initial cover idea were developed by Diane Mole who then relinquished the course to Debbie Crouch; their expertise has transformed our typescripts into this handsome series of volumes. The speed and accuracy with which the multiple drafts were turned round by Margaret Charters and Doreen Warwick also deserves our special thanks. Without their excellent secretarial support, the course would not be in any shape at all.

Lastly, in the collaborative style of work by which Open University courses are produced, the awesome task of co-ordinating the efforts of the Course Team and ensuring that the materials are produced to schedule, falls to that of the course manager. It is still a source of amazement to us how our course manager, Christina Janoszka, managed this task as if it were no task at all. We owe her probably more than she is aware.

John Allen
on behalf of
The Open University Course Team

Introduction

The current age is one in which globalization is posing a serious challenge to the meaning of 'place' and to the meaning of 'culture'. Even accepting that globalization is unequal, uneven and disjointed, there is no denying that in recent years there has been an acceleration in its pace and a deepening of its impact. Contacts, chains of command, personal interlinkages, and relations of social power and domination are increasingly stretched out around the surface of the planet. And in the midst of this global connectedness, places and cultures are being restructured; on the one hand, previous coherences are being disrupted, old notions of the local place are being interrupted by new connections with a world beyond; on the other, new claims to the – usually exclusive – character of places, and who belongs there, are being made. On the Baltic, in Central Asia, in what used to be Yugoslavia, new nationalisms arise along with claims to particular spaces. Economic relations are reorganized into trading blocs – new spaces with freer movement (for some) within, but tighter controls around them. While negotiations under the General Agreement on Tariffs and Trade open national borders around the world to trade and investment, to communications and cultural flows, and thereby to further cultural mixing, first world countries debate the possibilities of raising further the barriers to the international movement of people.

In such a context, what meaning can be retained, or rebuilt, around the concept of *place*? Are the alternatives limited to the end of the uniqueness of place on the one hand or a return to a (mythologized) exclusivity of place on the other? If places are thought of as settled, coherent worlds of their own, then they are surely under challenge in an age when everywhere seems to be being opened up to wider forces. The constant interconnections – of economics, culture, ecology – mean that any notion of an internally generated 'uniqueness of place' is hard to sustain. In this volume we begin to examine the disruption to place which is happening in these times and to explore the implications for our most commonly held definitions.

One of the things most centrally at issue here is the relation between place and culture. On the one hand there is the continuous mixing of cultures through the interconnections between places, especially though not only via migration. It is a reaction against this historical mixing, and an exercise of the power relations in which it takes place, which has resulted in the horrors of ethnic cleansing, the sporadic outbreaks of exclusivist nationalisms and a whole host of jingoistic parochialisms at smaller social and spatial scales. The alternative to such a reaction might be the imagination and living of a new form of cosmopolitanism – a different kind of geographical imagination.

The other side of the relations between place and culture, and of their non-conformity, is the holding together of cultures which have been dispersed over often vast spatial distances – the differentiated reproduction of a migrant culture in places far from 'home'. If a common notion of place, and perhaps especially of small-scale places, is often bound up with settledness, coherence and continuity, then any current talk of *dis*placement, most particularly through migration, depends likewise on a prior notion of cultures as embedded in place. Yet in today's world, this is either less and less true or – the more positive approach – it must be thought about in a different way. The simple relation between local place and local culture is not one which can be assumed. Perhaps the notion of local *culture*, too, must be re-thought.

If place and culture are two of the key terms in this book, then *identity* is a third. There is a multiplicity of threads in the relations between these terms. Cultural identity, as has been said, has often been interpreted as bound up with place, whether through notions of local culture or through the sometimes more calculated constructions of national identity, which often in their supporting imagery call up physical attributes (the rolling Downs of England, the outback of Australia). The relation with personal identity can be equally strong, as people identify with 'home-places' or feel themselves outsiders in places primarily claimed by others. And that, of course, raises a further thread – the identity and meaning of places themselves. One place-identity which is currently being constructed is that of Europe: to whose personal and cultural identity will this appeal? And who may be excluded?

In the argument of this book, the identities of places are frequently contested. The meaning of a place may vary between different groups and such meanings may be mobilized in battles over the material future of places – whether a new development should occur, whether new people should be allowed to move in, whether a place should remain 'unspoilt'. Rival claims about the potential futures of places are often based on rival interpretations of their pasts. *Contestation*, then, is a further term which weaves its way through all the chapters of this volume – and, with it, social *power*. For both globalization and the reconstruction of the meanings of places are happening within a world which is already unevenly developed, both socially and geographically. Battles over the meaning and the identity of places are waged in the context of, and between, unequal forces. These, then, are truly geographical questions, but they also link into and draw directly on much wider intellectual and social concerns.

This volume has been produced at a particular moment, and a moment in *space*–time rather than just time. That is to say, it reflects concerns, and probably theoretical and conceptual predelictions, which are primarily at issue in, and seen from the perspective of, first world and other industrial countries. Thus the way in which these questions are often couched implies that the relations between place and culture *were* once simple, that local places *were* settled, coherent and bounded, that cultures *were* internally generated and deeply embedded in spatial propinquity, in place. Yet in fact there has since the beginning of human existence always been movement, migration and settlement in new areas; for as long as is known and in most parts of the world, individual places have been open to, and partly constituted by, their contacts with 'outside'. Interconnection is not new, and diasporas are certainly not only a feature of the recent past. The conceptual arguments pursued in this book, therefore, although they may have been stimulated by current events, we would argue nonetheless have a more general relevance beyond this particular moment.

○   ○   ○   ○   ○

We use the process of international migration as our starting-point because migration is the process of globalization whereby people are 'spread' – moved and mixed – around the globe. Throughout human occupancy of the Earth, humanity has been restless and mobile, laying claims upon territory while yet still clinging, often strongly, to ideas of place and 'home'. This raises the issue of *meaning and imagining* in relation to place. When people lay claims to territory, when they grieve for home, when they construct and re-construct the meaning of place, they are 'imagining geography' – producing images and creating identities which then form the bases both of the future character of those pieces of space and of the behaviour of people towards them, be that acquisitive or defensive. By starting with migration, we are therefore immediately into questions of place, and the relations between cultures and places.

In this way, Chapter 1 raises questions for the rest of the volume. And the first one we tackle is: how do we conceptualize 'place' in these global, mobile times? If globalization does not, in fact, mean the end of place, it does pose serious questions about how we conceive of place, and how we explain how it is that places retain their uniqueness in a period of rapid and fundamental social change. This is the task of Chapter 2. By 'place' we mean any part of the Earth's surface, however large or small. Thus our questions about the construction and the identity of places relate both to the scale of, say, the village, or a small corner of the world known intimately to some, and to the scale of, say, the continent – the new 'Europe' which is now being built, for instance.

These issues lie at the heart of the notion of *geographical imagination*. As well as the material constructions of place through processes of interconnection and interdependence, we also consider the construction of the meaning of places, of 'senses of place', the construction of place through the production of meaning. Central to this argument is the issue of *identity*. Chapters 3 and 4 follow this line of discussion.

Chapter 3 is about the way in which place and identity are bound into our notion of 'sense of place'. We often identify with place as part of our own personal sense of identity; some sense of geographical locatedness in the world may be important to how we see ourselves. But this way of imagining geography – of defining and interpreting and representing place – may also rely on the exclusion of 'others'. This goes back to the rights to place and the claims which people make to place, raised in Chapter 1. We often call upon particular images, particular histories, to reinforce our own self-confidence. Chapter 3 looks at how we use geographically located 'others' to construct images of ourselves, to establish our own identity. There are important links here with culture and it also raises important issues of power and power relations.

Contests over place – the clash of rival claims to their meaning, their character and their future – are taken up in Chapter 4 where we explore a small number of specific cases of *conflict*. This allows the further exploration of the definition and representation of place and of how these representations are constructed and mobilized. What is at issue in each of these cases is a conflict over the material character of a place (what development should be allowed, what people allowed to settle and claim what rights). However, each of the protagonists in each conflict also bases their case on a particular interpretation of the identity of the place in question. The background battle is about characterizing the place, about the power to assure a particular identity for it and thus influence its future.

Chapters 2, 3 and 4, therefore, deal primarily with questions of place, although in all of them issues of culture are not far below the surface. But in Chapter 5 we turn to *culture* directly and pick up, from Chapter 1, some of the challenges to the notion of distinct cultures which have been raised by processes of globalization. This chapter explores different ways of conceptualizing cultures and cultural traditions. As Chapter 2 for place, so

Chapter 5 for culture argues that we need to reconsider some of our most taken-for-granted ways of thinking.

The construction of meanings of place, the contests over the identity of places, battles over the future of places, claims to rights over place, all occur within an already constituted social and geographical unevenness. Volumes 2 and 3 in the series have amply demonstrated that globalization is unequal. If it were not for political, economic, environmental and cultural unevenness, would we have major issues arising out of migration? Migration is essentially a product of *uneven development,* and contributes to it. Places which people leave are often places which are 'left off' our global map, their futures destined to decline further, until and unless they are suddenly seen as useful in some way for 'development' – low wages, no environmental controls, exotic cultures, new scenes of nature not yet exploited by tourism or other resource-users. Who leaves places is a matter of restrictions and rights – of *power.* Power and control over mobility is a major factor in globalization and uneven development. These are truly geographical questions but they link strongly with the kind of 'big political issues' which we mentioned at the beginning of this Introduction. The relations which construct uneven development compose the sets of forces within which spatial meanings are produced and we argue that it is only within this context that they can be evaluated. It is the role of Chapter 6 to spell this out. In Chapter 6 we draw together the main arguments of the book in relation to the concept of uneven development. Essentially, we rehearse the relations between space and place, global and local, to underline the importance of conceptualizing place in the context of globalization. By this means, we argue, the concept of the uniqueness of place can be re-evaluated. We then look again at issues of power and identity in relation to culture and place and argue for the close relationship of all these facets of shifting spatial relations.

o o o o o

In this volume we have used migration to problematize place but in fact it is globalization more generally that has challenged our ideas about the contemporary relevance of place and 'the local'. Lying behind the arguments and enquiries of this book is the assumption that the current era of intensified globalization is characterized not by the complete erasure of the importance of place (of whatever dimensions – the local village or the continent), but by a continuing tension between, and process of mutual construction of, 'the global and the local'. 'Places' – their characters and the differences between them – continue to matter: they matter to capital which exploits the different characteristics of place – in other words, uneven development; and they matter to people because of our senses of belonging and identification, and the quality of our geographical imaginations.

The series, *The Shape of the World,* uses ideas about space, nature, place and the tension between 'global' and 'local' to interrogate theses of globalization and what these ideas have to say about geography. In *this* volume we focus on *place* and on the *local* as part of the overall debate, on the construction of 'places' and the meaning of places within their wider contexts. At first sight this may seem quite straightforward but, as subsequent chapters show, many complex issues arise from our attempts to conceptualize and analyse place, culture and identity.

Doreen Massey and Pat Jess

Migrations, globalization and place

Chapter 1

by Russell King

1.1 Introduction

Goodbye rivers, goodbye springs
Goodbye little streams
Goodbye view from my eyes
I don't know when we'll see each other again

Goodbye glory, goodbye happiness
I leave the house where I was born
I leave the village that I know so well
For a world I have not seen

Goodbye also my loved ones
Goodbye forever, perhaps
I say this goodbye with tears in my eyes
Wherever I am overseas
Do not forget me, my love
If I die of solitude
So many leagues across the ocean
O for my little house, my home!

This poem, which I have translated from Gallego, the language of Galicia, is chiselled into the base of the 'emigrants' monument' overlooking the Atlantic at La Coruña in north-west Spain. It enables me to make several preliminary points about migration, global relations and place – points which will be recurrent throughout both the rest of this chapter and the rest of this volume.

First, there is the significance of the location of the monument itself, positioned at a point which expresses the long involvement of Galicians with transoceanic migration. How many tens of thousands of young men and women must have sailed out of that green, deep-fjorded coast bound for the Americas! Second, such long-distance migration can be regarded as an early expression of globalization. In the case of Spain's relationship with Central and South America, migration was a natural accompaniment of colonialism: an instrument for the diffusion of Spanish culture, for economic exploitation, and for Spanish settlement in the conquered lands. But behind the imperial project there lay a multitude of human dramas and feelings. This is the third element of the poem, and the one that comes over most strongly. The departing migrant takes with him or her a powerful vision of the place left behind. The Galician landscape retains a special place in migrants' hearts, no place more so than their ancestral village and bit of well-watered countryside. Finally, the poem demonstrates that there is more than one way of writing about migration. It shows that a 'subjective' view of migration, taken from the inside, can do much more to convey real feelings – for instance about the pain of departure, or the nostalgia for home – than the cold analyses of social scientists who tend to objectify migration under a series of statistical data and stereotyped behaviour.

The purpose of this chapter is to relate migration to three concepts that are central to this volume, and indeed to the series as a whole: globalization, uneven development and place. Accordingly, three key messages will be stressed.

- *Migration, particularly international migration, is intimately linked to the general issues of globalization.* It involves the stretching across space of both the social relations of production and the more personal social networks of individual people and ethnic communities. At a wider conceptual level, migration connects to many issues which are central concerns of social science such as the nature of capitalist development, the rise of industrialization, the creation of urban working classes from peasantries, and many more.

- *Migration is an expression – and often a reinforcement – of uneven spatial development.* This relationship can be observed at a variety of scales. Within British and North American cities the flight to the suburbs, particularly of middle-class white people, has accelerated the decay of the inner cities and paved the way for ethnic polarization between the prosperous white suburbs and the ghettoized inner areas where immigrants have concentrated. Within individual countries, rural–urban migration creates uneven development between burgeoning cities and depopulating rural areas. Such rural–urban population shifts have become less important now in highly-developed countries in Europe and North America, but the rush to the 'bright lights' of big cities is still a key migratory process in less developed countries. And, at the international level, heavy outmigration from areas like the west of Ireland to industrial Britain in the 1950s or southern Italy to Germany in the 1960s has hastened economic decline in these peripheral regions. Uneven development, in turn, is linked very much to international power relationships which can feed back to migration in terms of *who* controls migration flows or puts up immigration barriers.

- *Migration raises interesting questions about the changing nature of 'place'.* The places of origin experience abandonment and decay, but may be rejuvenated by return migration if the out-migrants decide to send money or come back home. The places of destination – typically urban areas – take on particular 'ethnic' characteristics as a result of mass migration from other countries and cultures. However, there is also a more subjective engagement between migration and place: the shifting meaning of 'place' for migrants themselves, as hinted at in the poem. Migration is a dislocation from one place and a physical attachment to another – although the emotional attachment may well remain with the place of origin. At an individual level, migrants' experience of *displacement* raises complex psychological questions about their own existence and self-identity.

displacement

A further point I should like to stress in this introduction is that migrants are not 'exceptional' people – 'others'. On the contrary, migration is something which touches the experience of most of us. Nowadays, in the western world, only a minority of people are born, live their entire lives and die in the same rural community or urban neighbourhood. Most of us have therefore had some experience of migration, albeit perhaps only a short-range move from one part of town to another. Some of you, on the other hand, will be international migrants, or perhaps your ancestors were. If you have made one or more migratory moves, you should realize that you have played a part in one of the major processes that continually reshape our cities, towns and rural communities.

What kind of migrant are you? Are you a rural–urban migrant, moving from the countryside to the city? Did you, or any members of your family, come from abroad, perhaps from India or the Caribbean or Eastern Europe? Why did they, or you, move to where you are living now? What was the attractiveness of the place that drew you to migrate there? Were your expectations fulfilled? What are your feelings towards the places you have lived in before? Maybe you cannot answer all these questions, but by considering some of them you should begin to realize how migration represents a critical engagement with the concept of place *and* reflects macro-scale forces which may be global in scope – such as the legacy of colonialism or the international distribution of economic opportunity.

This chapter is in four main parts. The next section will briefly review the history of migration. It will show how migration has helped to shape the world in different places in different ways at different times, and exemplify some of the extraordinary variety in types of migratory movements. Section 1.3 will then examine post-war labour migrations and evaluate their contribution to uneven development. Section 1.4 will look at today's 'post-industrial' migrations and link these to the restructuring of the global economy. A focus on Europe will enable us to introduce the notion of barriers to movement and to examine migration policies and controls. In the final major section of the chapter we turn our attention more explicitly to place and examine the various ways in which migrants preserve their sense of place within the tumult of globalization.

1.2   Migrations in history

Migration, even long-distance international migration, is by no means a new phenomenon. Migration is a fundamental, recurrent process of human mobility and mixing. The big migratory waves of people moving from one place to another have had an enormous impact in shaping the world. Throughout history, migration has created dislocated peoples. As the human expression of place, cultures have often been radically changed and shaped by migration: they have been transplanted, extinguished, fused.

The questions to be posed – and answered – in this section mirror those stated at the beginning of the chapter, but here they are cast in a more historical frame:

- What was the nature of the long-range migrations of the past?

- How have these migrations been expressions of early globalization processes and of the evolution of global uneven development?

- What have these migrations contributed to the changing nature of places?

The historical material on migration is colossal. A complete answer to these questions would be nothing less than a historical–cultural geography of the world. In one sense, we can do no more than skim the surface – to roam the world widely but inevitably briefly, concentrating mainly on 'big' migrations that did most to shape the world, but not neglecting a couple of the smaller and more intriguing ones which contributed a lasting uniqueness to certain places. However, beneath the kaleidoscope of examples and the curtness of the treatment of each, you should appreciate the deeper, more fundamental points: that the concept of a mobile global population is not new; that migration has always been part of structured inequality; and that hybridity in the creation of cultures, places and regions is likewise a long-established process nurtured by migration.

1.2.1 From earliest times

Migrations have been part of human history from the earliest times. Some scholars have speculated that migration has been such a universal phenomenon that it is part of human instinct, as it is in many animals, birds and fishes – like the reindeer that led the Lapps from the lichen of northern Sweden to the summer grass of northern Norway and back again (Scott, 1968, p. 2). Migration lies at the heart of a major controversy about the development of human life on this planet. The debate is between those who believe that *homo sapiens* evolved independently and in parallel in different parts of the globe – Africa, Asia, Europe – and those who believe that the early humans emerged first in Africa and radiated out from there to colonize the rest of the world (Fagan, 1990). At present the weight of evidence favours the latter interpretation, in which case it took about 150,000 years for the human species to migrate from its primal habitat in East Africa to occupy all the major continents and islands except the frozen wastes of Antarctica. Figure 1.1 shows the pattern and its approximate chronology.

These earliest migrations took place against a background of marked climatic changes: ice ages, glaciation, desertification as well as more localized climatic

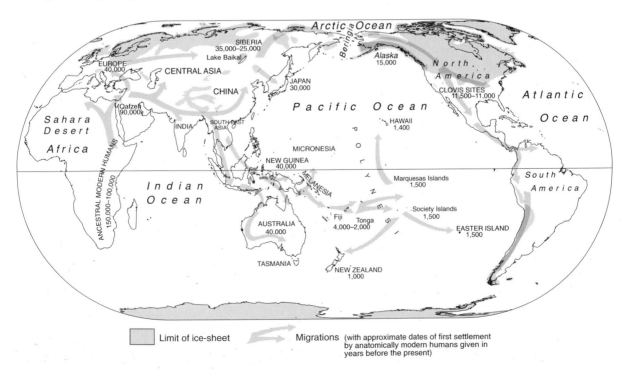

Figure 1.1 The earliest human migrations (Source: Fagan, 1990, pp. 234–5)

events. Geology and sea-level change also played a role: 20,000 years ago dry land joined the south-east Asian mainland to Sumatra, Borneo, the Philippines and the Malayan peninsula. Onward migration to New Guinea and Australia took place via the first great sea-faring migrations, perhaps 40,000 years ago. Much later came the original colonization of the Americas, across the land and ice bridge of the Bering Straits. Much controversy surrounds the date of this crossing into these hitherto uninhabited continents: probably it was around 15,000 years ago, but there are those who believe it was much earlier.

The story of this first great migration – the pre-colonial, pre-imperial Stone Age peopling of the world – is concluded by the development of long-distance, island-hopping, sea-faring migration, which took humans around 6,000 years ago to Melanesia, then Polynesia. As Figure 1.1 shows, Pacific sailors finally reached remote Easter Island about 1,500 years ago, Hawaii 1,400 years ago and New Zealand 1,000 years ago – by which time, new migratory processes and systems had evolved in the Old World.

In the river-fed plains of the Middle East, intensification of agriculture and the rise of urban civilizations about 5,000 years ago transformed the nature of migration. For the first time, organized societies were able to move thousands of people for purposes of either war or settlement. Human mobility was increased by the domestication and use of animals – horses, donkeys, camels and elephants.

Throughout the ancient world, captured slaves were transported to public works projects and mines and as agricultural labour. Commercial slavery was big business amongst the Romans, Egyptians and Arabs, all of whom were capable of shifting thousands of prisoners of war to distant places. The Greek city-states were probably the first to practise large-scale colonization – the deliberate, state-planned transfer of people for empire-building purposes. Overpopulation and over-farming of the Athenian homelands spurred the founding of Greek colonies elsewhere, notably in Sicily and southern Italy. Classical colonization also produced the first immigration policies. Rome used the granting of citizenship and other privileges to cultivate loyalty from non-Romans. Elsewhere in Europe – and later, between 600 and 900 AD – came the great Slavic tribal migrations. Perhaps the largest-scale migration of this era was the extraordinary expansion of Islam from Mecca and Medina to Syria, Iraq, Iran, across North Africa and thence into Spain. This ceased to be effective for the Arabs around 1280 but subsequently spread indirectly through the Ottoman Empire. Thus, for instance, 30,000 Muslim Turks settled on the island of Cyprus in 1571, sowing seeds of an ethnic conflict which since 1974 has partitioned the island into Greek and Turkish sectors. Outside of Europe great southward migrations were occurring in China during 300–900 AD, and in Central and South America pre-Columbian peoples were migrating through conquest and settlement.

1.2.2 Migration, colonialism and the development of the global labour market

Later, international migrations – both forced and voluntary – gathered pace. From the end of the Middle Ages, the development of European states and their colonization of most of the rest of the world gave a new impetus to

colonial migration   long-range migrations which can be termed *colonial migration*. Improvements in cartography, navigation and shipbuilding made transoceanic mass migrations possible. From the early sixteenth to the early nineteenth centuries, the principal routes were from Western Europe to North, Central and South America and the Caribbean. Overall numbers of migrants during this period are impossible to quantify precisely, but one estimate is that between 1500 and 1800 the expansion of Europe towards the New World transplanted about 2 million Europeans and 6 million African slaves (Emmer, 1993, p. 67). These two linked, but very different, migration streams enabled the consolidation of settler colonies in the New World, as well as the formation and expansion of plantation colonies in the Caribbean, north-east Brazil and southern North America.

Technical and financial constraints on intercontinental mass migrations were further relaxed after 1800 and it became possible to transport more migrants in one decade than in any of the previous three centuries. The forced migration of slaves from Africa continued during the early nineteenth century. Slavery continued to form the basis of commodity production in the plantations and mines of the New World until its progressive abolition during the middle decades of the nineteenth century. The production of sugar, cotton, coffee, tobacco and gold by slave labour was fundamental to the economic and political strength of Britain and France, and played a major role for Spain, Portugal and the Netherlands too. The slave migration system was organized in the famous 'triangular trade' (see Figure 1.2): ships destined for West Africa set out from ports such as Liverpool, Bristol and Le Havre laden with manufactured goods and guns; these goods were traded

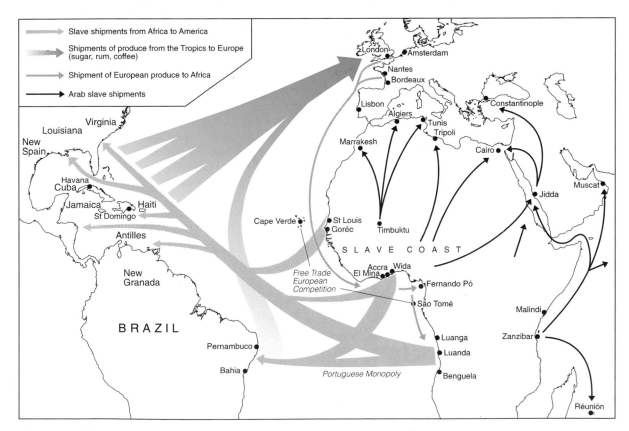

Figure 1.2 *The transatlantic slave trade triangle (Source: Potts, 1990, p. 42)*

with local African chiefs for slaves (who were also forcibly abducted by the crews); the ships then transported the slaves to North and South America and the Caribbean where they were sold for cash, used in turn to buy plantation products which were brought back for sale in Europe on the final leg of the trip – a trading system described by **Meegan** (**1995**)*.

The scale of the Atlantic slave migration was greater than any other long-distance migration, voluntary or involuntary, up to the early nineteenth century. Truly it was one of the greatest and most tragic events of world population history.

indenture As the African slave trade faded away, a new stream of migrants moved between continents: Asian indentured labourers, or 'coolies'. *Indenture* involved the mass recruitment, often by force, of Indian and Chinese workers and their transfer to another part of the colonial empire to exploit their labour power. The British colonial authorities extracted over 30 million people from the Indian subcontinent, shipped out via Madras and Calcutta. Some were taken to the Caribbean (especially Trinidad and Guyana) to substitute for the labour of emancipated slaves in the sugar plantations; others were sent to mines, plantations and railway-building projects in Malaya and East Africa; smaller British colonies such as Fiji and Mauritius also received Indian coolie migration. This was the 'new system of slavery' which ensured and expanded the overseas wealth of Britain by exploiting the raw materials of the tropical colonies (Tinker, 1974, p. *xiii*).

A parallel system of coolie migration developed from China, directed mainly by the Dutch towards construction projects in the Dutch East Indies. However, like the Indians, the Chinese were also used in many other parts of the world as cheap labour – in British Malaya, Queensland, South Africa, North America, Cuba and Peru. In fact, indentured workers were used in about fifty countries by all the major colonial powers.

Coolie migration is both a historical and a typological intermediary between the slave migration that preceded it and the twentieth-century labour migration that followed it. Indentured workers were bound by strict labour dues for a period of several years, but they were paid. However, wages and work conditions were very poor, and rigid, often brutal, discipline was imposed. The following extract from a Chinese coolie's contract reveals the utterly subservient nature of this form of migration:

A CHINESE COOLIE'S CONTRACT

I, the undersigned ... do ... agree to the following conditions.

1   I pledge that on a day following this I shall embark for Havana on the island of Cuba, on moreover any ship specified by the master named.

2   I shall both commit myself and submit myself to work in the named country for a period of eight years and undertake any work commonly carried out there in the fields, in the settlements, or wherever else I may be assigned on the orders of the colonizing society or any person to whom this contract shall pass.

---

* A reference in emboldened type denotes another volume, or a chapter in another volume, of the series.

3   The hours which I am obliged to work shall depend on the type of work to which I am assigned and on the attention which this requires as determined freely (arbitrio) by the master under whose command I am placed, provided that I am guaranteed several consecutive hours for rest every 24 hours and time for breakfast and lunch, as are the other paid workers in that country.

4   In addition to being guaranteed these hours of rest during the working day, I shall also not be obliged to do any more work on any Sunday than that which my employer deems necessary on that particular day.

5   I shall submit myself to the Disciplinary Code ... in force within the organisation to which I am assigned and also to the Penal Code in force ... in the same.

I furthermore declare that I am in complete agreement with the wage stipulated, even though I know and understand that the free wage workers and slaves on the island of Cuba earn far higher wages.

(reproduced in Potts, 1990, p. 89)

Indenture epitomized the colonial principle of divide and rule, pitting one subservient and exploited people against another. The workings of the emerging global labour market meant that indentured workers could be used to undercut the wages of 'free' workers, often former slaves. Most of the indentured migrants were men, but there were also some women, as both workers and dependants. The proportion of females was much higher amongst the Indian indentured migrants (about a third) than amongst the Chinese. Largely for this reason, the Indians tended to remain abroad and evolved into settled communities, whereas the Chinese had high rates of return. However, as happened under slavery, indentured women were regarded as little more than chattels and were subject to often horrific levels of abuse.

Slave sale, Charleston, South Carolina

Activity 2 The common features of slave, coolie and labour migration are brought
out in Reading A which is taken from Lydia Potts' (1990) study of the evolution of the
world labour market. This is an orthodox Marxist treatment of the topic: Potts sees
all forms of labour migration as manipulated by capitalism in either its colonial or
post-colonial guise. In this way the twentieth-century worker migrations within and
into Western Europe, or the brain drain flows that have developed from the 'third
world' in recent decades, are functionally similar to earlier forms of forced or semi-
forced migration such as slavery and coolie migration. Note also that Potts draws
attention to the female dimension of long-range migration, whereas many other
writings on migration seem to assume that all migrants are either male or
genderless. Now turn to Reading A, which you will find at the end of the chapter.
When you have read it, return to the text below.

To summarize, then, slave migration and indentured labour were part of
evolving, colonially controlled, global economic empires, *creating and
perpetuating uneven development between different parts of the world*. Slavery had
existed in many pre-capitalist societies but the colonial system integrated
slavery and indentured workers into a world market for labour dominated by
merchant capital. Worked first by slaves and then by coolies, the plantations
produced commodities for export as part of an internationally integrated
agricultural and manufacturing system. The same sources of labour were also
used for large-scale construction projects, such as railways or hydraulic works,
which required large gangs of mobile labour to follow the projects across
sparsely populated land.

This brief study of colonial migration also gives us some basis for
understanding the origins of many modern-day conflicts between peoples.
The roots of racist stereotyping – today directed against recent immigrants in
many countries – often derive from the historical treatment of slaves and
other colonized peoples, whereas several post-colonial inter-ethnic conflicts
(for instance, hostility against Asians in East Africa, or against Indians in Fiji)
have their origins in the divisions brought about by indenture. Nor should
we forget the devastating effects of migration on indigenous peoples, many
of whom were wiped out by violence and disease. As Castles and Miller
(1993, p. 46) have pointed out, the destruction of indigenous societies was
part of the construction of new national identities: images such as 'how the
West was won' and the struggle of the Australian pioneers against the
Aborigines became powerful myths.

There is a story about an Indian chief in the 1850s who was asked by his
braves what was the biggest mistake of the past generation's leaders. His
answer was simple: 'we failed to control immigration'. Bearing in mind the
destruction of the once-proud way of life of the native Americans and the
shameful expropriation of their tribal lands, you may have sympathy with the
chief's view. But when the same sentiments are expressed by far-right
politicians such as Enoch Powell or Jean-Marie Le Pen, or even by the
current policy-makers of the European Community, a moral dilemma is
exposed.

I shall return to the dilemmas of present European migration policy later,
but in the meantime let me try to convince you that there is a big difference
between the Indian chief and the anti-immigration stance of modern right-
wing parties in Europe. The difference lies in *who* controls migration events.
Under colonial regimes the imperial powers clearly had the control in their

hands, not the territories of immigration. The colonial masters decided who to move where, which lands were to be settled, and which peoples were to be displaced or even exterminated. Now the control over immigration has passed to the countries that play host to the migrants. It is they who determine the scale and structure of the migration flows, shaping their composition in terms of age, gender, origin, qualification and so on. This change in the structure of control over the global labour market took place in the second half of the nineteenth century, a period that we now move on to study a little more closely.

1.2.3   To seek their fortunes

After 1850 the volume of international migration started to increase in an explosive way and Europeans came to dominate intercontinental migration in numbers which were previously unknown. Between this date and the outbreak of the Great War in 1914 around 50 million Europeans participated in international migrations. Some 70 per cent of them went to North America, chiefly to the United States; 12 per cent migrated to South America and 9 per cent migrated to South Africa, Australia and New Zealand. Figure 1.3 shows the geographical pattern of this great European human outpouring.

Transoceanic migration from Europe to the Americas reflected economic and social conditions in both the sending and receiving countries, as well as the growing interdependence of the North Atlantic economy (spelled out in more detail in **Leyshon, 1995**). The famous economist, Brinley Thomas (1954), saw transatlantic emigration as a response to capital flows in the Atlantic economy, with alternating investment cycles in Europe and the United States. Thus emigration was lowest when there was relative prosperity in Europe and depression in North America, but swelled when Europe faced hard times and America rode a wave of prosperity. Changing transport technology also had a key role. Steamships were quicker and cheaper than

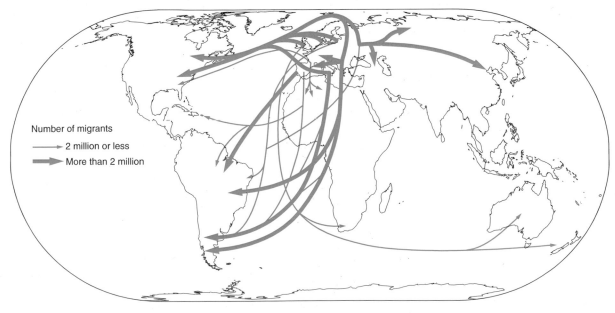

Figure 1.3   *European voluntary migrations, 1815–1914 (Source: Segal, 1993, p. 17)*

15

sailing ships. Railways enabled migrants from interior regions of Europe to travel much more quickly to ports, and facilitated their onward travel from the American ports of arrival.

For the sending countries, demographic factors had great importance. In many parts of Europe emigration was the only solution to rapid population growth brought on by early phases of the demographic transition when death rates fell more quickly than birth rates (Grigg, 1980). In Norway, for instance, which was one of the European countries to send the highest number of emigrants in proportion to its population, the population had doubled between 1800 and 1865.

The views of the Reverend Thomas Malthus on the dangers of overpopulation (outlined by **Hall, 1995**) had perhaps their greatest vindication in Ireland where the failure of the potato crop in the mid and late 1840s led to a tremendous surge in emigration. It is estimated that the Irish Famine resulted in the death of one million people and the emigration of 1.8 million. High levels of emigration from Ireland continued throughout the rest of the nineteenth century and for much of the twentieth century too. Indeed between 1845 and 1921 (the eve of Irish Independence) a total of 5.4 million people emigrated, virtually halving the Irish population in the process – from 8.2 million in 1841 to 4.2 million in 1921 (Smyth, 1992). No other country in Europe has been so deeply affected by the migratory experience.

Not all European countries were hit by 'emigration fever' at this time. There was relatively little emigration from France, Belgium and the Netherlands, and it was only at the end of the century that the countries of Eastern and Southern Europe came into the picture, with Italy dominant. In Germany emigration faded as industrialization got under way. In Britain, on the other hand, industrialization did not so much stem emigration as change its character. Emigrants increasingly came from industrial areas and were either ambitious artisans or the urban poor fleeing squalid working conditions (Grigg, 1980). Nevertheless the general conclusion is clear: the dramatic increase in the rate of economic growth in Europe in the nineteenth century was only sustained by using emigration as an 'escape hatch'. The exodus of 50 million people allowed the European economies to create a mix of the factors of production – land, labour, capital, industrial raw materials, enterprise – which promoted record growth, without having that growth swallowed up by population increase.

The arrows on Figure 1.3 obscure the fact that intensities of emigration varied greatly from region to region within countries. Some Italian data can be used to expand this point, and to demonstrate the key importance of the process known as chain migration.

The period 1901–13 witnessed the most intense emigration in Italian history. Nearly nine million left to go overseas during these years, an annual average of 20 per thousand or two per cent of the Italian population. The rates were heaviest in southern regions such as Calabria (37 per thousand per year), Basilicata (34), Abruzzi (34) and Sicily (26); elsewhere, in Sardinia and many of the northern regions, the annual rate was less than one-tenth of this at 2–3 per thousand (Baines, 1991, pp. 31–2). These rates are of gross migration and take no account of returns, for which the Italian authorities had only minimal records. Certainly there was much to-and-fro movement, but often the returns only served to provoke further emigration.

This continuity is the essence of *chain migration* whereby emigrants from one particular village or district tend to cluster in the same destination, often doing the same kind of work. Chain migration is also fostered by kinship links (one person who has already emigrated calling other family members such as brothers and cousins to follow) and the natural desire of emigrants to move to a place where there are friends and relatives already established. Thus American cities of large-scale immigration became ethnic mosaics with clearly defined Italian, Greek and Polish districts and so on, and, within these concentrations, more localized groupings of people from the same district or village in the 'old country'. This remaking of place and community via migration made the move less painful for the individual and enabled the migrant to fit in to a partly familiar setting where help could be offered to find a job and somewhere to live.

chain migration

Activity 3 To conclude this section on overseas emigration, I want to present you with a specific example based on two linked readings. The example – of turn-of-the-century emigration from rural Sicily to the Chicago slum known as Little Hell – uses two sources written in the 1920s. Reading B is from *The Italian Emigration of Our Times*, by the Harvard historian Robert Foerster (1924), one of the most complete surveys of its kind ever written. The extracts included in this reading outline some of the conditions which impelled so many Sicilians to seek their fortune in America. Reading C is from Harvey Zorbaugh's *The Gold Coast and the Slum* (1929). Written by a member of the famous 'Chicago School' of urban sociology which flourished in the 1920s and 1930s, this is a detailed study of the Lower North Side of Chicago, part of which was made up of 'Little Sicily' where 15,000 Sicilian immigrants were crowded into tenements and rooming-houses in appalling conditions. As well as describing some of these harsh conditions, the extracts from Zorbaugh's book bring out the meaning of chain migration and give insights into the reconstruction of 'place' and 'community' by an immigrant group. Now turn to Readings B and C and then return to the text below.

The readings from Foerster and Zorbaugh are 'dated', but they do have the value of being contemporary with the phenomenon being described. They give quite a good feel for the time and the places of Sicilian migration: from the overpopulated rural wastelands of central Sicily to the throbbing tenements of Little Hell. Foerster's text brings out some of the structural factors operating from the Sicilian end: population increase, poor diet, disease, ignorance, a history of colonialism, and class oppression through the monopolization of land by aristocrats and the bourgeoisie. Zorbaugh describes the transplantation of Sicilian cultural traits to Chicago where, to his evident exasperation, the Sicilians conserve their 'Sicilianness' and refuse to become 'Americans'. Today these readings appear at best patronising and at worst occasionally offensive. And they tend to assume that migrants are male. They are included here in order to demonstrate both the value and the limitations of older scholarly work on migration.

The experiences of Sicilians were by no means unique. They are the paradigm for other peasants who in the nineteenth and early twentieth centuries flocked to America from all over Europe: from western-most Ireland and the Russian plains in the east, and from the northern forests of Sweden and the sun-dried mountains of Greece. As Oscar Handlin wrote in his classic book, *The Uprooted*, these immigrants *were* American history (Handlin, 1951, p. 3).

Finally, let me remind you of the central pivot of this chapter: the counterpoint between global push and pull forces on migrants exerted by coercion, colonialism and economic gain; and their personal and place identities which are torn up and recreated through migration. From the melting-pots of Brazil and the Caribbean to the formation of long-standing ethnic mixes in port cities such as Liverpool and Cape Town, these past migrations have left powerful legacies of cultural hybridity. In a pre-1914 world dominated by sea trade and sea-borne colonialism, port cities were the key nodes in global relations, contact-points for layers of immigration which have enriched such places with peoples and cultures previously separated not only by geographical distance but also by historical phases of colonial and commercial development. This establishment of the fact that hybridity in the creation of places and regions is not new lays an important historical benchmark for what follows in the rest of this chapter, and in the rest of this book. Equally, our study of early long-distance migrations suggests that the interconnections, interdependences and unequal relations of the modern world have important historical antecedents.

Summary of section 1.2

o   The human world has very largely been shaped by past migrations; mass migrations are therefore not just a modern phenomenon.

o   Colonial migrations can be regarded as early expressions of globalization.

o   Historically, Europe has used emigration as a means of shedding surplus population.

o   Past migrations have contributed to the cultural hybridity of many places.

1.3   Post-war labour migration

The post-war era witnessed the changing nature of globalization from colonial and imperial expressions of the concept to the spread of economic empires based on the hegemony of capital. This rather high-sounding statement needs to be qualified in two ways. First, as my earlier account showed, colonialism was at base an early form of international capitalism, structured through conquest and international control. Second, with regard to migration, post-war international flows contain within them powerful echoes of the earlier colonial periods. How else can we explain the migration to Britain of so many Irish, West Indians, Indians and Pakistanis? However, the lack of a colonial empire did not prevent other countries from encouraging mass immigration when it was beneficial for them to do so – as the cases of Germany and Switzerland illustrate.

labour migration   *Labour migration* – movement purely for the purpose of finding work or a better rate of pay – boomed in the decades following 1945. The key factor was the demand for cheap labour from centres of capital accumulation. These were either fast-growing industrial economies in North America, northwest Europe and Australia, or regions based on mineral exploitation such as the Persian Gulf (oil) and South Africa (gold, diamonds, coal). Here we focus on the European case, paying particular attention to Germany where the characteristics of labour migration are present in their clearest form.

During the 1950s and 1960s a complex international system of mass labour migrations evolved, transferring millions of workers from the mainly rural peripheral regions of Europe to the industrial and urban 'core' regions. The sending countries were of two types: colonial and ex-colonial countries such as India, Pakistan and the British, French and Dutch Caribbean territories; and countries on the margins of Europe – Ireland to the west, Finland to the north-east, and the Mediterranean countries to the south. By the early 1970s about ten million migrant workers were living in Europe: a massive hidden, exploited and stateless group of people equivalent to the population of a medium-sized European country such as Belgium or Portugal.

Activity 4 The main factors responsible for this labour migration system are lucidly set out in Reading D from Castles and Kosack's *Immigrant Workers and Class Structure in Western Europe* (1973) to which you should now turn. This book remains the most thorough analysis of West European labour migration and was published in the same year that the whole system came to a shuddering halt as a result of the first oil crisis. Castles and Kosack neatly distinguish between *'push' and 'pull' forces* and conclude that the pull of labour demand was the decisive factor. They also point out that, despite their origin as temporary migrants, foreign workers have made themselves structurally indispensable to Western European economies.

'push' and 'pull' forces

1.3.1 The case of Germany

Germany provides a good example of the working out of the push and pull factors outlined by Castles and Kosack. After the erection of the Berlin Wall in 1961 cut off the supply of labour from Poland and East Germany, the West German economy, growing rapidly in its reconstruction and industrialization phases, sought labour elsewhere in Europe. Initially it found ready supplies in Italy, a fellow member of the fledgling Common Market. During the 1960s the provisions of the Common Market's free movement of labour policies made it progressively easier for Italians to enter and leave West Germany and avoid overt discrimination in the labour market. However, this period coincided with the rapid growth of the Italian economy, and the southern Italian peasants who might have migrated to German industrial jobs (or followed their ancestors overseas) found 'intervening opportunities' in factory jobs in northern Italian cities such as Milan and Turin. German capital had to search elsewhere for cheap labour, and during the 1960s a series of bilateral recruitment agreements was signed with Greece, Spain, Portugal, Yugoslavia, Turkey and Morocco. The post-war chronology of worker migration into West Germany illustrates this widening search for supplies of labour to feed the growth of German industry and perform the low-status service jobs (sweeping streets, cleaning offices etc.) that the German workers were not filling.

Activity 5 Examine the figures in Table 1.1 and see if you can find evidence of this geographically expanding international hinterland for migrant workers.

Table 1.1 Numbers of foreign workers in West Germany 1963–87, by nationality (percentages)

Year	Total (000s)	Italians	Greeks	Spanish	Portuguese	Yugoslavs	Turks	Others
1963	773	34.3	13.7	14.5	–	–	–	37.5
1966	1244	29.1	15.4	14.1	1.5	7.4	12.0	21.5
1970	1807	20.1	12.7	9.0	2.2	20.7	17.9	17.4
1973	2595	17.3	9.6	7.3	3.3	20.6	23.3	18.6
1976	1925	14.2	9.3	5.8	3.3	20.1	27.2	20.1
1979	1924	15.4	7.2	4.7	3.1	18.9	27.8	22.9
1983	1714	13.9	6.4	4.2	2.7	17.9	31.5	23.4
1987	1557	11.4	7.1	4.1	2.3	18.3	32.9	23.9

Source: Adapted from Potts, 1990, pp. 142–3

The West German policy was to use foreign labour as fuel for the engine of economic growth, but also as a cushion against unemployment for the German workforce. The German strategy of *Konjunkturpuffer* was quite explicit: migrant labour was to be used as a 'buffer' against 'conjunctures' or economic cycles. To this day, Germany officially denies that it is a country of immigration: the foreign workers are *Gastarbeiter* or temporarily residing guestworkers.

Konjunkturpuffer

Gastarbeiter

In fact the connection that foreign workers have with the 'place' that is Germany is highly ambivalent. Part of this ambivalence derives from the indelible fact that they are migrants and therefore have an attachment to the place where they were born and grew up. But part is created by the strangely contradictory policies of Germany towards foreigners. Compared to most other European countries, Germany has a liberal attitude towards admitting asylum-seekers fleeing persecution in other countries (though this attitude has hardened during the early 1990s). On the other hand, economic migrants, especially those from Turkey and North Africa, have been only partially integrated into German society. They are the victims of racist attacks and are denied rights of citizenship that they would have if they lived in other European countries such as Sweden or France.

Guestworker migration into West Germany occurred in its 'purest' form during the 1960s. Foreign workers were hired directly from their home countries by German recruitment offices set up all over the Mediterranean regions of supply. Many writers drew parallels with the past and called the *Gastarbeiter* the slaves of modern Europe (Cohen, 1987). The recruitment centres had medical units to ensure that only healthy young adults were admitted to perform what were widely called the 'shit jobs' of the German economy. Those passed fit were marked with a felt-tip pen like a piece of merchandise. A long train journey – three days from Turkey – transported them to start their 'other' life, where they were housed in single-sex dormitories close by their place of work. Both men and women were hired and accommodated in this way – the men for heavy industry and the women for light industry and cleaning jobs. By giving the migrants annual contracts which could be renewed or revoked at the whim of the employer, German capital was assured of a flexible labour supply which could be repatriated during a recession – as happened during 1966–67 and 1973–74. The constant 'rotation' of foreign workers minimized their ability to put down roots in

Turkish workers in a Volkswagen factory in Germany

West Germany. Thus the German economy was relieved of the costs of reproduction of labour – the feeding, clothing and upbringing of migrants had already been taken care of by their home countries. By admitting only single workers, social support costs for families were avoided; and by returning them to their home countries through the rotation policy, no costs of non-productive old age were incurred. Such was the theory and the practice of *Konjunkturpuffer*.

During the 1970s the *Konjunkturpuffer* thesis broke down. Partly stimulated by European Community legislation favouring the rights of immigrant workers, and partly driven by the realization that many migrants wanted to stay in Germany at all costs, a different attitude took hold and many migrants were allowed to bring in their families. Thus although worker migration tailed off after the 1973 oil crisis (see Table 1.1), the migration of family members increased, as did the total stock of foreign population, which reached 5.2 million in 1990.

1.3.2 The situation worldwide

Let us now highlight some key points about international labour migration worldwide (Castles and Miller, 1993, pp. 75–7; Potts, 1990, pp. 157–62).

First, the large scale of the phenomenon should be stressed. In the early 1980s the International Labour Office estimated that 25–30 million people were international labour migrants: this number should be doubled to 50–60 million to include family members. But the real figures are much larger, because the ILO did not enumerate illegal immigrants, refugees or asylum-seekers, most of whom are also migrants who work or seek work.

Second, there is the overwhelming relevance of economic factors. Economic motivation is paramount for the migrants themselves who see the opportunity to earn higher wages and to escape unemployment and drudgery; and it is equally important for the employers who can exploit a cheaper source of labour than indigenous workers.

Third, there is an interesting geographical trend to be noted: that is, the growing spatial spread and diversity of origins of the migrants and, as a result, the increasing cultural divide between them and the host populations. We saw this point most clearly in the case of West Germany, but it is also true of many other migrant-importing nations. As will be seen shortly, this increasing diversity of migrant source countries – a reflection of the progressive globalization of the labour market – has continued with the new 'post-industrial' migrations of the 1980s and 1990s.

Fourth, wherever the migrants come from, they have become overwhelmingly concentrated in manual employment, mainly in industry, construction and low-grade service jobs. Along with this occupational ghettoization in unskilled employment have come a spatial concentration in substandard housing and social marginalization involving limited contact or integration with host populations. This occupational and spatial ghettoization gives powerful expression to the nature of certain places – typically the inner cities of developed countries (discussed in **Hamnett, 1995**).

Finally, it is important to remember that labour migration is closely linked with international uneven development: development of the rich countries and underdevelopment of the poor countries. More than half of the world's post-war labour migrants come from the developing nations: in the USA it is two-thirds, in the Gulf 90 per cent. International labour migration can be interpreted in many ways: whilst there are some who believe that it can compensate for uneven development, increasingly it is being regarded as a form of development aid – the export of the finest and fittest – given by the poor to the rich countries.

Summary of section 1.3

o   Labour migration results mainly from the pull of labour demand exerted by capital.

o   Labour migration both reflects and exacerbates uneven development.

o   Labour migration creates 'occupational ghettoes', as well as spatial concentrations of culturally distinct, deprived and socially marginalized people.

1.4   Migrations today

The worker migrations of the 1950s, 1960s and early 1970s were very much mass phenomena: millions of more or less homogeneous workers mass-migrated from rural areas of poor countries to take jobs in industries in the prosperous countries where they contributed to the mass production of goods for mass consumption. Since the 1980s there have been fundamental changes (Castles and Miller, 1993, pp. 8–9, 77–8). Both the nature of international migration, and the driving forces behind it, have changed – in the following ways:

1   The first tendency is the *globalization* of migration: the incorporation of more and more countries into the global migration system. This means that

destination countries receive migrants from a wider spread of geographical origins and of economic, social and cultural backgrounds. This leads closely to the second trend …

2 Migrations are becoming more *differentiated*. Countries now receive a greater variety of *types* of migration – labour migrants seeking a long-term or permanent stay, highly educated skilled and professional migrants, refugees, illegal migrants, 'commuting' migrants who stay for a few days or weeks only, and so on.

3 The third tendency is the *acceleration* of migration. Migrations appear to be growing in volume in all major world regions.

4 The fourth trend is the *feminization* of migration. In the past, most labour migrations were male-dominated; now women are playing a leading role in many migration streams. Some examples are the Filipinos, Cape Verdians and South Americans who migrate to work as domestic helpers and carers in Italy and Spain. Many refugee movements, such as those from former Yugoslavia, are also female-dominated.

5 Both push and pull factors have changed. Generally speaking, there is a greater emphasis on *push pressures* from the 'third world'. Both in real terms and through the eyes of the potential migrants, poverty, overcrowding, political instability and environmental disaster are becoming ever more sharply contrasted with increasing knowledge of conditions in the 'West'. With the avenues of legal migration closed off, there is increasing resort to clandestine movement. Mass migrations of refugees and asylum-seekers have also been a feature of the late 1980s and early 1990s. At the same time the nature of the pull factor of *demand* has changed. The decline in manufacturing industry has reduced the requirement for traditional labour migrants. Meanwhile, the expansion of the service industries creates new demand for highly skilled migrants, whilst the growth in the informal sector draws in casual workers with little or no training.

1.4.1 Globalization and migration

Changes in the global economy, which feed through to the level of particular places and regions via restructured production processes and reshaped local labour markets, have tended to polarize labour demand into high-skill and low-skill categories. This polarization also reflects an emerging duality between a *primary labour market* of well-paid, secure and pensionable jobs and a *secondary labour market* of poorly-paid, insecure and often part-time employment. Migration processes are affected accordingly, so that the skill profile of today's international migrants tends to reflect the polarity between highly-trained professionals, scientists and technicians on the one hand and low-grade casual, flexible service labour on the other.

primary labour market
secondary labour market

Activity 6 Reading E explores in some depth the implications of globalization for international migration. The reading consists of selected extracts from Saskia Sassen's *The Mobility of Labour and Capital* (1988). Sassen's reference-point is the US economy and the emerging roles of New York and Los Angeles as 'global cities', a notion discussed by **Hamnett (1995)**. She describes two linked processes: first, how labour is 'dislodged' from sending countries by US foreign investment; and, second, how that labour fits into restructured labour markets in the US. Although her account is of the US, much of what she says is also valid for Europe, as we shall see.

One of the clearest expressions of the globalization of economic life, and of labour markets in particular, is the rapid growth of skilled international migration – a new breed of executive nomads who, whilst quantitatively much less important than the mass labour migrations of the past, nevertheless wield enormous influence over the functioning of the global economy.

Most of the migration of the highly skilled takes place amongst the advanced capitalist countries and consists of relatively balanced, two-way exchanges between pairs of countries in Europe or with Japan or North America. It is facilitated by improved transport and communications, especially between the key global cities of the world economy. Some of this executive migration, which is mainly of men, actually takes place *within* the labour markets of multinational companies who for reasons of business strategy, career planning or trouble-shooting, shift their high-status employees amongst the various countries in which they operate. Other movement of skilled labour is stage-managed by recruitment agencies specializing in particular regions of the world or in occupational sectors such as accountancy, economic planning, civil engineering and so on.

Obstacles to the movement of highly skilled migrants are much less than for low-skilled migrants. Special entry regulations and work permits have been introduced to facilitate their movement; indeed some countries, such as Australia and Canada, have actively courted skilled and professional personnel, recognizing their importance in improving the quality of the labour force. Footballers, entertainers and artists are also able to relocate quickly and easily to most countries of the world.

Not all skilled international migration takes the form of 'talent exchanges' amongst the advanced countries. Two other situations occur. The first is the move of technical and management experts from more to less developed countries as part of *contract migration* or aid and development policy. Often such a migrant is charged with setting up or managing a particular project, and training a cadre of local people who will eventually take over the running of the enterprise. The second is the reverse flow, or *brain drain*. Brain drains often move along channels defined by former colonial links and may be tied to particular shortages of skilled personnel, as, for example, the migration of Indian doctors and West Indian nurses to Britain. Brain drains are a reflection of sharp international differences in salaries for given professions. They also reflect intellectual unemployment in the country of origin whereby the education system has been expanded and distorted, often by colonial influences, beyond the capacity of the country to absorb its own graduates. India, Sri Lanka and Egypt are examples of countries with massive intellectual unemployment and long-established brain drains.

contract migration

brain drain

At the other end of the skill profile, current global labour market trends, and especially the restructuring of labour demand in major cities in advanced countries, have opened up new possibilities for migrant workers. These opportunities are very different from the factory jobs offered to migrants a generation ago. Most of the new low-skill jobs are in the service sector, many in the informal economy. Their essence reflects the very vulnerability and desperation of the migrants, most of whom come from 'third world' countries rather than countries of the European periphery, some of which have switched to being immigration areas now. This is the secondary labour market of casual, part-time, seasonal, insecure work where rates of pay are pitifully low by developed world standards, no social insurance contributions are paid, and not too many questions are asked. These waves of *post-industrial migrants* – often clandestine – have affected the United States, Japan, the Gulf and Europe. Their *raison d'être* is cogently explained in Reading E by Saskia Sassen: in a labour market which is becoming progressively deregulated and flexible, with strong pressures to reduce labour costs, they provide a pool of casual workers available for virtually any low-grade job at any time and at any place.

post-industrial migrant

1.4.2   Barriers to migration

Now consider a major paradox: the globalization of economic life – of capital, trade, culture, the labour market – does *not* include the right to migrate internationally. Capital is free to roam the world, labour is not. The much-publicized right to freedom of movement within the European Union is coupled with a more sinister erection of barriers around the EU. The epithet 'Fortress Europe' is often used to express this 'boundedness' of the European Union. Europe is thus a place for some, a non-place for others.

Here is another illogicality. For decades during the Cold War the 'West' derided the 'East' for not allowing its citizens to exercise a basic human right – to choose where to live by emigrating. East European border guards shot and killed many would-be migrants trying to cross to the 'West'. Now the position has been reversed. Faced with a tide of migrants from Eastern Europe, Western Europe's tolerance, humanity and charity are in short supply and much effort is put into keeping the migrants out. The Iron Curtain has become an ironic curtain!

Activity 7   Think about the issue of whether migration is a fundamental human right. It is, let me say, a desperately difficult question. Social scientists and philosophers have agonized over the complex ethical, political and practical issues involved (see, for example, Barry and Goodin, 1992). Few, it appears, have difficulty in supporting the right to emigrate. The right to immigrate is much more tricky. Why is this so?

Most first world countries are worried over uncontrolled immigration because of the likely numbers involved, because of threats to national security and cultural identity, and because of strains on housing, employment and welfare systems. But these concerns have been politicized and transformed into a vehicle for racial hatred which has itself emerged as a serious cultural problem in many societies, including Britain, Germany and France. The racialization of the politics of migration is massively assisted by statements by some mainstream political leaders. Here is Mrs Thatcher in an interview with the *Daily Mail*:

We joined Europe to have free movement of goods ... I did not join Europe to have free movement of terrorists, criminals, drugs, plant and animal diseases and rabies, and illegal immigrants ... How are you going to stop anyone from Bangladesh, from any country, coming for a holiday in Greece, coming right in, right across all borders, no controls, and settling in Britain and we would have no means of finding out?

(18 May 1989)

Yet many of the people to whom Mrs Thatcher refers are not migrants by choice: they are refugees. At the end of 1992, there were 19 million refugees worldwide. Most of them were in Africa and western Asia, not in Europe – contrary to what the European media and politicians would have us believe. Nevertheless it is true that the number of asylum-seekers entering Europe per year rose by ten times between the early 1980s and early 1990s (the figure was 700,000 in 1992). In the face of this pressure, many governments have stiffened their procedures on admitting refugees, looking for loopholes in UN guidelines in order to screen applicants more severely. The refugees streaming out of former Yugoslavia discovered this hardening attitude on the part of the 'West'. But many could not return: they had, quite literally, lost their place in the world, bombed and burnt out of existence by an opposing faction.

There are many processes forcing international migrations in the late twentieth century. Rapid population growth and consequent overpopulation, environmental degradation, ecological disaster, extreme poverty, famines and floods all combine greatly to increase the push pressures for migration from the less developed world. The reaction of the 'West' is usually to pull down the shutters and deny people who have lost their original place in the world the chance to find another. Once again the paradox of restrictions on the right to migrate in an apparently globalizing world is exposed. The rules of modern migration are clear. 'Desirable' migrants with skills, education and

'Ethnic cleansing' has displaced about 2 million people in the former Yugoslavia. Here, about 4000 Muslims leave Bossanski Nova in Serbian-controlled Bosnia for Croatia, in UNHCR trucks

capital are let in; 'undesirables', illiterates, poor people from different cultures, religions and 'races' are filtered out. Globalization is a process of social exclusion.

> **Summary of section 1.4**
>
> o   Migrations today are stimulated more by push factors than by pull factors.
>
> o   Modern mass migrations are highly differentiated into many types.
>
> o   Capital is free to migrate, people are not. The barriers to human migration are selective; therefore migration is a process of social exclusion.

1.5   Migration: an engagement with place

So far in this chapter we have touched upon many different types of migration. The movements have been differentiated with respect to scale, distance, historical period, level of development and other variables. Although at a statistical level migrations are often reduced to rather placeless flows of people, it is vital to keep in mind that such movements are always place-specific when studied as the personal experiences of individual migrants. In fact, migrants engage with place in several ways. At a basic level, migration is a human link between places – the place of departure and the place of arrival and settlement. Migration stretches particular forms of social relations across space: both the social relations of capitalist production (for example, between the owners of capital and the workers) and the personal social networks that reproduce migration chains through time.

The meaning of place for a migrant torn from his or her roots is indelible. For rural migrants, the start was the village where they were born, and which remains the fixed point from which progress is measured. Oscar Handlin conjures up what must have been a typical view of the millions of rural peasants who flocked to America in the first part of the twentieth century:

The village was a place. It could be seen, it could be marked on a map, described in all its physical attributes. Here was a road along which men and beasts would pass ... There was a church, larger than the other structures around it. The burial ground was not far away, and the smithy, the mill, perhaps an inn ... The fields were round about, located in terms of river, brook, rocks or trees. All these could be perceived; the eye could grasp, the senses apprehend the feel, the sound, the smell of them. These objects, real, authentic, true, could come back in memories, be summoned up to rouse the curiosity and stir the wonder of children born in distant lands.

Yet the village was still more. The aggregate of huts housed a community. Later, much later, and very far away, the Old Countrymen also had this in mind when they thought of the village. They spoke of relationships, of ties, of family, of kinship, of many rights and obligations. And these duties, privileges, connections, links, had their special flavour, somehow a unique value, a meaning in terms of the life of the whole.

(Handlin, 1951, pp. 8–9)

habitus

Handlin's words provide a good definition of what Pierre Bourdieu (1977) has termed the *habitus* of migrants: their personal accumulated space–time experiences and inheritances, their geographical background, cultural origins and social networks. Habitus gives people a sense of their place in the world, a sense which is carried with them and refashioned in the new context when they migrate. Gillian Bottomley in her study of Greeks in Australia has shown how migrants cling to their habitus: they preserve it, mould it and adapt it to their often very alienating experiences of being a migrant in a strange land on the other side of the world. Bottomley discusses the expression of the habitus of Greek migrants in Australia not only through their clubs and associations, but also through their literature, dance and music – what she calls the poetics of ethnicity. In a beautiful cameo she describes how an old woman, dancing in a bare hall in Sydney felt that, whilst dancing, she was 'at home', in her village, as a young girl; she could even smell the pine trees (Bottomley, 1992, p.141). For Greeks in Australia, and elsewhere in the Greek diaspora, dancing is a way of connecting to their past, both to the place of their past and to their youth. It is an expression of a landscape of small villages and small houses, of a life led out of doors with lots of informal gatherings, music and games. This idealization of the place left behind is very common amongst migrants and overlooks, of course, the hunger, poverty and fatigue of rural life – the conditions that turned them into migrants.

Such an idealized view of 'home' also overlooks the fact that these places have been changed by the migrants' act of leaving. The mass departure of migrants leaves places drained of their life-blood. It creates communities of old people and landscapes of empty farms and semi-derelict villages. Many regions have been denuded in this way: the west of Ireland and the mountain villages of Corsica are two examples. They are places of abandonment.

Sustained emigration from the west of Ireland causes much of the settlement to become abandoned, like this cottage on Inishbiggle island

For many migrants, however, the place of departure is also the place of return. Of course, not all migrants return to base. Many stay away for good, whilst others who do return to their native country do not go back to the place that they left but resettle elsewhere, perhaps in a nearby town or the national capital. For many migrants, however, the return only has meaning if it is to their place of birth and upbringing. Only there can they rediscover themselves, enjoy the warmth of family and kin, achieve some admiration and social prestige for what they have done and where they have been. As the final reading shows, the return is full of symbolic meaning. It is, above all, a return to the place and the people that were held in the memory whilst away.

Activity 8   Reading F, to which you should now turn, gives some moving human insights into the return of a migrant worker from Switzerland to the former Yugoslavia. The source is *A Seventh Man* by John Berger and Jean Mohr (1975). The trip, by train and car, is a journey between two places that are geographically relatively close but represent symbolically two different worlds.

Berger's words – clipped, direct, eloquent – sum up beautifully the dilemmas and tragedies of being born in one place and having to work in another. They describe the powerful meaning of place for the migrant who approaches his or her native village after a period abroad. They portray hopes for the future but also some of the objective difficulties of trying to resettle.

Whilst it may be the case that, as Berger says, the final return is mythical, it is also true that returning migrants, through their remittances and savings, have transformed many of the villages and districts of origin. The new house is the visible status symbol of the successful migrant. In southern Italy in the early twentieth century many towns and villages had whole streets of 'American houses' – new houses built by the *americani*, the local emigrants who went to America; in Hong Kong houses built with money earnt in England are called sterling houses; in the Punjab two-storey *pukka* houses stand out above the local dwellings as testimony to a certain level of success abroad on the part of their owners. Often architectural styles of the place of emigration invade the place of return: thus we find American-style ranches and bungalows in the west of Ireland, or Swiss chalets in rural Portugal. Houses may be decorated and furnished with mementos of the emigration place.

The examples described above show that the migrant's sense of place and of personal identity often involve a duality – 'here' and 'there' – which is an important aspect of their lives. When they are abroad they tend to identify with home, when they are back home they identify with abroad. When abroad, migrants often attempt to recreate their home environment in order not to feel alienated: they cluster together, clinging to their habitus, and thereby change the character of the places they settle in. Many large American cities had their 'Little Italies'; London and Liverpool had their Chinatowns. A perfect Little Italy still survives in the North End of Boston, bounded on three sides by a loop in the river and on the fourth by a road fly-over: here every shop, restaurant and business has an Italian name, there are saints' statues and shrines on street corners and the population is made up entirely of Italian immigrants and their descendants.

Recent Bangladeshi migration into the Brick Lane area of London's East End has given a very special character to this place – as shown here at the junction of Brick Lane and Princelet Street.

In many European cities too the mass migrations of the post-war era have transformed the nature of urban space. In Britain we can think of Brixton in south London, St. Paul's in Bristol, and many more. Within these areas what appears homogeneous to the outsider is highly variegated to the insider. The old Little Italies broke down into distinct quarters inhabited by migrants from the same region of Italy. Asian areas in British cities often divide into subdistricts on the basis of country of origin, religion and language.

Ethnic enclaves also function as a seed-bed for small businesses which further reinforce the character of the district by developing its ethnic economy. Some of these businesses – shops, travel agents etc. – serve the ethnic population only; others may cater to the wider population, particularly if they become 'fashionable', like Indian or Italian restaurants. This shows that migrants are not always the passive victims of capital and economic restructuring; sometimes they have contributed actively to economic change.

Activity 9 The final activity is intended to get you to relate as many features of this chapter as you can to an area you know or can visualize.

Think of your own town, or a city near you, and identify an area of that town where immigrants have settled. (You may, of course, be a recent immigrant yourself.) Now try to answer the following questions.

(a) Where do the migrants come from?

(b) What circumstances brought them to live there?

(c) What jobs do the immigrants do?

(d) What types of housing do they live in?

(e) Which migrant activities lend a special character to the place?

1.6   Conclusion

This chapter has shown that migration is part of the process of globalization – although, of course, not all migrations are global. Many international migrations closely reflect the global economic distribution of power, in particular the demand for particular types of labour by the centres of capital accumulation in North America and Western Europe. The links between places, in terms of their economic relationships and colonial histories, are expressed in different types of migration – slave and coolie migration, labour migration, colonial settler migration, brain drain, illegal migration and so on.

A study of migration exposes the social inequalities and often terrible human dramas that lie at the heart of the process of globalization. Such inequity is often made worse by international and national policies. Despite the world's apparently increasing concern for human rights in the post-colonial era, the growth of state regulation of international migration means that in many ways it is more difficult to migrate in the 1990s than in the 1890s. The constraints which have been shown to exist against the free movement of people contrast sharply with capital's liquid mobility to flow freely around the world.

Nevertheless these constraints are merely an attempt to control what is now an increasing volume of migration. According to Castles and Miller (1993, p. 5), 'international migration is part of a transnational revolution that is reshaping societies and politics around the globe'. They confidently predict that the rest of the 1990s and the first decade of the twenty-first century will be the 'age of migration'. What is new about the new forces of globalization, and the new mass migrations, is that the connections which bind people and places across the globe are now expressed at greater speed and intensity than ever before.

Summary points of the chapter

o   Migration has been an important global process since the dawn of time.

o   Migration is both a product and an agent of uneven development.

o   Although economic factors generally trigger migration, especially labour migration, the continuity of migration flows is often perpetuated by social factors.

o   Migration results from a blend of push and pull forces. In the past, under slavery, indenture and labour migration, the pull of labour demand was the major factor. Now the push of poverty, population pressure and environmental deterioration is more dominant.

o   Despite globalization there are many barriers to migration in the modern world. These barriers are selective: only the privileged can pass. Overall, people are less free to move than capital.

o   Discussions on whether migration is a basic human right founder on the conflict between moral principle and political possibility.

> ○ Migration shapes both the places of origin and the places of destination of the migrants. In particular, migrants have reshaped the nature of urban space in the cities in which they have settled.

References

ALLEN, J. and HAMNETT, C. (eds) (1995) *A Shrinking World? Global Unevenness and Inequality*, Oxford, Oxford University Press/The Open University (Volume 2 in this series).

BAINES, D. (1991) *Emigration from Europe 1815–1930*, London, Macmillan.

BARRY, B. and GOODIN, R. E. (eds) (1992) *Free Movement: Ethical Issues in the Transnational Migration of People and Money*, New York, Harvester Wheatsheaf.

BERGER, J. and MOHR, J. (1975) *A Seventh Man*, Harmondsworth, Penguin.

BOTTOMLEY, G. (1992) *From Another Place: Migration and the Politics of Culture*, Cambridge, Cambridge University Press.

BOURDIEU, P. (1977) *Outline of a Theory of Practice*, Cambridge, Cambridge University Press.

CASTLES, S. and KOSACK, G. (1973) *Immigrant Workers and Class Structure in Western Europe*, Oxford, Oxford University Press (2nd edn, 1985).

CASTLES, S. and MILLER, M. J. (1993) *The Age of Migration*, London, Macmillan.

COHEN, R. (1987) *The New Helots: Migrants in the International Division of Labour*, Aldershot, Avebury.

EMMER, P. C. (1993) Intercontinental migration as a world historical process, *European Review*, 1(1), pp. 67-74.

FAGAN, B. M. (1990) *The Journey from Eden: The Peopling of Our World*, London, Thames and Hudson.

FOERSTER, R. F. (1924) *The Italian Emigration of Our Times*, Cambridge, MA, Harvard University Press.

GRIGG, D. B. (1980) 'Migration and overpopulation' in White, P. and Woods, R. (eds) *The Geographical Impact of Migration*, London, Longman, pp. 60–83.

HALL, R. (1995) 'Stabilizing population growth: the European experience' in Sarre, P. and Blunden, J. (eds) *An Overcrowded World? Population, Resources and the Environment*, Oxford, Oxford University Press/The Open University (Volume 3 in this series).

HAMNETT, C. (1995) 'Controlling space: global cities' in Allen, J. and Hamnett, C. (eds).

HANDLIN, O. (1951) *The Uprooted*, Boston, Little, Brown.

LEYSHON, A. (1995) 'Annihilating space: the speed-up of commmunications' in Allen, J. and Hamnett, C. (eds).

MEEGAN, R. (1995) 'Local worlds' in Allen, J. and Massey, D. (eds) *Geographical Worlds*, Oxford, Oxford University Press/The Open University (Volume 1 in this series).

POTTS, L. (1990) *The World Labour Market: A History of Migration*, London, Zed Brooks.

SASSEN, S. (1988) *The Mobility of Labour and Capital*, Cambridge, Cambridge University Press.

SCOTT, F. D. (1968) 'Migration in the dynamics of history' in Scott, F.D. (ed.) *World Migration in Modern Times*, Englewood Cliffs, NJ, Prentice-Hall, pp. 1-8.

SEGAL, A. (1993) *An Atlas of International Migration*, London, Hans Zell.

SMYTH, W. J. (1992) 'Irish emigration, 1700-1920' in Emmer, P. C. and Mörner, M. (eds) *European Expansion and Migration*, New York, Berg, pp. 49-78.

THOMAS, B. (1954) *Migration and Economic Growth: A Study of Great Britain and the Atlantic Economy*, Cambridge, Cambridge University Press.

TINKER, H. (1974) *A New System of Slavery: The Export of Indian Labour Overseas*, London, Oxford University Press.

Reading A: *Lydia Potts, 'The historical development of the world market for labour power'*

The world market for labour power in its direct form emerged not as a result of present-day migration, but hundreds of years ago. Living labour power has been transferred in large quantities and over long distances since the end of the 15th century.

… The journey … span[s] the enslavement of the Indians that followed the conquest of America, the various forms of forced labour and forced migration in Latin America, Asia and Africa, African slavery, the coolie system used to despatch the people of Asia all over the world, and finally present-day labour migration and the brain drain, the exodus of academics from the developing nations.

Regarded thus, the world market for labour power appears to be a universal structure with a history of several hundred years. In the course of that history every inhabited continent and almost every society on earth has been drawn into the world market – although with differing, even opposing functions. For the original inhabitants of America and Australia, and the residents of Asia and Africa this has meant extermination, abduction, and exploitation. For at least part of the white people's world it has meant material wealth.

The systems under which the workers of the world are transferred across its surface appear, at first sight, very different. Closer inspection reveals that to some extent at least they build on each other and interlink both temporally and geographically, that experience of the one form is used to develop new forms, that time and time again, even in the recent past, humankind has reverted to older, apparently obsolete forms. The history of the world market for labour power – as we understand the term – is, of course, not primarily the story of free wage labour; often the worker concerned was neither 'free', nor paid a wage. Both in the 20th century and before, essentially compulsion and force have shaped its evolution.

Women play an important part in the labour market. Although in terms of labour migration, slavery, and coolie labour they constituted a minority (as a rule around one third), they were no less affected by the structures of the world market for labour power than men: their reproductive function and its control has been the subject of particular attention and has attracted various measures during every stage in the market's development. Women have suffered exploitation not only in the productive process, but also in the reproductive process, and this in the most extreme forms imaginable. Moreover, the women left behind in their country of origin have borne the brunt of often forced emigration in very specific ways.

[…]

The world market for labour power may be roughly divided into two main historical phases. The first encompassed the emergence and development of the world market for labour power under colonialism; the second began with industrialization and resulted in the direct incorporation into the world market of the capitalist metropole …

[…]

Those labour systems characteristic of the first phase of the world market for labour power – Indian slavery and forced labour, African slavery and forced migration, the export of the Chinese and Indians as coolies, and numerous forms of intra-continental forced and migrant labour, i.e. all the systems … by means of which workers from and in the colonies were exploited, in particular by the Europeans – are closely connected. For one thing they were all structural elements of European colonialism, for another those who deployed the labour power recruited under such systems, namely the European colonial rulers, regarded two or more of these systems during any one phase as being in competition with each other. As early as the sixteenth century the profitability of the forcible deployment of Indian labour was being compared to that of the deployment of African slaves. Later the

Caribbean planters debated the relative profitability of the various forms of slave ownership, and in the nineteenth century the costs of the coolie system were compared with those of slavery.

[…]

Between the colonial phase of the world market for labour power and the second phase, which extends into the present day and encompasses the import into the metropole of living labour, there have been a number of developments of a continuous nature. Present-day labour migration and the brain drain, like the slavery and the coolie systems and the fascist system of forced labour, are all methods of importing living labour. The fact that the calculations of profitability used by slave-traders as early as the sixteenth century have been further developed since then and are still common is a clear indication of this. The calculation of profitability for the hire of forced labour from Nazi concentration camps … is just one extreme illustration of the fact that the inhumanity which underlies the slave-traders' calculations is still intensifying.

Ultimately these calculations were forerunners of the markedly economics-orientated, often hugely mathematical cost-benefit analyses that were for a long time commonly used in the study of labour migration.

Competition between labour systems not only exists during the first phase of the world market for labour power, but also in the second. The debate surrounding various forms of labour migration conducted in West Germany primarily in the 1960s, which was characterized by catchwords such as 'rotation' and 'integration', was part of this trend.

Source: Potts, 1990, pp. 6–7, 200, 204, 206

Reading B: *Robert F. Foerster, 'Sicilian emigration: the source'*

In very few countries of the world do the causes of emigration show themselves in such prominence as in the south of Italy. There emigration has been well-nigh expulsion; it has been exodus, in the sense of depopulation; it has been characteristically permanent … The

South is a great laboratory in which emigration may be studied in its largest aspects …

[…]

What are the concrete terms of living in the South? What is the immediate form of things which the emigrant leaves behind him? ...

The setting is well enough known. Sometimes it is a desolate scene, or a pleasantly picturesque one, sometimes a landscape rising to an association of mountain, sky, and sea in a crystal and incomparable beauty. The houses of the contadini are small and simple, placed generally in a town upon an elevation, those of the more wretched day labourers (which rent for as little as 36 lire a year) being on the periphery. One storey is usual. Tuff, stone, brick, mud, and lava are the materials of composition; rarely wood. Washing facilities are meagre, drainage is absent. Oil or petroleum may be burned, but many a family has its evening meal in darkness. The street is the parlour, the resort for gossiping, odes and wooing; it is where the children romp, the women work and the men have their games. On the other hand the house itself, often of only one room, may contain during the night and part of the day, not only the entire family, with a demoralizing collapse of privacy, but the ass, goat, poultry, and other animals, all making assaults upon order and cleanliness; heroic is the rôle of many wives in keeping their households clean. It even happens that several families will occupy one room. When the work-place is far away, the worker may remain in the fields overnight, perhaps throughout the season, resting on the ground, or perhaps on straw, with a straw roof over his head. Worst off is the herdsman, who must sleep lightly. Here and there families live in caves or dens... braving the dampness – true troglodites.

During unemployment, whether of a normal sort or exceptional, hunger or at least privation is not uncommon ... Dry bread, soaked in oil and salt, is the staple diet of many a labourer. Chestnut bread has become rare. In general meat is seldom eaten, or only on grand occasions, or when a sick animal has died. Women and children never or rarely, depending upon the region, taste wine; men may do so on days of hard work.

Physical robustness is not general and is particularly wanting in the lower districts. In stature the men of the southern compartments rank lowest in Italy, and they have poor chests. Undoubtedly inferior physique has made for the frequency of malaria, just as it has been a consequence of malaria. Tracoma, as a filth disease, has prevailed in many sections ...

Life in the South exalts the family. It has been said of Sicily that the family sentiment is perhaps the only deeply rooted altruistic sentiment that prevails. Gallant to his wife, the husband has almost complete power over the members of the family; the wife's affection tends to be slavish ... Nearly a third of Sicilian brides are between the ages of fifteen and twenty ...; the men are generally older than twenty. Four or six children are commonly born, eight or ten sometimes. It is a region where earning capacity demands first of all a strong arm, and where the question of the scattering of a patrimony does not usually arise because there is no important patrimony to scatter. Among the better-to-do, *contadini* children are less numerous.

In this population children have grown to adult life unlettered. Three out of four of the inhabitants six years of age or older, in the first years of the twentieth century, could neither read nor write. It is a situation with few parallels in civilized countries ...

[...]

So grave has been the economic maladjustment which has come to rule in South Italy that one need not long ask why it should prompt to emigration. And yet our account is still incomplete ... [A] further word regarding historical forces is necessary.

For several centuries a blight has lain upon the South. An ancient greatness there was, under the Greeks, a medieval greatness under the Normans; fourteenth-century Frederick made Sicily one of the freest lands of Europe. Under Spaniard and Bourbon, however, the life of the region declined. Neglect, weakness, and oppression in varying degrees characterized the rulers. There was no encouragement of artisanry and bourgeoisie. There was no government which the people could call their own. From the powerful hold of feudalism no relief could come save by external pressure, and such a pressure the Spaniards did not exercise, nor the Bourbon Charles ... When [Bourbonism] gave way to the government of Italy, a stupendous task of reform was in waiting. But the reform came not. The Mezzogiorno was promptly regarded more as a conquered region than as a participating entity in the new government. Its people were too backward to count as equals with those of the North ...

So economic ills remained uncorrected. Institutions were suffered to exist which the world in its progress had sentenced to death. Landed proprietors, who could afford to, kept away from their estates ... Feudal class lines gave way grudgingly. When the investigators of the *Inchiesta Agraria* inquired into the relations subsisting between proprietors and labourers, they found everywhere a servile homage on the part of the peasants, the attitude of the man who appreciates that the gulf between him and another is impassable ...

[...]

...The act of emigration begins as a renunciation of country, a preference for another land's social ladder. It easily 'grows upon itself', because later emigrants find cherished social ties awaiting them in the new country, and because, also, the picture of better things allures more insistently when, through emigrated friends abroad and common rumour at home, it is the oftener presented to the mind.

[...]

With surprising slowness, considering its adjacency to Calabria, Sicily became a land of emigration, and when that happened it was upon terms which suggested an independent impulse. Remoteness of destination was no bar, and Argentina and Brazil were favourite early goals, the United States soon supervening as the goal *par excellence*. It was mainly a permanent emigration, of day labourers, small proprietors, and tenants... The beginnings were in the province of Palermo, substantially distant from the Calabrian shore; the rest of the island was in the early eighties not yet aroused from its age-long lethargy. From Palermo it continued with vigour, so that of all the Sicilian emigrants of the last quarter of the nineteenth century, nearly half came from that province. Next it began in Messina where probably the contagion of Reggio, across two miles of straits, was more potent than that of Palermo. Only with the twentieth century, however, did the great outburst come. Then all provinces were swept into a resistless current. In their ratio to population other South Italian compartments continued to show a stronger movement than Sicily, but nowhere was its growth so prodigiously rapid as in the island. In the year 1906 the astonishing total of 127,000 Sicilian emigrants was reached. In some regions the annual emigration has been five per cent of the population; these are especially the regions of the interior where emigration began late and the past weighed most heavily ...

Source: Foerster, 1969, pp. 49, 94–6, 98–9, 102–4

Reading C: Harvey Warren Zorbaugh, 'Sicilian emigration: the destination'

... Little Hell, or Little Sicily, is a world to itself. Dirty and narrow streets, alleys piled with refuse and alive with dogs and rats, goats hitched to carts, bleak tenements, the smoke of industry hanging in a haze, the market along the curb, foreign names on shops, and foreign faces on the streets, the dissonant cry of the huckster and peddler, the clanging and rattling of railroads and the elevated [railways], the pealing of the bells of the great Catholic churches, the music of marching bands and the crackling of fireworks on feast days, the occasional dull boom of a bomb or the bark of a revolver, the shouts of children at play in the street, a strange staccato speech, the taste of soot, and the smell of gas from the huge 'gas house' by the river, whose belching flames make the skies lurid at night and long ago earned for the district the name Little Hell – on every hand one is met by sights and sounds and smells that are peculiar to this area, that are 'foreign' and of the slum.

Two generations ago this district was an Irish shanty-town called Kilgubbin. A generation ago it was almost equally Irish and Swedish. Then the 'dark people' began to come …

[…]

… Industry was demanding cheap labour. Sicilians came in great numbers, especially in 1903–4, the tremendous Italian immigration year. In this river district of the Near North Side they found cheap living quarters. It was the old story of a competition of standards of living, coloured somewhat by national antagonisms. The Irish and Swedish, more prosperous, moved out of the district and northward. And by 1910 Kilgubbin and Swede Town had become Little Sicily.

Little Sicily this district has remained. It now has a population of about 15,000 Italians of the first and second generations. Save for a few Genoese in the south of the district, this population is almost solidly Sicilian …

[…]

From the various towns of western Sicily they have come, settling down again with their kin and townspeople here, until the colony is a mosaic of Sicilian towns. Larrabee Street is a little Altavilla; the people along Cambridge have come from Alimena and Chiusa Sclafani; the people of Townsend from Bagheria; and the people on Milton from Sambuca-Zabut. The entire colony has been settled in like fashion.

[…]

Because of its isolated situation, due to poor transportation and the barrier of river and industry, Little Hell remained until the war relatively untouched by American custom, a transplantation of Sicilian village life into the heart of a hurrying American city.

"We are contadini." This phrase from the lips of the immigrant Sicilian is most revealing as to his social attitudes. The Chicago Sicilians have come largely from the villages and open country of Sicily, where they were poor, illiterate peasants, held down by the gabelloti or landlords in a state little better than serfdom. Generations of this condition have led them to look upon this status as fixed, and as the horizon of their ambitions. Why should contadini send their children to schools to bother their heads with letters? And besides, in Sicily the boys go to work in the fields at fourteen. Why should they not go to work here? The peasant attitudes and devices that sufficed for the primitive agriculture of Sicily, moreover, are utterly inadequate to adjust the Sicilian to the labouring conditions of the industrial city.*

The spirit of campanilismo, of loyalty to paesani, is another trait of the Sicilian significant for his attempts to adjust to city life. The Sicilian peasants' interests are literally limited by the skyline. His only interests are the local interests of his village. The man from even the adjoining town is a foreigner. The government is a vague something that collects taxes. The spirit of campanilismo, of dwelling under one's own church tower, of jealous loyalty to his … fellow villagers, circumscribes the Sicilian's social, religious, and business life. Social control in the village is largely in terms of gossip; one must not be sparlata – spoken badly of. The old men, too, occupy a respected and influential position in the life of the family and the village.

But the family is the centre of the Sicilian's life and interests. The Sicilian's virtues are domestic virtues. The events of his life centre about the birth, christening, marriage, and death of members of his family. The man is head of the house, and exacts obedience from his wife and children. He even has a say in the affairs of his grown-up sons and grandchildren; it is a custom with force of law that the first child be named for the paternal grandfather or grandmother. The family becomes almost a clan. Even the godfather and godmother are looked upon as blood relations. The interests of the family take precedence over those of the village. Its honour is jealously guarded, and upheld by feuds that endure for generations. Within the family the status of each member is fixed. The women and daughters are carefully protected and much secluded. The young girl is kept in the home until her marriage. The marriage and dowry are arranged by the parents. Grief over a death in the family is genuine and violent. But the funeral must have the proper degree of pomp to maintain the family's status in the community.

[...]

Individually, Sicilians seem to vary as much in their manner and ideals as Americans, but as a group they have certain very marked characteristics: reserve, suspicion, susceptibility to gossip, timidity, and the desire to fa figura. Intense family pride, however, is the outstanding characteristic, and as the family unit not only includes those related by blood, but those related by ritual bonds as well ..., and as intermarriage in the village groups is a common practice, this family pride becomes really a clan pride.

The extent to which family loyalty goes is almost beyond belief; no matter how

disgraced or how disgraceful a member may be, he is never cast off; the unsuccessful are assisted; the selfish are indulged; the erratic patiently borne with. Old age is respected, and babies are objects of adoration. The self-respect of a man can be gauged by the number of his children, and the women seem to accept the yearly bearing of a child as a privilege. Both children and adults seem satisfied with the social opportunities offered within the family itself. The births, baptisms, christenings, betrothals, marriages, and deaths furnish the occasion for ceremonial visits and festivities. Traditional religious forms and superstitions are observed on these occasions, but the church and the priest seem adjuncts rather than the centre of the various rites.

(Helen A. Day, 'Sicilian traits', Document 41)

Source: Zorbaugh, 1929, pp. 159–61, 164–5, 162–3, 166–7

Reading D: *Stephen Castles and Godula Kosack, 'Migration to Western Europe since 1945'*

Since 1945, millions of people have migrated from the underdeveloped parts of Southern Europe, Africa, Asia, and the Americas to Western Europe, in search of employment and better living standards. Nearly all the developed countries of Western Europe have experienced large-scale immigration at the same time. Immigrant workers have become a structural necessity for the economies of the receiving countries.

The causes of the migratory movements which have taken place since 1945 are far too varied and complex to examine adequately here. But we may note certain general features which apply in nearly all cases. It is necessary to differentiate between the 'pull' factors which have attracted migrants to certain Western European countries and the 'push' factors which have caused them to leave their home countries.

The 'pull' factors are a combination of economic, demographic, and social developments in Western Europe during the post-war period. There has been very rapid and almost continuous economic

growth in most countries. Post-war reconstruction rapidly absorbed the returning soldiers and any existing pockets of unemployment. There was soon a marked shortage of labour. At the same time, the demographic situation has been unfavourable to rapid increases in the domestic labour forces. In fact population has tended to grow faster than the labour force, so that there have in several cases been declines in the percentage of the population at work. In other words, each worker has had to support a growing number of inactive persons. There are several reasons for this. One is that with increased life expectancy and falling birth rates, old people form an increasing proportion of the population. In countries which took part in the Second World War, many men were killed or incapacitated, leaving gaps in the active population. Another important factor has been the increasing length of full-time education, which postpones the entry of young people into the labour force ...

An important social factor which has helped to bring about a need for immigrant workers has been one which has not affected the size of the labour force, but rather its structure. In a situation of full employment, indigenous workers have been able to take advantage of opportunities to move into better-paying, more pleasant jobs, usually in the white-collar or skilled sectors. Many workers have been able to obtain vocational training, and young people entering the labour market have had far higher average levels of education than in the past. Few indigenous workers have been willing to remain in unskilled manual jobs, but the often-voiced expectation that such jobs would be swept away by mechanization and automation has not been realized. The result has been an increasing need for labour in areas deserted by indigenous workers. Every period of economic expansion since the war has led to labour shortages, which have been alleviated through the recruitment of immigrant workers. The relationship between labour demand and immigration has been shown by analyses in several countries. Thus the demands of the Western European labour market may be regarded as the dynamic factor which has determined the volume of migratory flows.

The 'push' factors which cause migrants to leave their countries of origin are unemployment, poverty, and underdevelopment. These conditions are more or less constantly present. They form a 'permissive' factor, which leads to migration once the dynamic factor of labour demand elsewhere becomes known ... Immigrants come to Western Europe from highly diverse areas. The clearest distinction is between the Southern European and the non-European countries of origin. But for all the disparities there are important common characteristics. Firstly, the high rates of natural increase in population: Algeria is the extreme case with an increase of 3.4 per cent annually, but other countries are not far behind – Jamaica 3.1 per cent, Pakistan 3.1 per cent, Turkey 2.7 per cent. The Southern European countries have lower rates of increase: Greece 1 per cent annually, Spain 1.2, Portugal 1.1 – but these rates are still higher than those typical for the immigration countries: Switzerland 0.9 per cent, United Kingdom 0.6, Germany 0.6, France 0.6. Secondly, the sending countries all have low levels of per capita income. In 1967 the per capita gross national product at market prices in some emigration countries was as follows: Pakistan US $125, Jamaica US$520, Turkey US$353, Spain US$822, Italy US$1,279. By comparison the per capita GNP in the main immigration countries ranged between US$1,977 (United Kingdom) and US$2,324 (France). Moreover, economic growth rates per capita tended to be slowest in the poorest countries like India, Pakistan, Tunisia, Senegal and fastest in the rich countries of Western Europe. Of course, it is not just the average level of income which is decisive, but rather the inequality of distribution between different regions, between town and country, and between different social classes. For instance Italy has a prosperous and fast-growing industrial economy in the north, but in the south there is a stagnant backward agricultural economy; it is from southern areas like Calabria and Sicily that the overwhelming majority of Italian emigrants come today.

To understand fully the causes of emigration would involve studying the causes of underdevelopment in the contemporary world. The disparity between fast demographic growth and comparatively slow development of the resources available to the population is due on the one hand to the uneven development of the capitalist economy within Europe, and on the other to Europe's imperialist exploitation of the Third World. In both cases the industrial revolution has destroyed traditional systems of production, but has at the same time brought about a population explosion by drastically reducing the death-rate. The result is a surplus of people who cannot find employment in their own countries, and who are faced with a choice between poverty and near starvation at home, or emigration to Western Europe where industry urgently needs labour.

Source: Castles and Kosack, 1985, 2nd edn, pp. 25–8

… The current migration to the US shares a number of general traits with earlier migration phases. But it is also predicated on specific conditions that arise out of the reorganization of the world economy over the last two decades …

… The fact that not all countries became large-scale senders of immigrants points to the need for specifying the manner in which countries are incorporated into this transnational space. A key assumption in much thinking about immigration in the US is that poverty, overpopulation and a stagnant economy are the central causes for emigration. Most countries in the Third World have one or more of these conditions; yet most do not have significant emigration flows. We need to understand whether there are specific kinds of linkages between the US and those countries that do become major senders of immigrants to the US. It may well be that particular forms of incorporation into the internationalization of production coalesce with basic conditions such as poverty or unemployment to promote a migration inducing situation.

[…]

Precisely because these countries [sending migrants to the US] have had large-scale direct foreign investment and considerable growth rates in employment, particularly manufacturing employment, traditional migration push factors seem inadequate to explain the high levels of emigration registered over the last decade and directed to areas with much lower overall growth rates. Apparently there are a number of intervening factors that along with considerable employment growth, transform the situation and promote emigration. While one can understand that the direct displacement of small farmers by commercial agriculture can generate out-migration, this is less clear in the case of labour-intensive manufacturing which creates jobs.

Do these developments induce emigration in the areas where they take place? That is to say, besides conditions inducing emigration among population sectors not affected by such

developments, can we *infer* here the existence of a specific dynamic that facilitates emigration both as an objective process and as a culturally viable option? New and highly labour-intensive export manufacturing conceivably could contribute to solve the unemployment problem, particularly among prime-aged males. Instead, the evidence overwhelmingly shows that it has drawn new segments of the population into the labour force: mostly young women who under conditions of a more gradual industrialization would not so massively have entered the labour force. Large-scale creation of jobs concentrated in a few areas has rapidly and extensively mobilized young women into the labour force. This effect has been further accentuated by high turnover rates due to employment practices in the plants and the mental and physical fatigue associated with these jobs. This results in ongoing recruitment of new cohorts of young women.

The absence of expected outcomes and the creation of new, undesirable outcomes have to be taken into account when examining the employment implications of the development of export industries. First, the large-scale mobilization of young women into wage labour has had a disruptive effect on traditional waged and unwaged work structures. Second, employment in the new industrial zones has brought about a cultural distancing between the women and their communities of origin. Together these two processes pose objective and ideological barriers to these women's return to their family homes and the work they would traditionally perform there for the household or the local market. At the same time, long-term employment in export factories is highly unlikely. All the evidence points to average tenure being around five years. After that, for a number of reasons, women are laid off with little possibility of being employed in another firm, given the preference for women between sixteen and twenty-five years of age. These women, laid off and westernized, have few options. They add to the ranks of the unemployed. The disruption of traditional work structures due to the extremely high levels of young female emigration has further contributed to increase the pool of unemployed. It has stimulated male emigration and the emigration of women who may not have planned on doing so.

Under these conditions, emigration for both women and men may be the only option. At this point the fact of a strong foreign presence becomes crucially significant. The foreign investment presence is concentrated in a few areas and foreign firms also dominate the zones objectively and culturally. Finally, it is the fact that the workers employed in export manufacturing and associated services are applying their labour to goods or services that are geared to foreign countries. Year after year, day after day, these manual and service workers are engaged in activities that meet demand in the US, or West Germany, or Japan. In other words, they make things of use to people and firms in countries with much higher levels of development than their own. One could infer, then, that these workers may feel capable of using their labour power effectively in these developed countries as well.

[...]

The new industrialization in several Asian and Caribbean countries is in good part the other side of what the US experiences as deindustrialization. These shifts are one aspect of the territorial decentralization of economic activity generally. Decentralization and the technical transformation of work have contributed to the development of a new core economic base in highly industrialized countries. This new core consists of highly specialized services, the corporate headquarters complex, and high technology industries, and it promptly evokes images of high-level, specialized jobs. However, this is only part of the actual situation: the new economy has also generated a massive expansion in the supply of low-wage jobs.

For a number of reasons, these new trends are particularly accentuated in major urban centres, which are also the destination of the vast majority of new immigrants. They have intensified the role of major cities as producers and exporters of specialized services and of high-level managerial inputs. The technological transformation of the work process, the shift of manufacturing to less-developed areas domestically and abroad, in part made possible by the technological transformation of the work process, and the ascendance of the financial sector in management, have all contributed to the consolidation of a new kind of economic centre – the global city from where the world economy is managed and serviced ...

The locational concentration of this expanding sector of specialized services and corporate headquarters in major cities has emerged as an important source of low-wage jobs, both directly and indirectly. The direct effect is through the occupational structure of these sectors. The indirect effect is through the ancillary sectors and the consumption structure underlying the lifestyles of the new high-income professional/technical workers.

To this source of low-wage jobs we need to add (a) the ongoing growth of the consumer services sector catering to the population at large and (b) the growth of certain types of manufacturing, notably electronics, and certain forms of reorganized manufacturing, notably the proliferation of sweatshops and industrial homework. For various reasons, large cities tend to facilitate the growth of ancillary services, consumer services generally, and sweatshops. Thus also in these sectors we see a tendency towards locational concentration. The overall outcome is a large supply of low-wage jobs in major cities like New York and Los Angeles.

[...]

The concentration of these activities in major cities and the corresponding internationalization in the economic base of such cities has brought about a pronounced reorganization in the capital–labour relation. The manufacturing sector, once the economic base and key export sector in major cities, no longer shapes the organization of this relation. One indication of this reorganization is the increasing polarization in the occupational and income distribution of the labour force.

The evidence shows a sharp expansion in a stratum of very high-income workers, including as a key component what I call the new cadres in control, management and servicing operations. Secondly, it shows a shrinking of middle-income workers, a function of the expulsion from the production process of a wide range of white and blue-collar middle-income jobs, a function not only of declining sectors – as is often believed – but primarily of growth sectors.

[…]

Several trends that contribute to an additional expansion in the supply of low-wage jobs particularly in global cities, bring about greater income polarization. First, the existence of a critical mass of very high-income workers provides the conditions for a rapidly expanding process of high-income residential and commercial 'gentrification'. This entails not only a physical upgrading, but also a reorganization of the consumption structure, both of which generate a demand for low-wage workers. Many components of high-income gentrification are labour intensive: residential building attendants, workers producing services or goods for speciality and gourmet food shops, dog walkers, errand runners, cleaners of all sorts, and so on. The demand for low-wage workers to service the high-income lifestyles of the rapidly expanding top-level workforce is one key factor in the expansion of an informal sector in cities like New York and Los Angeles. Part of the goods and services produced in the informal sector circulate through the modern sector of the economy that caters to these high-income lifestyles. It would explain why the expansion of an informal sector is most developed in major urban centres experiencing very dynamic growth and not in cities like Detroit.

Second, there has been an expansion of low-wage jobs in the manufacturing sector as a result of (a) the social reorganization of the work process, notably the expansion of sweatshops and industrial homework; (b) the technological transformation of the work process that has downgraded a variety of jobs; and (c) the rapid growth of high-technology industries which are characterized by a large share of low-wage production jobs. These three trends have resulted in what I call a downgraded manufacturing sector. It is important to note that the *downgrading* of the manufacturing sector is part of major *growth* trends: the development of high-tech industries, the technological transformation of the work process (which has also upgraded a large array of jobs), and the growth of an informal sector that contains a large number of sweatshops. Sweatshop work and electronics production are often considered to be two very different if not opposing developments, one representing backwardness and the other modernity. Yet both have a similar outcome: an expansion in the supply of dead-end low-wage jobs …

[…]

The large influx of immigrants from low-wage countries over the last fifteen years which reached massive levels in the second half of the 1970s cannot be understood apart from this restructuring.

Source: Sassen, 1988, pp. 3–4, 115–17, 126, 127, 136, 144–6

Reading F: John Berger and Jean Mohr, 'The migrant's experience'

A Yugoslav: To go home? Of course. As soon as I can. You can see I live out of a suitcase. I buy nothing. What should I do with the things I bought? You can't cart them around from lodging to lodging. It would be different if I was going to stay here, if we were going to settle. But I could never do that. I'd always choose the life at home in my own country. One day it will be better at home than abroad and, when I go back there, I'll be able to work for myself and I'll build myself a house. It'll be a kind of paradise. If only the wages at home were a bit higher and if everyone could find work there, nobody would leave to go abroad.

Most legal migrants are able to return home for about a month every year. The timing of their release usually depends upon the convenience of production. For example most French factories close down during August and so the migrant workers go home. In Switzerland and Germany building and construction work becomes difficult or impossible during the two coldest winter months, and so it is then that the migrant workers are dismissed – with pay for one month only.

[...]

For weeks he has plotted how to smuggle three watches through. Customs officials discriminate against migrant workers in accordance with the international convention that: WHEN THE POOR HAVE MONEY IT POINTS TO A CRIME. It will be the last contest of the year and he believes he has won it already. When he boarded the train, with his suitcase and packages, all that had been taken away from him was returned to him: independence, manhood, private address, voice, proclivity to love, right to age. Nobody handed these things over to him like the confiscated contents of his pockets, but they were returned to him by his destination.

[...]

When he shaves in the train corridor he looks at the face in the mirror critically; for months the face has only looked at him slyly, with complicity. He is returning to himself at last acknowledged. What he has had to hide for eleven months will now be evident to everyone who sees him: that he is not inferior but superior.

He gets off the train in the capital of his province. When he left, its new unfamiliar sights impressed him. Now he looks at it with a kind of familiar astonishment. He knows all the words he hears. If a passer-by, a stranger, stopped him and said: You should be ashamed of yourself! his first reaction would be of delight at being addressed by a stranger in his own language. The glances he receives, however, suggest a very different greeting. Nobody in the large square outside the station knows his name, but everybody knows where he has come from, and their glances, far from speaking of shame, are admiring and envious.

He has changed faster than his country. The economic conditions which formed his decision to leave have not improved; they may have deteriorated.

[...]

According to his calculations, his annual return is a preparation for his final return. None of his experience has ever led him to doubt the power of money in hand. He is nearer to fulfilling his plan.

To be one's own master in the economic as well as the social sense.

To receive all the money which the finished job brings in.

To have a shop.

To run a taxi service.

To start a garage.

To buy better land and cultivate it. To buy a tractor.

To become an independent mason.

Sometimes:

To become a tailor.

To work in an office.

To mend radios.

To buy land and rent it to somebody else to work.

To start a photography business.

To sell goods from the city.

[...]

Near the bus station he finds a car, driven by two compatriots who have come from Zurich. They are going near his village. A beggar asks for money. He gives it.

As they drive off, they light up cigarettes with their lighters from the city. They pass the sentinel of the first animal. Pass Friend.

Along the road are carts and boys holding out small pears to sell.

Sitting back in the car, manufactured in the metropolis where he works, he has become the latest rumour of the city. He is wearing its clothes. He has its shoes on his feet. He has three of its watches keeping perfect time.

The trees are in their place.

From within the rumour, its window rolled down, he watches his village approach. To here, for eleven months, he has sent its money.

His mother frail and tiny in his arms.

For a whole month now the photographs will become redundant.

His uncle, who is still alive, looks at him with a different look. It is hard to know whether this look is out of respect for the honour he has acquired or because his uncle has come closer to death.

For the first time for a year he is recognized as a desirable. For the first time for a year he can afford to be gentle. For the first time for a year he can choose to be silent.

They talk of his final return.

The final return is mythic. It gives meaning to what might otherwise be meaningless. It is larger than life. It is the stuff of longing and prayers. But it is also mythic in the sense that, as imagined, it never happens. There is no final return.

Because the village has scarcely changed since he left, there is still no livelihood there for him. When he carries out one of his plans, he will become the victim of the same economic stagnation which first forced him to leave.

He will join the already swollen and parasitic service sector. The economy of the village or the nearest town is incapable of supporting him. Two or three years after his final return he or other members of his family will be compelled to go abroad once more.

Unchanging as the village is, he will never again see it as he did before he left. He is seen differently and he sees differently.

His prestige as a returned and successful migrant is considerable. (Given this prestige, it would be unseemly for him to take on a menial local job.) The villagers now respect him as a man of different experience. He has seen and received and achieved things which they have not. He is the interpreter, the transmitter, the conveyer of these things to them; the things range from money through commodities to information. They seize upon them to put them to their own use. Gradually he is stripped of what he came back with. Not because his family or the friends of his family are ruthless, but because nothing else is possible. Neither he nor they, whilst remaining in the village, can re-produce any of the things he brought back. His different experience is not applicable to the village as it is. It belongs elsewhere. The village can only use what the time-units of his experience can be exchanged for. He has become a wage earner. They have become the dependants of his wage. Yet he must always accept their judgement. And they cannot allow for his experience of the metropolis. If they knew of them, they would call his deprivations there shameful. The village behaves like a beggared king. If he questions its judgement too openly, not even his newly-won prestige will save him from being condemned as an agitator.

An assured place for him no longer exists in his village.

Such an end can be subsumed under several generalizing categories in order to render it normal: The Road to Development: The Unification of Europe: The History of Capitalism: even The Oncoming Revolutionary Struggle. But the categories do not make him less homeless. In space and time.

Source: Berger and Mohr, 1975, pp. 205, 208, 209, 213–21

The conceptualization of place

Chapter 2

by Doreen Massey

2.1   The question of place

2.1.1   The future of place in the face of globalization

home

The migrants in Chapter 1 remembered with nostalgia the places they had come from and saw them as *home*. The man described by Berger and Mohr (in Reading F) who actually makes his way by train and car back to his village in a province of Yugoslavia finds himself, in fact '... homeless. In space and time'.

place

Very often, when we think of what we mean by a *place*, we picture a settled community, a locality with a distinct character – physical, economic and cultural. It is a vision which has entered the English language in phrases such as 'a sense of place', 'no place like home' and – perhaps most tellingly of all – the notion of things being on occasion 'out of place', meaning that they do not fit in with some pre-given coherence of character. Places are unique, different from each other; they have singular characteristics, their own traditions, local cultures and festivals, accents and uses of language; they perhaps differ from each other in their economic character too: the financial activities of the City of London mould the nature of that part of the capital; the wide-open arable fields of East Anglia give a particular feel that 'it couldn't be anywhere else'.

Yet in the latest era of globalization, of worldwide communications, of time–space compression and convergence, and of major flows of international migration, all this is challenged, thrown into doubt. Migrants arrive and settle, bringing with them different cultures and different connections around the world. The old, settled coherence of 'the locals' may seem to be disrupted. Everywhere seems to become 'a melting-pot'. Regions see their old economic specializations go into decline: their jobs are increasingly in the branch-plants of multinationals whose head offices are perhaps on another continent, and whose activities are scattered over a dozen countries. The goods in the shops come from producers in every continent; the films at the local cinema (and the ones on television) seem always to be from the United States; the restaurants in the town centre provide food from around the globe. Little of this is new but, it is argued (see **Allen and Hamnett, eds, 1995**), the speed of it all – and its intensity – have increased dramatically in recent years.

The question therefore arises: what happens to the notion of place now, in this age of globalization? Do individual places still have their own distinctiveness within 'the global village' and, if so, is this distinctiveness still constructed in the same way as it was before? With the mixing of cultures, the migration of peoples, and the increasing internationalization of economic structures, does the notion of distinct local places make any sense at all? *How can we think about – that is, conceptualize – 'place' in these global times?*

This question, and our responses to it, matter in quite practical, and often political, ways. In Hampstead, London, in 1993 McDonald's finally opened one of their restaurants. This was long after they had opened branches not only throughout Europe and Latin America and elsewhere, but also in Moscow and Beijing. In Hampstead, however, the chain had for years been resisted. There were a number of reasons cited for this resistance, but among them was clearly a sense that this would be an alien importation. Many local residents conducted a vociferous and highly articulate campaign against the siting in their 'village' of what they saw as an icon of a certain type of the brasher sort of Americanism. It just wouldn't fit; it would be completely out of place; it would spoil the character of the area. (However, it did eventually arrive; it did open; but it did so with the compromise of an acceptably genteel frontage.)

In 1993 the British National Party won a seat in elections for the local council in Tower Hamlets on the Isle of Dogs in London's Docklands. Behind this victory – and defeat for the Labour candidate – lay again a long argument about 'the character of the local area'. In this case a crucial issue was housing. This is an area of predominantly public housing and of housing shortage and there had been much argument about whether 'non-locals' were being given priority in allocation over 'locals'. The Liberal Democrat local council had devised a 'sons and daughters' policy whereby the older-established population, many though not all of whom were white, could maintain some intergenerational continuity in where they lived: grandchildren could be brought up near to grandparents, the policy argued. But another effect was to keep out other people, many of them of Bangladeshi background, and who were newer arrivals in the area. The arguments for the local policy drew out, and were reinforced by, racism. And this in turn was bound into arguments about the nature of the place. Much of the popular argument, and especially the rhetoric of the British National Party candidate, revolved around an idea of the 'real' local character of the area, of 'the real local people'; around arguments that the character of areas

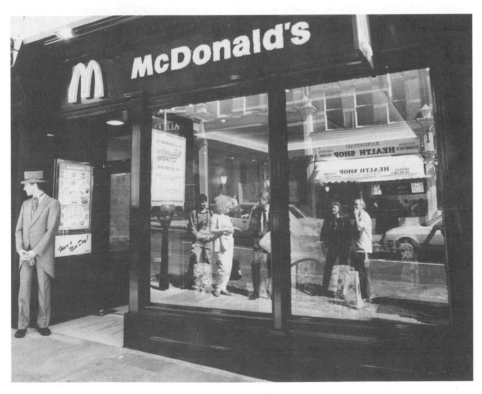

McDonald's in Hampstead, London

should in some way be maintained and given some degree of continuity; and around an assumption – often implicit, sometimes explicit – that local people had more rights in and to the place than did newcomers.

The way in which we define 'places', and the particular character of individual places, can be important in issues varying from battles over development and conservation to questions of which social groups have rights to live where. As I write this chapter (in mid 1994) the media are full of news of the break-up of Yugoslavia and battles over the designation of parcels of land as 'Serb' and 'Croat', or as 'Bosnian Muslim'. And in South Africa, as that society struggles to emerge from apartheid, an Afrikaaner group is claiming a piece of the territory for its own – ethnically defined – region. Moreover, in an era of globalization, when the challenges mount to what is often seen as the old settled coherence of place, these issues become more urgent. The paradox is, of course, that – if these arguments are valid – people are searching after, and trying to establish, such an interpretation of place at the very time when the fact of increasing, and increasingly stretched, spatial flows makes any such notion much more difficult to maintain.

Thus, David Harvey (1989), in his major study of the increasing globalization and time–space compression of the present era, has argued that not only does the growing mobility and internationalization of these times make our old notions of places as settled, coherent communities more difficult to sustain but the very fact of heightened spatial mobility, and the feeling – which he sees as a product of it – that we live in an increasingly unstable and uncertain world, also makes us *need* even more strongly that notion of place as secure and stable. 'A place called home' can, then, be a blessed haven of retreat from an uncontrollable world. This need for a settled place which carries with it a feeling of continuity and coherence may, he argues, be part of what lies behind the recent resurgence of exclusivist nationalisms (for instance in Eastern Europe and the old Soviet Union), regionalisms and localisms. The same kind of argument can also be drawn upon at a more individual level, touching upon the need for settledness and coherence that people might feel in their personal lives. The retreat at night to the fantasy of an 'olde worlde' English country village after a day of international 'phone-calls and faxes in the office of a multinational enterprise can be interpreted in the same light. Or again, Kevin Robins (1991a) has written of the increasingly popular 'heritage centres' that 'the driving imperative is to salvage centred, bounded and coherent identities – placed identities for placeless times' (p. 41). In this sense, we actively *make* places, both in imagination (the 'olde worlde' village) and in material practice (perhaps by keeping out things and people whom we argue do not belong).

Activity 1 Turn now to Reading A which is a short extract from David Harvey's *The Condition of Postmodernity* in which he addresses some of these issues.

Harvey is focusing quite specifically on the globalization of capitalist economic relations, and he points to the kind of reactions which, he argues, it tends to provoke. Important here is the defensive reaction of the assertion of place-bound identity. In other words, since people are relatively immobile in comparison with the global fluidity of capital, they are in various ways pressured to defend their local communities. This immediately links us to two points which have already been established in this volume (and in earlier volumes of this series). First, that globalization is unequal – in this case capital is, in general, far more mobile than labour. But second, as Chapter 1 pointed out, this inequality is in part produced by rules and regulations: while 'free trade' and free movement of capital are frequently applauded, the barriers to migration are formidable. Moreover, people may simply *wish* to stay where they are. As Berger and Mohr's migrant worker reflected, 'If only the wages at home were a bit higher and if everyone could find work there, nobody would leave to go abroad.' For all these reasons, then, people may be more committed to particular local places than is industry. Yet, argues Harvey, this relative place-boundedness leaves working-class communities, for instance, having to construct 'place-bound' identities, and this in turn can have serious dangers. It can divide people in different localities from each other, by obscuring connections which might otherwise unite them. It forces people into uniting around a notion of tradition, as a unifying place-related theme. Yet such 'traditions' are often themselves hard to grasp in an increasingly globalized world, and may be reduced to the 'commodified', 'pastiche', 'often romanticized' and 'partially illusory' presentations of, for instance, the heritage industry. Worse, and bringing his two criticisms together, they can result in jingoistic forms of localism and nationalism.

Building walls and place: identities in the face of time–space compression

Activity 2   What 'defences' have been noted so far that people may build against the threat to place of time–space compression?

The present chapter, and the remaining ones in this book, will be exploring different aspects of this problem and how we might approach it. The main focus of the present chapter is on the challenge which, it is argued, has been posed to our idea of place by the facts of globalization and time–space compression. Anthony Giddens, a sociologist who is particularly aware of geographical issues, has written of places as specific, familiar and enclosed, and has argued that 'in pre-modern societies, space and place largely coincided, since the spatial dimensions of social life were, for most of the population, dominated by "presence" – by localized activity' (1990, p. 18). Such a description might be seen to apply to what Chapter 1 called 'the spirit of *campanilismo'* where 'the Sicilian peasants' interests are literally limited by the skyline'. However, argues Giddens, 'modernity increasingly tears space away from place by fostering relations between "absent" others, locationally distant from any given situation of face-to-face interaction' (op. cit.).

The most general question at issue for us here, then, is whether and how we can continue to work with a notion of place in these internationalized times.

2.1.2   Refining the question

However, before we begin to try to answer this question directly, let us explore a little further its form and its implications. One thing which is made immediately clear by the very formulation of this question is that our notions of place, and the meanings which the term carries, can vary. In this book part of what we are exploring is what might be a more adequate understanding of place *for these times*. Implicit in the question, therefore, is that – unless we have lost any sense of place altogether (a possibility which some might argue and which must be held open) – our understanding of place may vary over time. It will vary in part because the world itself is changing and it will also vary because of shifts in the way in which different groups in society think about place – how the idea of place is *represented*. What is at issue, then, is another aspect of how we both construct and imagine the world.

Our views of place, in other words, are products of the society in which we live, and to that extent the future of those views, even if constrained by circumstances, is in our hands. Should we build a future world in which distinct groups of people, however defined (by ethnicity – the South African case; by culture and political affiliation – as in the Nationalist/Loyalist divisions within Belfast; or by social class – as with the sharp divisions within our major cities), protect exclusive rights to control who should live in a particular place and what should be – because, they say, it always has been – the cultural character of the area? Or should we imagine a future of endless mixing, of peoples, of cultures, of economic activities; a future in which – it might be argued – places would entirely lose their individuality, absolutely everywhere would have a burger restaurant, and there would be no point in travelling since you could get it all quite easily within a few miles of 'home' (only differences in natural features might remain). Or are there different approaches to the problem altogether?

The fact that our currently dominant ideas of places are socially constructed can be emphasized by looking at groups whose idea of place is different. In a minor way, we could think of peoples who do not equate place with any idea of settledness, or of home – the many groups of nomadic peoples which there have been, and which still to some extent exist today, or Romanies, or even today's phenomenon of 'new-age travellers'. The very different, spatially mobile, cultures of such groups does not mean they have no sense of place, but it does mean that this sense is not so intimately related to settledness, to enclosure, or to home, as is the one which is currently so prevalent in the western world. What is interesting and important to note is just how disturbing such mobility, such apparent lack of attachment to a single place, can be both to state authorities which prefer to be able to keep tabs more easily on people's whereabouts, and to other people's sense of what is 'right and proper' – such wandering is a challenge, perhaps, to their own priorities of settledness and establishment. In the seventeenth century in Britain there were strict laws against vagrancy, and a very definite attempt by government to get people to 'settle down'.

But there are also far greater differences between cultures in the notion of place and the relation of that idea to cultural identity. The aboriginal peoples of Australia, for example, have a notion of their geographical place in the scheme of things which, while it is not defined in terms of their *ownership* of territory, is very clearly concerned with the mutual identification of a particular piece of land and its people. Here the notion of *home-place* is utterly tied to particular rocks and paths and dunes and mountains: the attachment is to the natural features of the area; the people belong to and are defined by them. The same is true in many pre-Columbian cultures in North America.

home-place

Here, then, there *is* a sense of the absoluteness of place, of 'time immemorial' and of a mutual belongingness between a place and a people, but it is tied to the natural–physical environment. In the case of Australian aborigines, their very myths of creation are tied to the stories woven from and around the natural features of the land. Recent legislative changes in Australia have begun to recognize these culturally specific claims to particular areas as having validity, and new laws have been drawn up that define greater rights for Aboriginal peoples in these designated areas and that lay down procedures and conditions for the actions of certain categories of 'non-locals', such as mining companies.

These, then, are very different conceptualizations of the relation between a place and its people, between a local area and a local culture, of the sources of the specificity of place.

The question we are addressing in this chapter is not primarily concerned with these views of place, although it does relate to them. Primarily it is concerned with the disruptions to the notion of place which have occurred in recent years in many countries of the first world as a result of increasing globalization and time–space compression. It is, therefore, a *culturally specific* enquiry.

It is also culturally specific in another sense which allows us to push further our exploration of the precise terms of the question at issue. All the authors who have been cited so far – Harvey, Robins and Giddens – point out very clearly that the question of the construction and the meaning of place arises for us now because of particular developments. They refer to the greater spatial extent of social relations, time–space compression, globalization and so forth. Most particularly they refer to the feeling of a local culture's being 'invaded'. Such a feeling may result from the in-migration of peoples who have their roots elsewhere, it may be because of the take-over of the 'local' economy by 'foreign' interests, or it may simply be the arrival on the High Street of cultural imports (from banks to restaurants) from around the world. Kevin Robins has articulated this feeling most clearly; thus he has written:

Globalization, as it dissolves the barriers of distance, makes the encounter of colonial centre and colonized periphery immediate and intense.

(1991a, p. 25)

and

Whereas Europe once addressed African and Asian cultures across vast distances, now that 'Other' has installed itself within the very heart of the western metropolis. Through a kind of reverse invasion, the periphery has infiltrated the colonial core. The protective filters of time and space have disappeared, and the encounter with the 'alien' and 'exotic' is now instantaneous and immediate. The western city has become a crucible in which world cultures are brought into direct contact ... Time and distance no longer mediate the encounter with 'other' cultures.

(Robins, 1991a, pp. 32–3)

Now, clearly there have been other 'invasions' too, for instance by companies from other parts of the first world, but let us stay for a moment with the particular point that Robins is making. Part of what is at issue, he argues, and what – it is hypothesized – may have triggered this concern with the identity of place is what has been referred to, in general terms, as the arrival of the margins at the centre (see **Allen and Hamnett, 1995**).

And it is indeed social scientists at 'the centre' who have been primarily responsible for raising the question. It is important for us, therefore, at least briefly to ask how this question sounds when posed in other parts of the world.

Activity 3 Look again at those last quotations from Robins, but this time as you read them think of them from the point of view of, say, the indigenous peoples of Latin America, black people living in South Africa, or people in areas anywhere that have been subject to external colonialism and/or imperialism.

From this perspective, how new is the encounter between centre and margins? How new is the shrinking of distance, and the invasion of place?

Don't read on until you have thought about this seriously.

From the point of view of the colonized periphery, the encounter between it and 'the centre' has for centuries been 'immediate and intense', as missionaries, settlers, companies and administrative officials arrived and quite deliberately changed the local culture. To those living in the periphery at that period it cannot at all have seemed that Europe was addressing it only 'across vast distances'. The centre was installed, to reverse the phrasing in the quotations, at the heart of the periphery. There were no 'protective filters of time and space' for the indigenous societies of the periphery as the 'alien' forces of the centre imposed their presence. 'Time and distance', even then, in these parts of the world, were 'no longer' able to 'mediate the encounter with "other" cultures.'

In other words, although the feeling of being invaded – whether by US and Japanese multinationals, by the products of the world, or by people from the so-called 'margins' – is today a new and important phenomenon in many countries (for instance, in the first world), it is a feeling which has been known for centuries in many parts of the globe.

This is by no means to invalidate the question. What it means is simply that the issue which faces us in this chapter is one quite specific in its significance to particular times and places. (It does also raise important issues about our role as social scientists in the first world, and how all too frequently the questions which first world social scientists think are significant – and which give rise to new theories – are exported to intellectuals in other countries as the burning issues and new paradigms of our day, when in fact the questions which might be more significant to those countries' experience, and indeed relevant to ours, and from which other theoretical avenues might be opened, are quite different.)

We have, then, clarified our question in two ways: it is a question about problems raised for an interpretation of place, which is culturally produced and culturally specific, by developments – such as globalization and time–space compression – which are currently having a particular impact in a number of countries of the first world, perhaps particularly those of Europe, Canada and the USA. These clarifications matter: being absolutely clear about the question you are asking is just about as important as the way you answer it.

Summary of section 2.1

o   Processes such as time–space compression/convergence pose issues about the nature of place.

o   These issues concern both how places are changing materially as a result of these processes and how we represent to ourselves what a place is.

o   Such questions are being raised now in the first world. In that way, they are particular to these times and to certain parts of the world: they are historically and culturally specific.

o   In that context, can we continue to conceive of places as settled and coherent, or must we re-imagine them in ways which take account of their changing nature?

2.2   Space and place: the global in the local

2.2.1   Space and place

The relation between space and place is at the heart of what we are examining here. What both Robins and Giddens are arguing is that, by the late twentieth century, *spatial* movement, interaction, influence and communication have become so extended, so fast, and so available, that the borderlands and boundaries which once used to define *places* as distinct and in some degree separate from each other are so often crossed that the notion of place which was previously viable has to be re-thought. That is, they are positing a previous notion of 'places' as different, separable, probably bounded, areas within a wider whole called 'space' and where those places historically developed in some important degree separately from each other. The changing social organization of *space* has, it is argued, disrupted our existing forms of, and concepts of, *place*.

Thus Manuel Castells, a leading theorist of the city and of urban form, has written of the emergence of what he calls 'the informational city' and has argued that what we are witnessing is 'the historical emergence of the space of flows, superseding the meaning of the space of places' (1989, p. 348) and

The fundamental fact is that social meaning evaporates from places, and therefore from society, and becomes diluted and diffused in the reconstructed logic of a space of flows whose profile, origin, and ultimate purposes are unknown.

(p. 349)

(By a 'space of flows' Castells is getting at something like the approach in **Allen and Hamnett (eds, 1995)** of thinking of social space as a complexity of social relations stretched out and meeting and intersecting with each other.) Cultural theorist Peter Emberley has written that,

... the possibility of space being invested with human meaning, such that it could be interpreted as 'place', has evaporated.

(1989, p. 754)

David Harvey, analysing the spatial flexibility of multinational corporations, talks of 'a world that capital treats as more and more place-less' (1989, p. 14). And, finally, Kevin Robins comments:

With these developments the holding tension between settlement and movement is broken apart. We have the 'disarticulation of place-based societies'.

(1991b, p. 13)

In **Allen and Hamnett (eds, 1995)** the notion was introduced of social space as being formed out of 'stretched out' social relations. That is, social space consists of all the networks and complexities of social interaction and interconnection, whether these be very small-scale or global in their reach. The argument being made by the authors we have just cited is that, in these times, social relations have become *so* stretched out and interconnected that it is difficult any more to distinguish within social *space* any coherent areas which might be called *places*. But that, of course, implies that we continue to think of places – to represent them – in that way. (The reading from Harvey, for instance, asserts that 'any place-bound identity has to rest at some point on the motivational power of tradition'.) If we think of space as stretched-out social relations, then perhaps we also need to re-think our idea of places – to question our representation of them as coherent, bounded and settled.

activity space   One way of approaching this systematically is to think in terms of the *activity spaces* of different phenomena. The activity space of something is the spatial network of links and activities, of spatial connections and of locations, within which a particular agent operates. Thus the activity space of a small firm might be just its single plant and its set of links to suppliers or customers; it might well be all contained within, say, a single region. The activity space of a multinational company would be vastly different. Not only would its tentacles spread out around the world linking branch-plants and marketing offices, research and development labs and design studios, but there would also be a *geography of power* within it. In the simplest of cases, the power of ownership and of strategic decision-making might radiate outwards from head office. The effects of decisions taken, say, in some world city would be felt in the daily lives of people working in a free-trade zone in South East Asia. The idea of activity spaces is not a precise theoretical concept: there are no rules about where to draw the cut-off point around a company's activities or influence, for instance. Rather it is a 'heuristic device' (a useful tool) to help us into a particular way of thinking about the spatial organization of society. Taken in that general way, all agents in society have activity spaces, and they come in highly varied shapes and sizes. The 'local' cinema, for instance, may on its customer side have quite a restricted reach. But on its film-industry side it may be linked into organizations which are thoroughly internationalized: through the chain of distributors of which it may be part, through the links from there into the film-producing industry itself. The 'local Roxy' may thus be a significant link between a place and the wider world. How that link functions, and how it is interpreted, may be the subject of contestation: is it a window on the world letting a breath of fresh air into local parochialism, a connection to people and places which might otherwise remain unknown? Or is it the purveyor of unwanted intrusions into a (supposedly) locally grown culture, bringing nothing but endless Rambos and Kung Fu?

geography of power

Each of us, as individuals, also has our own activity space. You could think of your own and then compare it with that of other people. The basic shape is probably a set of fairly local paths and places as normal daily life is lived between home, school, work, church and club, with occasional trips further afield to a neighbouring town, or to a hospital maybe. This pattern may in turn be punctuated by forays much further afield – to friends or relatives for a visit, for weekend excursions, or to follow your team to an away match. Maybe once a year there is a dramatic break-out for the annual holiday. The detail is not important; what matters is the basic range and shape. For not only does the idea of activity spaces give access to thinking about the spatial organization of society, it also points to a little recognized aspect of social inequality.

Activity 4 Try your hand at comparing, in a rough and ready way, some contrasting activity spaces. Select two from the following:

o   a social centre or school which you know

o   a (relatively rich) inhabitant of Hampstead village

o   the local garage

o   Janu, at the Niceview Lodge in the Annapurna District of Nepal (see **Cater, 1995**, section 5.4.1)

o   the Misquito Indians of the Honduran coast (**Massey, 1995**; also Chapter 4 in this volume).

Activity spaces always tend to be more complex – and to stretch further – than you think. And you can often 'push' them further by continuing to pursue connections beyond the most immediate and obvious ones. So give yourself a few minutes on each of the ones you choose in order to explore them a bit.

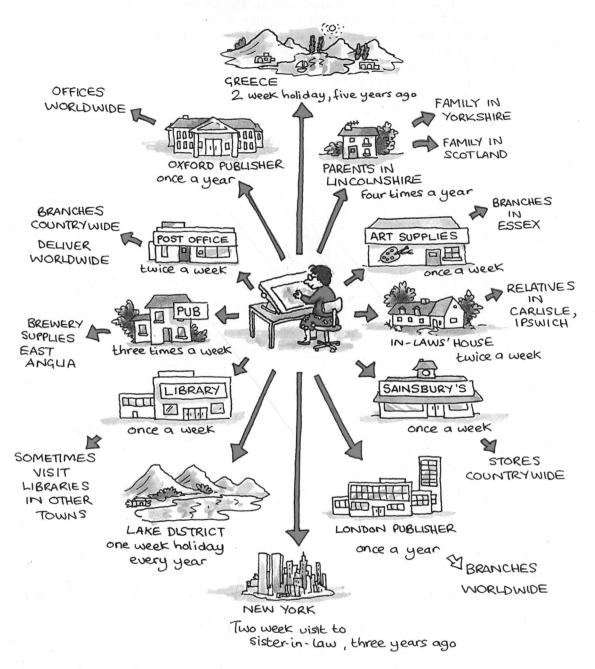

The cartoonist's immediate activity space

The argument of the theorists whose work we have been examining is that the present era (usually seen as beginning in the second half of this century) is witness to two major changes in the nature of activity spaces. *Firstly*, they are in general increasing in their spatial reach. *Secondly*, they are increasing also in their complexity and in the complexity of the linkages between them. Let us take each of these, briefly, in turn.

The evidence for the increasing spatial reach of activity spaces is considerable. **Leyshon (1995)** has analysed the globalization of the finance sector and **Allen (1995)** the international organization of production in the hands of multinational companies. The same argument could be made about the media and about culture, as cable television increases in importance in comparison with national, as international exhibitions tour the world, and as so-called world music grows in popularity. As **Cater (1995)** points out, the phenomenon of tourism is also experiencing this constant stretching of the distances which it covers, its boundaries being pushed ever outwards. And in the environmental field the increasing spatial spread both of problems and of the organizations to tackle them have been analysed by **Yearley (1995)** and **Sarre (1995)**. As all these authors have emphasized, the situation is not a simple one of uniform globalization. There is some movement in opposite directions: some lives are becoming more spatially circumscribed. Some would argue that in many ways the inequalities between groups in terms of spatial access and spatial mobility are increasing. Nor are the phenomena of globalization and its associated effects entirely new. Yet the bulk of the evidence would seem to support the thesis of increasing time–space compression, of growing time–space distanciation: that is, a general expansion of activity spaces. The social relations which form social space are becoming increasingly 'stretched out'.

'First world' lifestyle

There is also considerable evidence for growing complexity. This occurs both within individual activity spaces as they grow in size and in the variety and multiplicity of types of spaces. It also occurs in the complexity of the links between them. The local company may be confined to a single region in its suppliers and customers (although that in itself, of course, becomes less and less likely), but those suppliers and customers may themselves be locked into systems of economic linkages which have a far greater spatial spread. We as individuals today live lives which are linked into far more complex and multifaceted systems than used to be the case. As two social theorists have put it, 'each of us operates in a universe of disparate, fragmented and discontinuous spatial references, between which there is no necessary coherence and unity' (Bonetti and Simon, 1987, p. 55).

Activity 5 Think about your own life, and the geographies which go into sustaining it:

o the geography of production of your consumer durables, clothes, food

o the spatial links of your place of paid work if you have a job

o the cultural background of your friends and associates, and of the children at the local school

o the geographical source of the material on your television or radio, and the music that you listen to

o the spatial reach of any religious or other organizations to which you belong

o the geographical spread of your bank and/or building society

o other aspects you can think of.

You are linked into all these activity spaces. Your daily life makes these worldwide connections. Imagining this for all the people and activities in any given place – whether small village, major city or a nation – gives some idea of the spatial complexity and interconnections of the lives we lead today.

What these two developments (increasing reach and increasing complexity) mean for 'places', then, is firstly that their boundaries are far more open than they have been in the past and, secondly, that the complexity of interconnections which link places together, and thus which meet in any one of them, has increased dramatically.

identity Now, one possible response to these developments is to abandon the notion altogether of the uniqueness of place, and particularly of place as a source of *identity*. This would seem to be Manuel Castells' position in the quotation cited at the beginning of this section – 'social meaning evaporates from places, and therefore from society, and becomes diluted and diffused in the reconstructed logic of a space of flows ...' (1989, p. 349). But another approach is to re-think that notion, *to re-think the relationship between space and place.* This is what is being attempted in the notion of 'a global sense of place' (Massey, 1991) and when Kevin Robins reflects on an ideal which would be 'to match community and security with the kind of openness that can stimulate a positive sense of challenge and contestation' (1991b, p. 17). What is proposed by these authors (and by others whom we shall meet at the end of this chapter) is a questioning of the notion of places simply as settled, enclosed and internally coherent (representing 'community and security' in the quotation from Robins) and its replacement or supplementation by a concept of place as a meeting-place, the location of the intersections of particular bundles of activity spaces, of connections and interrelations, of influences and movements.

Contrasting place as security with place as a meeting-place

2.2.2 The openness of places

Let us explore this idea further by using recent research carried out at The Open University and which involved looking at some small villages set in the countryside around the city of Cambridge. What became clear as we examined these villages was the enormous complexity and variety of the activity spaces which intersect with each other even in such tiny places as these.

In these small villages there are considerable contrasts in the spatiality of different lives and different economic activities. There are high-tech scientists, mainly men, whose work is based in Cambridge, though they often have computers with modem links at home as well. The companies they work for operate in a highly internationalized part of the economy, and these employees spend their time in constant contact with, and physically travelling between, colleagues and customers all around the world. Their activity spaces, and those of the companies where they work, are thoroughly multinational. At the other extreme are people who have never been to London and only rarely have made it as far as Cambridge. When they have done so, it is usually in order to go to the shops or maybe to the hospital. These are the people who would probably call themselves 'locals', and are certainly so termed by the new arrivals. They work locally – some on the farms, some in the village shops and services. On the whole they are older, they have known one another for years, they – certainly the men – gather most evenings in a particular pub. They are based, rooted, in this area in a way the high-tech scientists are not.

There are other groups, too, in a sense in-between these two in terms of their immediate, personal spatiality. There are people who work more or less locally – in the village or nearby or in Cambridge – maybe as cleaners or caterers, but for firms which are multinational; for such firms this is just one group of workers among many scattered over the globe. There are women who are the partners of the high-tech men, some of them presently at home with small children, occupied in a daily round of nurseries and child-minders, often being the heart and soul of local meetings and charities. For shopping, they are more likely to drive into Cambridge than are some of 'the locals'; for holidays they may fly off to somewhere exotic; and they may have family in other parts of the country, whom they visit regularly and who visit them.

Let us stop this description here, and pull out some more general thoughts from this specific example.

(a) Perhaps the most evident point is the considerable variety of activity spaces which meet here, even in a small village in a relatively rural part of the country. There are clear differences, some of which may be interpreted as inequalities, between different groups of people. In the case briefly outlined here the sharpest contrasts would seem to be along lines of class, age and gender.

(b) It should be emphasized though that, in spite of the descriptions above, few people's lives, even their daily lives, can be described as simply local. Even the most 'local' of the local people here have their lives touched by wider events, are linked into a broader geographical field. The farms where they work may be affected by European legislation passed in Brussels; as they talk in the pub or do the dusting, their thoughts may travel to children who have left the village, who now live in a city somewhere and who may sometimes come home to stay. It is probably true to say that nobody in the first world these days lives their daily lives completely locally, entirely untouched by events elsewhere, by time–space compression and globalization. This does not mean that the importance of place has necessarily declined. But it does mean that each person, or each group of people, is placed very differently in relation to the phenomena of globalization.

(c) These very different lives, with their contrasting activity spaces, touch each other. They intersect and sometimes interact. Some of the cleaners and caterers work in the companies where the high-tech scientists are based. House prices are affected by the in-migration of new people, and thus indirectly by the high-technology economic growth in Cambridge. Issues – and conflicts – may arise in the village *because* of the juxtapositions; new social processes, in other words, may be set in motion. There may be ironies here. The high-tech scientists, whose lives are so international, may be seeking in the village a rural 'retreat' (the word is precisely chosen), peace and quiet, the whole image of a local village life as 'home', as a place to go back to after the rush and bustle of the day, that was referred to in section 2.1.1. Yet, of course, it may be that their arrival has itself disrupted what in their mind's eye they were seeking: the settled localness of the place.

(d) These contrasts mean also that different groups have very different views of the place, very different senses of its identity. And they have, too, very different ways of participating in, using and contributing to the place. This is an issue – this notion of a sense of place and its identity – which will be taken up centrally in the next chapter.

(e) Moreover, if we link all these local insights back into our wider discussion of space and place, then even more general conclusions can be drawn. For if we think of space as social relations stretched out then a place – this Cambridgeshire village or any other place – may be seen as the location of particular sets of intersecting social relations, intersecting activity spaces, both local ones and those that stretch more widely, even internationally. And every place is, in this way, a unique mixture of the relations which configure social space.

(f) Finally, thinking of space and of places in that way makes it very difficult to see places as naturally bounded. Drawing boundaries in space is always a social act.

This way of thinking about places has been discussed in **Hamnett (1995)**, where major cities such as London, Tokyo and New York were described as 'sites at which many lines of global interconnection meet and intersect'. Any place, of any size, could be examined in this way. Liverpool has seen a succession of interconnections over time, from the links of the 'triangular trade' in the eighteenth century, through all its interconnections as a port city, through that other triangular connection with Ireland and the USA from the nineteenth century, and so on (**Meegan, 1995**). And, as each new set of links is established, so new elements are added to the character of the place (in the case of Liverpool from profits of trade, to street names, to music), mixing with and in turn being moulded by, the place's existing features.

International connections and the 'openness' of places is thus not a new phenomenon, just as globalization itself is not; what is argued in the thesis of time–space compression is that we are in a qualitatively new and dramatically intensified phase.

2.2.3 Inside places

There are, moreover, two further steps in the argument which it is important to take at this point. Both of them concern what happens, in a sense, 'within places'. For to say that we can view places as the locus of intersecting social relations/activity spaces is only to set the stage, establish the framework, for the effect which this intersection can have.

First of all, the wider connections influence the very character of the place itself. In some cases this is plainly evident. The character of Liverpool – or any other major port city – is clearly based on connections with the world beyond. From the international trade in which the profits were made to finance the municipal architecture and the displays of private wealth, to the names of roads and the accents on the streets, the fact of this place being, and having been for a long time, a meeting-place, cannot be missed. But the same is true in less obvious ways and less obvious places. In England the areas of semi-countryside stretching around the capital city are referred to as 'the Home Counties'. The name is significant: this is the area from which so much of the imagery of Englishness is taken. It is an area in which the middle and upper classes have been, at least historically, relatively wealthy. It is a countryside dotted with small (and larger) stately homes and genteel country mansions. Yet when one comes to ask on what is all this established security built, in those villages and that countryside so redolent precisely of that older sense of place as community, security and enclosure, the picture changes. For probably one of the most important sources of income for these social strata historically has been 'rentier income' – earnings derived in one way or another from investments, a very large proportion of which have been either directly or indirectly derived from abroad, and certainly from beyond the south and east of England, beyond the Home Counties. Thus Edward Said (1992) points out how the material comfort of Mansfield Park, in Jane Austen's famous novel, rests in no small measure on the return from investments made in a slave plantation in Antigua. The very character of the area, *the very possibility of its being as it is*, rests on relations with a place on the other side of the world.

The second point is that, if we do think of places as 'meeting-places', then out of the very fact of these encounters new effects will emerge. This has already been suggested in the example of the Cambridgeshire village. As was argued there, each place is the focus for its own particular mix of activity spaces, of social relations, and of social groups. And out of each unique mixture new processes will arise. These may take an antagonistic form: the in-migration of new groups may be met with racism or lead to inter-group conflict, the new development may spark a campaign against it. Or it may lead, more harmoniously, to yet another influence being added to the long history of influences which goes to make up the particularity of any given place. Either way, these new processes and interactions are yet a further contribution to the uniqueness of each individual place.

The heart of England: what made this landscape possible?

Summary of section 2.2

o   An activity space is the spatial form of the links and activities, connections and locations, within which a particular agent operates. The activity spaces of different social groups/agents vary greatly.

o   The consensus is that, in recent decades, activity spaces (or, more generally, the spatial reach of social relations) have been both extending spatially and increasing in complexity.

o   Thinking in terms of (a) space as social relations and (b) activity spaces enables places to be imagined as the location of particular sets and intersections of such places and relations.

2.3   More reflections on the question

In section 2.1.2 the argument was made that the current urge to think anew about place has been provoked, at least in part, by material changes that are occurring in the world, especially time–space compression, globalization in its various forms, and so forth. This, it was pointed out, means that this is a question quite specific in its resonance to particular periods of history and particular geographical areas. It was also pointed out that the question is culturally specific in the sense that the understanding of place which currently seems under challenge is in fact only one among many that are possible – indeed that is why we can seek to ask if it is now necessary to change it.

Both of these arguments imply that the critique of the existing dominant notion of place – as a secure haven, as culturally relatively coherent, as bounded – is one which arises as a result of the changes going on in the world around us.

At the same time, however, some writers have questioned the notion of place even more fundamentally. What they have raised is the issue of whether the old notion of place is not just inappropriate to deal with these new times but was always inappropriate. Before we go on, then, let us examine some of these more fundamental critiques, for they raise some fascinating issues. We shall concentrate on two types of critique: empirical and theoretical.

2.3.1   Empirical critique

In the argument of this chapter so far, we have been implicitly accepting that, while current global changes put the meaning of place on the agenda today, 'in the past' it was perfectly correct to think of places – to represent them – as essentially separate and, relatively speaking, autonomous from each other. Yet is this so?

This point may well have struck you when reading of Liverpool in section 2.2.2. What this stressed was that the 'openness' of Liverpool as a place is by no means new. What has changed is the *nature and geography* of its interconnections with the world beyond it, but not the *fact* of those interconnections. As the theorists of time–space compression and globalization point out, it is not that interconnection is a new phenomenon, but that what we are currently experiencing is its *intensification*.

What that points to is the fact that while places may be more open now, less bounded than they were, and more interconnected, this too is not a new phenomenon. Maybe those notions of a coherent settled place were always inaccurate; maybe more attention should always have been paid to their openness and interconnectedness.

One reply, of course, is that this example concerns a city and moreover a port. And such 'places' have always been more historically open and hybrid than elsewhere. Maybe they were just 'ahead of their times'. In one sense this is true. But what, then, of the example of Mansfield Park, discussed in section 2.2.3? Jane Austen's setting is not a major metropolis; far from it: it is a single house, set apart within its grounds, in a settled part of rural England. Yet from this spot, even some two centuries ago, ran lines of connection not only to the watering places and society towns where the denizens of these places went for 'seasons', but also across the Atlantic to the Caribbean, to Africa, and to the sugar trade and processing in the great ports such as London and Liverpool. Or think of the Cambridgeshire village. Quite apart from its more recent history, integrated in to a rich agricultural trade, it stands in an area which in its ancient past has been invaded by Celts and Belgae, which was part of a Roman Empire which stretched from Hadrian's Wall to Carthage, from (what was to become) Portugal to Asia. The village church itself links this quiet place into a religion which had its birth in the Middle East, and arrived here via Rome.

The point is not that the pace and intensity of interconnection have not increased– for they certainly have – but that such interconnections are not new. This means that *in principle* the conception of places as bounded and undisturbed is incorrect. The identities of places which people campaign to defend are themselves the product, in part, of a long history of connections with the beyond, with other places.

2.3.2   Theoretical critique

There have also been more theoretical critiques of the idea of places as stable, settled and bounded. Above all, it has been feminists who have raised these questions (Rose, 1993; Massey, 1994). For, it can be argued, that old – even rather romantic – notion of place may have within it many connections, if only implicitly, to the (unequal) construction of gender – of masculine and feminine – in current western society. There are a number of distinct threads in the series of arguments here.

To begin with, integral to ideas of places as stable and settled, such as those outlined at the beginning of the chapter, is often – explicitly or implicitly – a notion of place as 'home', as a haven of peace and quiet and of retreat. This was clearly, for instance, a strong element in the migrants' view of their place of origin, discussed in Chapter 1. There are two elements to this way of thinking: first, there is the explicit analogy between the concepts of place and of home; second, there is the assumption that both are places of rest. Yet, as feminists have often pointed out, for many women home may be the place, not of rest, but of work. Neither is home necessarily a haven of peace and quiet: intra-family relations may be the source of just as much conflict as external social relations. Indeed, some feminists, such as Michèle Barrett (1980), have argued that the social organization of home is the central key to women's oppression. Thus, it may be argued, to characterize 'no place like home' in this way is to ignore a range of important social issues. The analogy with this notion of home, it is therefore argued, is an ill-chosen one. Moreover, the same points can be made directly about places themselves. To imagine, as some of the Cambridgeshire high-tech scientists did, that the old English village is a place free of problems is to avoid looking at its reality. That whole notion of the settled, happy village as a place of retreat belies the fierce inequality of the social relations on which such societies were in fact built: between master and servant, between landowner and labourer. Moreover, and to return more directly to issues of gender, the 'local community', precisely because of its assumption of settled social relations, may often be particularly restricting of any woman's desire to break out of the patriarchal norms of behaviour (see, for instance, Wilson, 1991).

Moreover, it is asked, who is it who has these romantic views of place (of the village, or of the region one comes from …), if not those who have the ability to leave? Consider the novels written of the northern home by those who have migrated south, songs sung by the migrant about the place they have left, the scientists who choose to 'live' in a village but in fact only spend evenings and weekends there. Such views may not be held by those confined to the place, or by those who more actively participate in its affairs, it is argued. (You may wish to question this – are romantic views of place *only* held by those who leave or who have the power to leave?) In many cases it may be men who are more able to leave, and return to, a place; and women whose lives are more enclosed there. Here again, though, there is variation: long-distance migration is most certainly not an all-male affair, as we saw in Chapter 1. Yet, as that chapter also pointed out, in the past most labour migrations have indeed been male-dominated; it is only recently that women have come to play a leading role in many migration streams. And in the Cambridgeshire village it was – and is – indeed the men who participate less in the daily business of the village.

Moreover, it is not necessary to the argument for it always to be the case that men are more mobile in relation to place than women (Irigaray, 1987; Rose, 1993; Massey, 1994). The deeper point made by these critics is that this *way* of characterizing place as home, as an unchanging stability to be looked back on, to be returned to, is itself masculine. It is so for two reasons. First, it is argued that this characterization so often takes the form of an actual female person. Thoughts of home frequently centre on 'mother', seen as an unchanging fixity, whom you left and may visit again. Yet mother has her own life, she is not in fact unchanging, and may even herself want to leave. This relates to the second point. For, it is argued, what is going on here is a much deeper and more general characterization of 'a place called home' in female terms, as Mother/Woman, as an unchanging point of reference from which one sets out on life. But this is to deny both the desire of women themselves for mobility and the fact that places change. As we have seen in Chapter 1, you may leave and dream of the places you once knew, but meanwhile they have themselves moved on. They no longer conform to the static picture that you retain of them.

All of this in turn raises the issue of the power which can lie in voluntary mobility. The ability to leave, to travel, to return, may be as important in establishing an identity – especially a powerful and independent identity – as may be the attachment to place. This aspect of the relationship between place and identity is explored in the next chapter, but for some a chosen identity may be best established by *escaping* the confines of place: Victorian 'lady travellers', striking free of the constraints of nineteenth-century social rules, are a good case in point. Indeed, it has often been argued that the net of social conventions which has in western society so long and so frequently confined women much more than men to the 'private' sphere of the home, while men much more than women had the freedom to enter the public sphere, was precisely a means of tying women down in place, effectively of controlling them. The Victorian lady travellers were not 'typical women': most of them had the advantages of class and material resources on their side.

With such a set of connections, and such a history, it becomes clear that to romanticize places as settled, coherent and unchanging is highly dubious.

Finally, it has often been argued by feminists of a psychoanalytic persuasion that, in societies such as ours where most child-rearing is done by women, boy and girl children establish their identities in different ways. Boys, since one of their tasks is in growing up to establish their difference from their carer, tend to draw a boundary between her and themselves. Girls, with no such task at the centre of their identity-formation, form identities which are much more interrelational, much more open and porous. To think of identities, and in our case specifically the identities of places, as necessarily bounded may therefore reflect a particularly masculine way of thinking. Certainly, some feminists have argued, whatever the psychoanalytic basis, the concept of identity (whether of place or of person) as constructed out of *interrelations with others* rather than by being cut off by hard lines of demarcation, is a way of thinking which enables us to see not only our individual specificity but also our connectedness to others. (To explore this in more detail, see articles in Harding and Hintikka, 1983, and Nicholson, 1990.) The same argument can be made about places. To see places as bounded can lead to their interconnections being ignored, and thus may result in parochialism. To see them, as some of the theorists we have looked at here have tried to see them, as particular sets of interconnections in a wider field might hold open the possibility of both appreciating their local uniqueness and recognizing their wider interlinkages.

Activity 6 Turn now to Reading B which is a brief passage from Kevin Robins' article, 'Tradition and translation: national culture in its global context'. The article as a whole is concerned with the development of enterprise and heritage cultures, and in this way and a number of others it picks up on themes developed in Reading A by Harvey.

The passage begins from globalization, and the challenge it poses to the established relations between space and place (see section 2.2.1), and in particular the challenge to notions of place as enclosure. It also challenges the notion of place-identity as necessarily founded upon tradition, as proposed by Harvey.

Robins then raises a question which has been gradually emerging through our discussions: 'Is not the very category of identity itself problematical?' Certainly, Robins argues, it is so if the identity of place must be purified and exclusive, where each group draws lines of demarcation between itself and other groups. This, he says, using a term of Sibley's, is a *geography of rejection*. (It is this approach to place-identity, in other words, which produces the divisiveness of which Harvey writes in Reading A.)

geography of rejection

The geography of rejection

But perhaps identities can be thought of in another way. Certainly, any identity is based on differentiation from others. But must it necessarily be a differentiation which takes the form of opposition, of drawing a hard *boundary* between 'us' and 'them', in other words the geography of rejection, the geography of separate spheres for antagonistic communities which each in themselves remain pure? For, as we have seen, the identities of places are *never* 'pure' (section 2.3.1) – the identities of the villages of Hampstead and of Cambridgeshire, for instance, are always already 'the product, in part, of a long history, of connections with the beyond, with other places'. They are always already hybrid places. Maybe, then, we can think of places as more essentially open, porous, and the products of links with other places, rather than as exclusive enclosures bound off from the outside world.

boundary

2.4 The interdependence of places

2.4.1 Boundaries

There are thus strong arguments for incorporating the interconnections of places into the very way in which they are conceptualized. That is, at the same time as recognizing the individual uniqueness of each, places may be conceptualized as essentially open and porous, as interlinked. These arguments have been made in this chapter from – at least – three positions: first, that current developments make a recognition of this interconnectedness simply impossible to evade; second, that in fact places have for long been open and porous even though it may only have been in more recent years that a recognition of the implications of this has been forced upon our theoretical consciousness; and, third, that there are anyway significant reservations to be made of any concept of identity (whether of person or place) which sees it as essentially bounded in the sense of closed off from the outside.

But – you may well have been objecting as this argument proceeded – places *do* have boundaries around them. There are nation-states and counties; there are the lines drawn around the European Union and there are the boundaries of the local parish. This is indeed true. But there are a number of points to be made about boundaries.

First, the point which would be made by some of the theorists being discussed in this chapter is that *these lines do not embody any eternal truth of places*; rather they are lines drawn by society to serve particular purposes. The county boundaries in the United Kingdom, or those of départements in France or Länder in Germany, do reflect long historical variations between different parts of their countries but they are also lines drawn for the purposes of administration: for regional government maybe, or for the delivery of services. All of the boundaries, whether the national borders on the world atlas or the lines marking property and parish on a local map, are socially constructed. They are just as much the product of society as are the other social relations which constitute social space. Moreover, this point applies just as much to boundaries which follow physical features of the landscape. Natural features are not naturally boundaries. Mountain ranges may form frontier barriers or be the unifying basis for a mountain state; rivers may be boundaries between nations, or their valleys may be the uniting feature of a social community.

Second, boundaries inevitably cut across some of the other social relations which construct social space. The places they enclose are not pure. They gain, and have gained, their character by links with elsewhere.

Boundaries cut across other social relations

Third, boundaries matter. Where you live in relation to them determines the level of your local taxes and the services you receive, where you were born in relation to them determines your nationality, determines which boundaries you may cross and those which you may not (the carving up of the world into politically bounded entities which are obstacles to migration was discussed in Chapter 1). Boundaries, in a sense, are one means of organizing social space. They are, or may be, part of the process of place-*making*. And indeed, as Chapter 3 explores, an enormous amount of effort may go into constructing a sense of identity within these bounded areas, whether it be national identity or the current moves towards the building of a European identity.

Finally, the drawing of boundaries is an exercise of power. This is true in the big issues of the determination of national boundaries but also in, for instance, the constant debates in the United Kingdom about what is the most appropriate shape for the units of local government. Boundaries may be constructed as protection by the relatively weak; they may also be constructed by the strong to protect their already privileged position. Boundaries are thus an expression of the power structures of society. They are one among the many kinds of social relations which construct space and place.

2.4.2   Linked fortunes

Places can therefore be conceptualized as formed out of numerous social relationships stretched over space. And many of these social relations link places together. Places, represented in this way, are thus *not* isolated from each other, each with its own internal history. Their very characteristics are formed, in part, through their links with one another.

This implies in turn that their fortunes, too, are linked together. **Allen (1995)** suggests that different parts of the world economy are today both more interconnected and more interdependent than previously has been the case. By interconnection he means that different parts of the world experience similar changes, that all may be affected by shifts which are international in scope. And by interdependence he means that the social relations which stretch between places bind the fortunes of those places together.

Places are both interconnected and interdependent. Their economic fortunes and general well-being can in no way be completely determined by events or actions within the place itself. **Blunden** (1995, Box 4.2) gives a neat example of how the fortunes of Amazonia, and the way in which it has been linked into wider social relations, have both changed over time and changed largely in response to events, agencies and centres of power located in other places (this is a case of thorough interdependence). Closer to home, a national government frequently has recourse to 'international conditions' to explain what might otherwise be seen as a lack of success in economic policy – for example, the international recession which is characterized as holding back the UK's recovery; this might be seen as an appeal to a more general interconnectedness.

2.4.3   Unequal interdependence

Places are not simply linked together, however; they are linked together in unequal ways. The social relations which bind them together are relations of power, and the geography of that power can be traced.

Thus, in the discussion of the increasing complexity of activity spaces in section 2.2.1, it was pointed out that there is a very definite geography of power within the activity space of a multinational company. The form that this takes will vary from company to company, but we may imagine a centre of power at the world headquarters, from which radiates control of a variety of sorts to the different branch-plants, marketing offices, development laboratories and so forth. There may be continental, regional and national 'headquarters', too, which function as relay-stations for the overall decisions of head office but which also have power to take certain kinds of decisions for themselves. There may also be a form of power relation between, say, the R&D laboratories and the production factories, with the former providing the more strategic ideas and the prototypes for the latter to take into full production. The global factories (discussed in **Allen, 1995**) and the various forms of organization of international companies, all represent different ways in which the relations of economic power may be arranged at the world scale. Each of them has a different geography of power and each of them draws places differently into the unequal geographies which they create.

However, the unequal geographies of power are not only embodied in such obvious things as multinational corporations. The unequal interdependence between places is certainly much easier to see when, for instance, you know that the decision to close or to expand the plant in your area is being taken in New York or Tokyo. It is then clear that control over events lies elsewhere. But the unequal interdependence between places does not have to be so clearly embodied in a particular person, headquarters or place for it to be real. Even when there is no direct institutional connection, the power of market forces can link places together in a competitive struggle for economic growth. The decline of, for instance, shipbuilding in the first world did not happen because of multinationals shifting investments around the world. In the United Kingdom the long-term decline took place for two main reasons (though there were many others as well). First, it reflected the much wider and more general shift in the international geography of power as Britain slipped down from its old imperial position in which it had controlled, and built the vessels for, a large part of world trade. Second, it reflected the increasing competitiveness in other parts of the world, and especially in newly industrializing countries. Thus as power, both political and in the market-place, shifted, so the fortunes of people in Glasgow, Tyneside and Merseyside were linked with those of people in Inch'on and Pusan in South Korea.

Neither, of course, is the unequal interdependence between places purely economic. The military and political inequalities of power between nation-states is evident (and is discussed in **Anderson, Brook and Cochrane, eds, 1995**). In the case of the media, a few major corporations increasingly dominate the transmission of the news and thus, very often, a particular first world understanding of it. And while some of the concerns from which this chapter began arose from the increasing mixing of cultures in every place in the world (or so it seemed) the directions of that are also unequal. There is, as I write, a major exhibition of Australian aboriginal art on display at a gallery in London. It has been a significant event, and much reviewed. Yet, as a cultural flow, it emphasizes by its very form the inequalities in relations between societies. The people of London, at the heart of the first world, visit the exhibition to learn something of a society they possibly know relatively little about, or they go because they are fascinated by aboriginal ways of thinking, or they go to get a taste of something exotic on a wet Sunday afternoon. But that relation to another culture is very different from the one which travels in a reverse direction. UK and US cultural influences are part of the infrastructure in many a 'peripheral' society. People in Papua New Guinea do not have to go to an exhibition to learn about UK and US culture. Their world is partly framed by it.

There is, then, a geography of power which structures the inequalities of uneven development. And individual places – whether trading blocs, or nation-states, or regions or small villages – are each positioned in different relations to that geography. The notion of an *international division of labour* (discussed in **Allen, 1995**) refers to the way in which different areas of the world play different roles within a wider system.

It is, undoubtedly, a complex geography. Not all the flows of power run in the same direction. For instance, in relation to the international economy, not all multinational corporations are based in the first world. There are long-term changes, too, in the geography of uneven development as individual places rise and fall in prosperity and influence. The rise over recent decades of Japan and of the 'tigers' of South East Asia (Taiwan, South Korea, Singapore, Hong Kong) is a clear case in point. Nonetheless, there are broad, systematic lines: from 'West' to 'rest', from the United States of America (although increasingly under challenge) to other first world societies, from global cities outwards. Within the United Kingdom the unequal geography of power – economic, cultural, symbolic and political – is strongly dominated by London and the South East of England.

This fact of power further problematizes the alternatives laid out at the beginning of section 2.1.2. For while we might want to reject a future in which local cultures protect their distinctiveness by resisting any invasions from outside (since that distinctiveness is itself partly a product of such 'invasions' in the past, and since anyway such a future is simply not feasible), it is necessary to remember that the alternative of 'endless mixing' will be a mixing on unequal terms. And each form of mixing will have its own geography of power: the power of multinationals to remake everywhere in their own homogenized image; the unequal powers of cultural exchange; and the inequality of power in different forms of migration (see Chapter 1). Maybe there is no general answer: each aspect of 'mixing' must be evaluated in its own terms, and in the context of the power relations in which the identity of place is established. You will get a chance to think about this for yourself in Chapter 4.

Power is one of the few things you rarely see a map of. Yet a geography of power – that is, of social relations stretched over space – is what sustains much of what we experience around us in any local area – from the nervousness of going down a particular street at night, to the financing of the local company down the road, to the arrival of the latest US movie at the multiplex. And it is out of the intersections of all these geographies that each 'place' acquires both its uniqueness and its interdependence with elsewhere.

Summary of section 2.4

o 'Boundaries' are socially constructed phenomena; they do not define 'essential places'. They are, however, an important aspect of social space; and they have effects.

o The linkages between places mean that their fortunes are also both interconnected and interdependent.

o However, these interdependencies are unequal: there are important geographies of power.

- o Such geographies of power exist in all spheres of life, for instance in economic and cultural relations.

- o Individual places occupy particular positions in these wider geographies of power, that is within the overall contours of uneven development.

- o This geography of power structures the inequalities of uneven development.

2.5 What kind of place for the future?

This chapter began from some representations of place which have been common, probably dominant, in western societies. A number of different kinds of challenge to that notion of place have been explored. Sections 2.1 and 2.2 examined the challenges posed by current developments and section 2.3 examined some more *in-principle* critiques. The result of both types of challenge is to argue that places must be conceptualized in ways which take account of the social relations which link them together. This means reconceptualizing places, re-imagining them so as to recognize more fully their interconnections. However, while it is all very well for us as social scientists to elaborate on time–space compression and its meaning for places, or for us to explore the constitution of the concept of identity, the question remains as to how we might re-think *and experience* places in our lives. In Reading A, Harvey writes of the danger of our mental maps not keeping pace with current realities. In section 2.2.1 Kevin Robins was cited as reflecting upon an ideal which would be 'to match community and security with the kind of openness that can stimulate a positive sense of challenge and contestation' (1991b, p. 17). A whole range of authors have examined this issue. We are going to focus here on the work of Iris Marion Young,

The places which are – and have for long been – most clearly open and interconnected, and which are often at the centre of current discussion, and often held up as a sign of what might be possible, are *cities*. For cities are simply too big and complex for anyone to know everyone. You *have* to live alongside people – thousands of them – about whose lives and cultures you may know very little. And cities have rarely been closed to the outside world, or homogeneous in their cultures. They have almost always been sites of cultural mixing, through trade, politics and migration. And so it is often in the context of cities that people have begun to think about how we might re-imagine places.

We shall turn now to the reading from Iris Marion Young which is an extract from her article 'The ideal of community and the politics of difference'. Young lays out the grounds of a possible future way of imagining the places in which we live. Reading C consists of two sections, 'Denial of difference as time and space distancing' and 'City life and the politics of difference'. The first of these is really quite difficult but it lays out some of the essential groundwork for the second section, which is directly about cities. Take this first section slowly and note down the basic steps (not every point) in the argument.

Activity 7 Read now the first section of Reading C by Iris Marion Young, then return to the text below which recapitulates the main points.

1   Young begins from a particular notion of community as requiring face-to-face interaction. This has much in common with notions of 'place as community'. Such face-to-face contacts are said to be 'authentic'. If there is no distance between people, the reasoning goes, then their communication can be immediate and direct – unmediated. In other words, it is argued, the very lack of spatial distance can give a community-in-one-place an authenticity which would otherwise not be possible. This relates to our own debate in this chapter: has the expansion of spatial movement and the time–space distancing of social relations made the authenticity of places – 'real' places – impossible? Or can it only be reconstructed in small, face-to-face communities?

2   Young criticizes this approach, however. She argues two things: (a) that there are no 'unmediated' interrelations, even face-to-face ones. In every interaction we always have to interpret each other; and (b) that *all* societies are structured across time and space. As she says 'all social interaction takes place over time and across space'. There is thus always some element of distancing.

3   Young is not arguing that the fact of greater distancing in our social relations makes no difference at all – clearly it does. But she is arguing that there is not such a sharp break between some supposedly authentic face-to-face, and some unauthentic distanced, sociability.

4   She also points to the problems which can exist even in small, and supposedly homogeneous and coherent, communities: 'For both face-to-face and non-face-to-face relations are mediated relations, and in both there is as much the possibility of separation and violence as there is communication and consensus.' (Think of our earlier discussion of 'home'.) What this means is that there must be some possibility both of constructing a way of thinking which brings us in some sense 'close' to people a long way away and of recognizing the always distanced nature even of those who are close. It is on the latter point that Young builds in her second section, on the city, in which she writes of 'the "being-together" of strangers'.

5   We have, she argues, to start from where we are, not posit some ideal society (and thereby 'detemporalize' our idea of social change).

6   Putting all this together, she argues in favour of towns and cities rather than isolated small communities. It is to cities that she turns in the second section.

Activity 8 Now read the second section of Reading C, 'City life and the politics of difference'.

Here Young is arguing that we cannot go back to *purified communities*, even if such things ever existed. We have to start from the interconnected world in which we live. Her vision of a future for the idea of 'place' in such a world is *the unoppressive city*. This would be a place in which the fact of difference between peoples would be accepted – it would be 'open to unassimilated otherness'. And it would be an open place, not enclosed against the world outside: it would be a city 'without walls'.

purified community

the unoppressive city

Pause now, and think back to Reading B. There, too, the search for purification was discussed, and the authors cited were critical. It is the search for purified identities, it was argued, which results in a geography of rejection. What Young is doing is trying to imagine, if you like, a geography of acceptance. And just as the geography of rejection is based on a particular notion of identity (bounded, closed), so this more welcoming geography must be based on a concept of identity which is open and interactive. The quotation from Sibley (1992) in Box 2.1 makes a similar argument. Note, as you read it, how geography itself is argued to be a factor in the designation of some people as 'outsiders'.

Box 2.1 Strongly and weakly classified spaces

'More generally, spaces which are homogeneous or uniform, from which non-conforming groups or activities have been expelled or have been kept out through the maintenance of strong boundaries, can be termed pure in the sense that they are free from polluting elements and the purification of space is a process by which power is exercised over space and social groups. The significance of such purified spaces in the construction of the 'other' is basically that difference is more visible than it would be in an area of mixed land use and social diversity. Residents in a socially and economically homogeneous suburb, for example, may erect barriers to those who are different because they pose a threat to the homogeneity which the residents have been conditioned to value …

Strongly classified spaces have clear boundaries, their internal homogeneity and order are valued and there is, in consequence, a concern with boundary maintenance in order to keep out objects or people who do not fit the classification. Weakly classified spaces will have weakly defined boundaries because they are characterized by social mixing and/or mixed land uses. Difference in this instance will not be obvious and if mixture and diversity are accepted, policing of the boundaries will be unnecessary. Generally, strongly classified spaces will also be strongly framed, in that there will be a concern with separation and order, as there is, for example, in many middle-class suburbs. Weak framing would suggest more numerous and more fluid relationships between people and the built environment than occur with strong framing. Buildings may have multiple uses, either simultaneously or at different times of day, for example. Using this schema, it is possible to see how space contributes to the social construction of the outsider …

I would argue, therefore, that there is a connection between the strong classification of space and the rejection of social groups who are non-conforming.'

Source: Sibley, 1992, pp. 114, 115

The proposal Young is putting forward is an ideal, as she admits. It is not, on the whole, a vision of place which is very common today. But others have written in a similar vein. Is it a conceptualization of place which is worth aiming it? Do you find it attractive, or possibly frightening? There are a number of points worth pondering. For instance, Young's city could still end up being a patchwork of differentiated groups, each with their own space. So a first question is whether even this small-scale exclusivity is what we should be aiming at. Of course, in Young's city the boundaries between the groups'

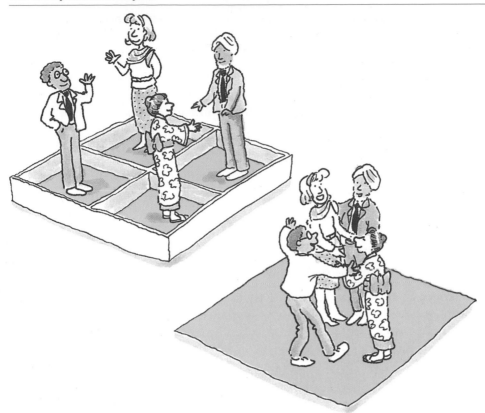

Two possible geographies of acceptance

spaces are not boundaries of antagonism; the differences between groups are tolerated easily. But there is still a further question – which Young herself acknowledges – which is how such groups themselves are to be defined. For, as we have seen, there are no 'pure' identities – the character of each of the groups will itself be mixed.

The following chapters pursue these issues further. In particular, Chapter 5 takes up this last question and explores the construction of group cultures themselves and the relation between place and culture. Meanwhile, the very next chapter steps back from these ideal visions to examine 'the identity of place' as we tend to construct it today.

References

ALLEN, J. (1995) 'Crossing borders: footloose multinationals?' in Allen, J. and Hamnett, C. (eds).

ALLEN, J. and HAMNETT, C. (1995) 'Uneven worlds' in Allen, J. and Hamnett, C. (eds).

ALLEN, J. and HAMNETT, C. (eds) (1995) *A Shrinking World? Global Unevenness and Inequality*, Oxford, Oxford University Press/The Open University (Volume 2 in this series).

ALLEN, J. and MASSEY, D. (eds) (1995) *Geographical Worlds*, Oxford, Oxford University Press/The Open University (Volume 1 in this series).

ANDERSON, J., BROOK, C. and COCHRANE, A. (eds) (1995) *A Global World? Re-ordering Political Space*, Oxford, Oxford University Press/The Open University (Volume 5 in this series).

BARRETT, M. (1980) *Women's Oppression Today: Problems in Marxist Feminist Analysis*, London, Verso.

BLUNDEN, J. (1995) 'Sustainable resources?' in Sarre, P. and Blunden, J. (eds).

BONETTI, M. and SIMON, J.-P. (1987) 'Du municipal à l'urbain', *Annales de la Recherche Urbaine*, Vol. 34.

CASTELLS, M. (1989) *The Informational City*, Oxford, Basil Blackwell.

CATER, E. (1995) 'Consuming spaces: global tourism' in Allen, J. and Hamnett, C. (eds).

EMBERLEY, P. (1989) 'Places and stories: the challenge of technology', *Social Research*, Vol. 56, No. 3, pp. 741–85.

GIDDENS, A. (1990) *The Consequences of Modernity*, Cambridge, Polity Press.

HARDING, S. and HINTIKKA, M. B. (eds) (1983) *Discovering Reality*, Dordrecht and London, D. Reidel Publishing Company.

HARVEY, D. (1989) *The Condition of Postmodernity: An Enquiry into the Origins of Cultural Change*, Oxford, Basil Blackwell.

IRIGARAY, L. (1987) 'Sexual difference' in Moi, T. (ed.) *French Feminist Thought: A Reader*, Oxford, Basil Blackwell, pp. 118–30.

LEYSHON, A. (1995) 'Annihilating space: the speed-up of communications' in Allen, J. and Hamnett, C. (eds).

MASSEY, D. (1991) 'A global sense of place', *Marxism Today*, June.

MASSEY, D. (1994) *Space, Place and Gender*, Cambridge, Polity Press.

MASSEY, D. (1995) 'Imagining the world' in Allen, J. and Massey, D. (eds).

MEEGAN, R. (1995) 'Local worlds' in Allen, J. and Massey, D. (eds).

NICHOLSON, L. (ed.) (1990) *Feminism/Postmodernism*, London, Routledge.

ROBINS, K. (1991a) 'Tradition and translation: national culture in its global context' in Corner, J. and Harvey, S. (eds) *Enterprise and Heritage: Crosscurrents of National Culture*, London, Routledge.

ROBINS, K. (1991b) 'Prisoners of the city, whatever could a postmodern city be?', *New Formations*, No. 15, Winter, pp. 1–22.

ROSE, G. (1993) *Feminism and Geography*, Cambridge, Polity Press.

SAID, E. (1992) *Culture and Imperialism*, London, Chatto and Windus.

SARRE, P. (1995) 'Paradise lost, or the conquest of the wilderness' in Sarre, P. and Blunden, J. (eds).

SARRE, P. and BLUNDEN, J. (eds) (1995) *An Overcrowded World? Population, Resources and the Environment*, Oxford, Oxford University Press/The Open University (Volume 3 in this series).

SIBLEY, D. (1992) 'Outsiders in society and space' in Anderson, K. and Gale, F. (eds) *Inventing Places: Studies in Cultural Geography*, Melbourne, Longman Cheshire, pp. 107–22.

WILSON, E. (1991) *The Sphinx in the City: Urban Life, The Control of Disorder, and Women*, London, Virago.

YEARLEY, S. (1995) 'Dirty connections: transnational pollution' in Allen, J. and Hamnett, C. (eds).

YOUNG, I. M. (1990) 'The ideal of community and the politics of difference' in Nicholson, L. J. (ed.).

Acknowledgement

The research projects referred to at the beginning of section 2.2.2 are funded by the Economic and Social Research Council (R00233004 and R000233008).

Reading A: David Harvey, 'The experience of space and time: the postmodern condition'

But it is exactly at this point that we encounter the [...] reaction that can best be summed up as the search for personal or collective identity, the search for secure moorings in a shifting world. Place-identity, in this collage of superimposed spatial images that implode in upon us, becomes an important issue, because everyone occupies a space of individuation (a body, a room, a home, a shaping community, a nation), and how we individuate ourselves shapes identity. Furthermore, if no one 'knows their place' in this shifting collage world, then how can a secure social order be fashioned or sustained?

There are two elements within this problem that deserve close consideration. First, the capacity of most social movements to command place better than space puts a strong emphasis upon the potential connection between place and social identity. This is manifest in political action. The defensiveness of municipal socialism, the insistence on working-class community, the localization of the fight against capital, become central features of working-class struggle within an overall patterning of uneven geographical development. The consequent dilemmas of socialist or working-class movements in the face of a universalizing capitalism are shared by other oppositional groups – racial minorities, colonized peoples, women, etc. – who are relatively empowered to organize in place but disempowered when it comes to organizing over space. In clinging, often of necessity, to a place-bound identity, however, such oppositional movements become a part of the very fragmentation which a mobile capitalism and flexible accumulation can feed upon. 'Regional resistances', the struggle for local autonomy, place-bound organization, may be excellent bases for political action, but they cannot bear the burden of radical historical change alone. 'Think globally and act locally' was the revolutionary slogan of the 1960s. It bears repeating.

The assertion of any place-bound identity has to rest at some point on the motivational power of tradition. It is difficult, however, to maintain any sense of historical continuity in the face of all the flux and ephemerality of flexible accumulation. The irony is that tradition is now often preserved by being commodified and marketed as such. The search for roots ends up at worst being produced and marketed as an image, as a simulacrum or pastiche (imitation communities constructed to evoke images of some folksy past, the fabric of traditional working-class communities being taken over by an urban gentry). The photograph, the document, the view, and the reproduction become history precisely because they are so overwhelmingly present. The problem, of course, is that none of these is immune from tampering or downright faking for present purposes. At best, historical tradition is reorganized as a museum culture, not necessarily of high modernist art, but of local history, of local production, of how things once upon a time were made, sold, consumed, and integrated into a long-lost and often romanticized daily life (one from which all trace of oppressive social relations may be expunged). Through the presentation of a partially illusory past it becomes possible to signify something of local identity and perhaps to do it profitably.

The second reaction to the internationalism of modernism lies in the search to construct place and its meanings qualitatively. Capitalist hegemony over space puts the aesthetics of place very much back on the agenda. But this, as we have seen, meshes only too well with the idea of spatial differentiations as lures for a peripatetic capital that values the option of mobility very highly. Isn't this place better than that place, not only for the operations of capital but also for living in, consuming well, and feeling secure in a shifting world? The construction of such places, the fashioning of some localized aesthetic image, allows the construction of some limited and limiting sense of identity in the midst of a collage of imploding spatialities ...

[...]

This should alert us to the acute geopolitical dangers that attach to the rapidity of time–space compression in recent years. The transition from Fordism to flexible accumulation, such as it has been, ought to imply a transition in our mental maps, political attitudes, and political institutions. But political thinking does not necessarily undergo such easy transformations, and is in any case subject to the contradictory pressures that derive from spatial integration and differentiation. There is an omni-present danger that our mental maps will not match current realities. The serious diminution of the power of individual nation states over fiscal and monetary policies, for example, has not been matched by any parallel shift towards an internationalization of politics. Indeed, there are abundant signs that localism and nationalism have become stronger precisely because of the quest for the security that place always offers in the midst of all the shifting that flexible accumulation implies. The resurgence of geopolitics and of faith in charismatic politics (Thatcher's Falklands War, Reagan's invasion of Grenada) fits only too well with a world that is increasingly nourished intellectually and politically by a vast flux of ephemeral images.

Time–space compression always exacts its toll on our capacity to grapple with the realities unfolding around us ...

Source: Harvey, 1989, pp. 302–4, 305–6

Reading B: Kevin Robins, 'The burden of identity'

... Globalization is profoundly transforming our apprehension of the world: it is provoking a new experience of orientation and disorientation, new senses of placed and placeless identity. The global–local nexus is associated with new relations between space and place, fixity and mobility, centre and periphery, 'real' and 'virtual' space, 'inside' and 'outside', frontier and territory. This, inevitably, has implications for both individual and collective identities and for the meaning and coherence of community. Peter Emberley describes a momentous shift from a world of stable

and continuous reference points to one where 'the notions of space as enclosure and time as duration are unsettled and redesigned as a field of infinitely experimental configurations of space-time' [1989, pp. 755–6]. In this new 'hyperreality', he suggests, 'the old order of prescriptive and exclusive places and meaning-endowed durations is dissolving' and we are consequently faced with the challenge of elaborating 'a new self-interpretation' [ibid., p. 748].

It is in this context that both enterprise and heritage cultures assume their significance. Older certainties and hierarchies of British identity have been called into question in a world of dissolving boundaries and disrupted continuities. In a country that is now a container of African and Asian cultures, the sense of what it is to be British can never again have the old confidence and surety. Other sources of identity are no less fragile. What does it mean to be European in a continent coloured not only by the cultures of its former colonies, but also by American and now Japanese cultures? Is not the very category of identity itself problematical? Is it at all possible, in global times, to regain a coherent and integral sense of identity? Continuity and historicity of identity are challenged by the immediacy and intensity of global cultural confrontations. The comforts of Tradition are fundamentally challenged by the imperative to forge a new self-interpretation based upon the responsibilities of cultural Translation.

Neither enterprise nor heritage culture really confronts these responsibilities. Both represent protective strategies of response to global forces, centred around the conservation, rather than reinterpretation, of identities. The driving imperative is to salvage centred, bounded and coherent identities – placed identities for placeless times. This may take the form of the resuscitated patriotism and jingoism that we are now seeing in a resurgent Little Englandism. Alternatively, as I have already suggested, it may take a more progressive form in the cultivation of local and regional identities or in the project to construct a continental European identity. In each

case, however, it is about the maintenance of protective illusion, about the struggle for wholeness and coherence through continuity. At the heart of this romantic aspiration is what Richard Sennett, in another context, calls the search for purity and purified identity. 'The effect of this defensive pattern', he argues, 'is to create in people a desire for a purification of the terms in which they see themselves in relation to others. The enterprise involved is an attempt to build an image or identity that coheres, is unified, and filters out threats in social experience' [1971, p. 15]. Purified identities are constructed through the purification of space, through the maintenance of territorial boundaries and frontiers. We can talk of 'a geography of rejection which appears to correspond to the purity of antagonistic communities' [Sibley, 1988, p. 410]. Purified identities are also at the heart of empire. Purification aims to secure both protection from, and positional superiority over, the external other …

[…]

Is it, then, possible to break this logic of identity?

References

Emberley, P. (1989) 'Places and stories: the challenge of technology', *Social Research*, Vol. 56, No. 3.

Sennett, R. (1971) *The Uses of Disorder*, Harmondsworth, Penguin.

Sibley, D. (1988) 'Purification of space', *Environment and Planning D: Society and Space*, Vol. 6, No. 4.

Source: Robins, 1991, pp. 40–2

Reading C: Iris Marion Young, 'The ideal of community and the politics of difference'

Denial of difference as time and space distancing

Many political theorists who put forward an ideal of community specify small-group, face-to-face relations as essential to the realization of that ideal. Peter Manicas expresses a version of the ideal of community that includes this face-to-face specification.

Consider an association in which persons are in face-to-face contact, but where the relations of persons are not mediated by 'authorities', sanctified rules, reified bureaucracies or commodities. Each is prepared to absorb the attitudes, reasoning and ideas of others and each is in a position to do so. Their relations, thus, are open, immediate and reciprocal. *Further, the total conditions of their social lives are to be conjointly determined with each having an equal voice and equal power. When these conditions are satisfied and when as a result, the consequences and fruits of their associated and independent activities are perceived and consciously become an object of individual desire and effort, then there is a democratic community.*

[Manicas, 1974, p. 247]

Roberto Unger [1975, pp. 262–3] argues that community requires face-to-face interaction among members within a plurality of contexts. To understand other people and to be understood by them in our concrete individuality, we must not only work together but play together, take care of children together, grieve together, and so on. Christian Bay [1981] envisions the good society as founded upon small face-to-face communities of direct democracy and many-sided interaction. Michael Taylor specifies that in a community, relations among members must be direct and many-sided. Like Manicas, he asserts that relations are direct only when they are unmediated by representatives, leaders, bureaucrats, state institutions, or codes [Taylor, 1982, pp. 27–8]. While Gould does not specify face-to-face relations as necessary, some of her language suggests that community can only be realized in such face-to-face relations. In the institutionalization of democratic socialism, she says, 'social combination now becomes the *immediate* subjective relations of mutuality among individuals. The relations, again become *personal* relations as in the pre-capitalist stage, but no longer relations of domination and no longer mediated, as in the second stage, by external objects' [Gould, 1978, p. 26].

I take there to be several problems with the privileging of face-to-face relations by theorists of community. It presumes an illusory ideal of unmediated social relations and wrongly identifies mediation with alienation. It denies difference in the sense of time and space distancing. It implies a model of the good society as consisting of decentralized small units, which is both unrealistic and politically undesirable.

Finally, it avoids the political question of the relation among the decentralized communities.

All the writers cited previously give primacy to face-to-face presence because they claim that only under those conditions can the social relations be *immediate*. I understand them to mean several things by social relations that are immediate. They are direct, personal relations, in which each understands the other in her or his individuality. This is an extension of the ideal of mutual understanding I have criticized in the previous section [not reproduced here]. Immediacy, also here means relations of co-presence in which persons experience a simultaneity of speaking and hearing and are in the same space, that is, have the possibility to move close enough to touch.[1]

This ideal of the immediate presence of subjects to one another, however, is a metaphysical illusion. Even a face-to-face relation between two people is mediated by voice and gesture, spacing and temporality. As soon as a third person enters the interaction, the possibility arises of the relation between the first two being mediated through the third, and so on. The mediation of relations among persons by speech and actions of still other persons is a fundamental condition of sociality. The richness, creativity, diversity, and potential of a society expand with growth in the scope and means of its media, linking persons across time and distance. The greater the time and distance, however, the greater the number of persons who stand between other persons.

The normative privileging of face-to-face relations in the ideal of community seeks to suppress difference in the sense of the time and space distancing of social processes, which material media facilitate and enlarge. Such an ideal dematerializes its conception of interaction and institutions. For all social interaction takes place over time and across space. Social desire consists in the urge to carry meaning, agency, and the effects of agency beyond the moment and beyond the place. As labouring subjects we separate the moment of production from the moment of consumption. Even societies confined to a limited territory with few institutions and a small population devise means of their members communicating with one another over distances, means of maintaining their social relationships even though they are not face to face. Societies occupy wider and wider territorial fields and increasingly differentiate their activity in space, time, and function, a movement that, of course, accelerates and takes on qualitatively specific form in modern industrial societies [Giddens, 1979, pp. 198–233].

I suggest that there are no conceptual grounds for considering face-to-face relations more pure, authentic social relations than relations mediated across time and distance. For both face-to-face and non-face-to-face relations are mediated relations, and in both there is as much the possibility of separation and violence as there is communication and consensus. Theorists of community are inclined to privilege face-to-face relations, I suggest, because they wrongly identify mediation and alienation.

By alienation, I mean a situation in which persons do not have control either over their actions, the conditions of their action, or the consequences of their action, due to the intervention of other agents.[2] Social mediation is a condition for the possibility of alienation in this sense; media make possible the intervention of agents between the conditions of a subject's action and the action or between a subject's action and its consequences. Thus, media make domination and exploitation possible. In modern society the primary structures creating alienation and domination are bureaucracy and commodification of all aspects of human activity, including and especially labour. Both bureaucracy and commodification of social relations depend on complex structures of mediation among a large number of persons.

That mediation is a necessary condition of alienation, however, does not entail the reverse implication: that only by eliminating structures of mediation do we eliminate alienation. If temporal and spatial distancing are basic to social processes, and if persons always mediate

between other persons to generate social networks, then a society of immediacy is impossible. While mediation may be a necessary condition for alienation, it is not sufficient. Alienation is that specific process of mediation in which the actions of some serve the ends of others without reciprocation and without being explicit, and this requires coercion and domination.

By positing a society of immediate face-to-face relations as ideal, community theorists generate a dichotomy between the 'authentic' society of the future and the 'inauthentic' society we live in, which is characterized only by alienation, bureaucratization, and degradation. Such a dichotomization between the inauthentic society we have and the authentic society of community, however, detemporalizes our understanding of social change. On this understanding, social change and revolution consist in the complete negation of this society and the establishment of the truly good society. In her scheme of social evolution, Gould conceives of 'the society of the future' as the negated sublation of capitalist society. This understands history not as temporal process but as divided into two static structures: the before of alienated society and the after of community.

The projection of the ideal of community as the radical other of existing society denies difference in the sense of the contradictions and ambiguities of social life. Instead of dichotomizing the pure and the impure into two stages of history or two kinds of social relations, a liberating politics should conceive the social process in which we move as a multiplicity of actions and structures which cohere and contradict, some of them exploitative and some of them liberating. The polarization between the impure, inauthentic society we live in and the pure, authentic society we seek to institute detemporalizes the process of change because it fails to articulate how we move from one to the other. If institutional change is possible at all, it must begin from intervening in the contradictions and tensions of existing society. No telos of the final society exists, moreover; society understood as a moving and contradictory process implies that change for the better is always possible and always necessary.

The requirement that genuine community embody face-to-face relations, when taken as a model of the good society, carries a specific vision of social organization. Since the ideal of community demands that relations between members be direct and many-sided, the ideal society is composed of small locales, populated by a small enough number of persons so that each can be personally acquainted with all the others. For most writers, this implies that the ideal social organization is decentralized, with small-scale industry and local markets. Each community aims for economic self-sufficiency, and each democratically makes its own decisions about how to organize its working and playing life.

I do not doubt the desirability of small groups in which individuals have personal acquaintance with one another and interact in a plurality of contexts. Just as the intimacy of living with a few others in the same household has unique dimensions that are humanly valuable, so existing with others in communities of mutual friendship has specific characteristics of warmth and sharing that are humanly valuable. Furthermore, there is no question that capitalist patriarchal society discourages and destroys such communities of mutual friendship, just as it squeezes and fragments families. In our vision of the good society, we surely wish to include institutional arrangements that would nurture the specific experience of mutual friendship, which only relatively small groups interacting in a plurality of contexts can produce. Recognizing the specific value of such face-to-face relations, however, is quite a different matter from proposing them as the organizing principle of a whole society.

Such a model of the good society as composed of decentralized, economically self-sufficient, face-to-face communities functioning as autonomous political entities is both wildly utopian and undesirable. To bring it into being would require dismantling the urban character of modern society, a gargantuan physical overhaul of living space, work places,

places of trade and commerce. A model of a transformed better society must in some concrete sense begin from the concrete material structures that are given to us at this time in history, and in the United States these are large-scale industry and urban centres. The model of society composed of small communities is not desirable, at least in the eyes of many. If we take seriously the way many people live their lives today, it appears that people enjoy cities, that is, places where strangers are thrown together.

One final problem arises from the model of face-to-face community taken as a political goal. The model of the good society as usually articulated leaves completely unaddressed the question of how such small communities are to relate to one another. Frequently, the ideal projects a level of self-sufficiency and decentralization which suggests that proponents envision few relations among the decentralized communities except those of friendly visits. But surely it is unrealistic to assume that such decentralized communities need not engage in extensive relations of exchange of resources, goods, and culture. Even if one accepts the notion that a radical restructuring of society in the direction of a just and humane society entails people living in small democratically organized units of work and neighbourhood, this has not addressed the important political question: how will the relations among these communities be organized so as to foster justice and prevent domination? When we raise this political question the philosophical and practical importance of mediation re-emerges. Once again, politics must be conceived as a relationship of strangers who do not understand one another in a subjective and immediate sense, relating across time and distance.

City life and the politics of difference

I have claimed that radical politics must begin from historical givens and conceive radical change not as the negation of the given but rather as making something good from many elements of the given. The city, as a vastly populated area with large-scale industry and places of mass assembly, is for us a historical given, and radical politics must begin from the existence of modern urban life. The material surroundings and structures available to us define and presuppose urban relationships. The very size of populations in our society and most other nations of the world, coupled with a continuing sense of national or ethnic identity with millions of other people, all support the conclusion that a vision of dismantling the city is hopelessly utopian.

Starting from the given of modern life is not simply necessary, moreover, it is desirable. Even for many of those who decry the alienation, massification, and bureaucratization of capitalist patriarchal society, city life exerts a powerful attraction. Modern literature, art, and film have celebrated city life, its energy, cultural diversity, technological complexity, and the multiplicity of its activities. Even many of the most staunch proponents of decentralized community love to show visiting friends around the Boston or San Francisco or New York in which they live, climbing up towers to see the glitter of lights and sampling the fare at the best ethnic restaurants. For many people deemed deviant in the closeness of the face-to-face community in which they lived, whether 'independent' women or socialists or gay men and lesbians, the city has often offered a welcome anonymity and some measure of freedom.[3] To be sure, the liberatory possibilities of capitalist cities have been fraught with ambiguity.

Yet, I suggest that instead of the ideal of community, we begin from our positive experience of city life to form a vision of the good society. Our political ideal is the unoppressive city. In sketching this ideal, I assume some material premises. We will assume a productivity level in the society that can meet everyone's needs, and a physical urban environment that is cleaned up and renovated. We will assume, too, that everyone who can work has meaningful work and those who cannot are provided for with dignity. In sketching this ideal of city life, I am concerned to describe the city as a *kind of relationship* of people to one another, to their own history and one another's history. Thus, by 'city' I am not referring only to those huge metropolises that we call cities in the United States. The kinds of relationship I describe obtain also ideally in those places we call towns, where perhaps 10,000 or 20,000 people live.

As a process of people's relating to one another, city life embodies difference in all the senses I have discussed in this chapter. The city obviously exhibits the temporal and spatial distancing and differentiation that I have argued, the ideal of community seeks to collapse. On the face of the city environment lies its history and the history of the individuals and groups that have dwelt within it. Such physical historicity, as well as the functions and groups that live in the city at any given time, create its spatial differentiation. The city as a network and sedimentation of discretely understood places, such as particular buildings, parks, neighbourhoods, and as a physical environment offers changes and surprises in transition from one place to another.

The temporal and spatial differentiation that mark the physical environment of the city produce an experience of aesthetic *inexhaustibility*. Buildings, squares, the twists and turns of streets and alleys offer an inexhaustible store of individual spaces and things, each with unique aesthetic characteristics. The juxtaposition of incongruous styles and functions that usually emerge after a long time in city places contribute to this pleasure in detail and surprise. This is an experience of difference in the sense of always being inserted. The modern city is without walls; it is not planned and coherent. Dwelling in the city means always having a sense of beyond, that there is much human life beyond my experience going on in or near these spaces, and I can never grasp the city as a whole.

City life thus also embodies difference as the contrary of the face-to-face ideal expressed by most assertions of community. City life is the 'being-together' of strangers. Strangers encounter one another, either face to face or through media, often remaining strangers and yet acknowledging their contiguity in living and the contributions each makes to the others. In such encountering people are not 'internally' related, as the community theorists would have it, and do not understand one another from within their own perspective. They are externally related, they experience each other as other, different, from different groups, histories, professions, cultures, which they do not understand.

The public spaces of the city are both an image of the total relationships of city life and a primary way those relationships are enacted and experienced. A public space is a place accessible to anyone, where people engage in activity as individuals or in small groups. In public spaces people are aware of each other's presence and even at times attend to it. In a city there are a multitude of such public spaces: streets, restaurants, concert halls, parks. In such public spaces the diversity of the city's residents come together and dwell side by side, sometimes appreciating one another, entertaining one another, or just chatting, always to go off again as strangers. City parks as we now experience them often have this character.

City life implies a social exhaustibility quite different from the ideal of the face-to-face community in which there is mutual understanding and group identification and loyalty. The city consists in a great diversity of people and groups, with a multitude of subcultures and differentiated activities and functions, whose lives and movements mingle and overlap in public spaces. People belong to distinct groups or cultures and interact in neighbourhoods and work places. They venture out from these locales, however, to public places of entertainment, consumption, and politics. They witness one another's cultures and functions in such public interaction, without adopting them as their own. The appreciation of ethnic foods or professional musicians, for example, consists in the recognition that these transcend the familiar everyday world of my life.

In the city strangers live side by side in public places, giving to and receiving from one another social and aesthetic products, often mediated by a huge chain of interactions. This instantiates social relations as difference in the sense of an understanding of groups and cultures that are different, with exchanging and overlapping interactions that do not issue in community, yet which prevent them from being outside of one another. The social differentiation of the city also provides a positive inexhaustibility of human relations. The possibility always exists of becoming acquainted with new and different people, with different cultural and social experiences; the possibility always exists for new groups to form or emerge around specific interests.

The unoppressive city is thus defined as openness to unassimilated otherness. Of course, we do not have such openness to difference in our current social relations. I am asserting an ideal, which consists in a politics of difference. Assuming that group differentiation is a given of social life for us, how can the relationships of group identities embody justice, respect, and the absence of oppression? The relationship among group identities and cultures in our society is blotted by racism, sexism, xenophobia, homophobia, suspicion, and mockery. A politics of difference lays down institutional and ideological means for recognizing and affirming differently identifying groups in two basic senses: giving political representation to group interests and celebrating the distinctive cultures and characteristics of different groups.

Many questions arise in proposing a politics of difference. What defines a group that deserves recognition and celebration? How does one provide representation to group interests that avoids the mere pluralism of liberal interests groups? What are institutional forms by which the mediations of the city and the representations of its groups in decision making can be made democratic? These questions, as well as many others, confront the ideal of the unoppressive city. They are not dissimilar from questions of the relationships that ought to exist among communities. They are questions, however, which appeal to community as the ideal of social life appears to repress or ignore …

Whatever the label, the concept of social relations that embody openness to unassimilated otherness with justice and appreciation needs to be developed.

Radical politics, moreover, must develop discourse and institutions for bringing differently identified groups together without suppressing or subsuming the differences.

Notes

1 Derrida discusses the illusory character of this ideal of immediate presence of subjects to one another in community in his discussion of Lévi-Strauss and Rousseau. See *Of Grammatology*, pp. 101–140.

2 For a useful account of alienation, see Richard Schmitt (1983), especially Chapter 5. In this book Schmitt, like many other of the writers I have cited, takes community to stand as the negation of the society of alienation. Unlike those writers discussed in this section, however, he does not take face-to-face relations as a condition of community. To the degree that he makes a pure/impure distinction and exhibits the desire for unity I have criticized, however, the critique articulated here applies to Schmitt's appeal to the ideal of community.

3 Marshall Berman (1982) presents a fascinating account of the attractions of city life ... George Shulman (1983) points to the open-endedness of city life as contrasted with the pastoral vision of community ...; for a similar critique, see David Plotke (1984).

References

Bay, C. (1981) *Strategies of Political Emancipation*, South Bend, IL, Notre Dame Press.

Berman, M. (1982) *All That Is Solid Melts Into Air*, New York, Simon & Schuster.

Derrida, J. (1976) *Of Grammatology*, Baltimore, MD, Johns Hopkins Univesity Press.

Giddens, A. (1979) *Central Problems in Social Theory*, Berkeley, CA, University of California Press.

Gould, C. (1978) *Marx's Social Ontology*, Cambridge, MA, MIT Press.

Manicas, P. (1974) *The Death of the State*, New York, Putnam and Sons.

Plotke, D. (1984) 'Democracy, modernization, and democracy', *Socialist Review*, Vol. 14, March–April, pp. 31–56.

Schmitt, R. (1983) *Alienation and Class*, Cambridge, MA, Schenkman Publishing.

Shulman, G. (1983) 'The pastoral idyll of Democracy', *Democracy*, Vol. 2, pp. 43–54.

Taylor, M. (1982) *Community, Anarchy and Liberty*, Cambridge, Cambridge University Press.

Unger, R. M. (1975) *Knowledge and Politics*, New York, The Free Press.

Source: Young, 1990, pp. 312–20

Place and identity: a sense of place

Chapter 3

by Gillian Rose

Activity 1 Before you read this chapter, take a few minutes to evoke a place that is, or has been, particularly significant for you in some way. Describe it to yourself, and think about why it is so important to you. Write down a few notes on it, or perhaps collect a few photographs that remind you of it, or play yourself a piece of music that brings it to mind. Keep this record of a place, because you will be asked to return to it later in the chapter.

3.1 Introduction

'Place' is one of the most theoretically and politically pressing issues facing us today. The previous two chapters of this book have stressed the importance of global flows of people, data and products; yet we also live in a world which seems every day to be fragmenting into smaller and smaller places. Nationalism is perhaps the most obvious form this fragmentation is taking; as the certainties of the Cold War era fade, many new nations are insisting on their right to their own territory. This often involves terrible violence, yet, even in areas not torn by civil war, local places seem to be becoming more and more important. Increasingly, the tradition and continuity of particular places is stressed, whether by local pressure groups, regional political parties, entrepreneurial developers or regional tourist boards. You will be able to think of many examples of the increasing salience of the local from other parts of this series.

As Chapter 2 in this book argued, 'place' is a concept which can address this contemporary tension between the local and the global very directly. This chapter will focus on only one aspect of place, however: it will examine the
sense of place way people feel and think about places. Its subtitle – *a sense of place* – is the phrase used by many geographers when they want to emphasize that places are significant because they are the focus of personal feelings. Many geographers thus use 'place' in this quite specific sense, to refer to the significance of particular places for people. These feelings for 'place' are not seen as trivial; geographers argue that senses of place develop from every aspect of individuals' life experience and that senses of place pervade everyday life and experience. Following this convention, this chapter will also refer to 'a sense of place' as a way of indicating that places are infused with meaning and feeling. Section 3.2 of this chapter will examine different ways of relating to place in these terms.

In their discussions of senses of place, geographers have emphasized that place is something created by people, both as individuals and in groups. This chapter will address the connection between place and people by thinking
identity about *identity*. Identity is how we make sense of ourselves, and geographers, anthropologists and sociologists, among others, have argued that the meanings given to a place may be so strong that they become a central part of the identity of the people experiencing them. But when used in the kinds of debates with which this chapter is concerned, the term 'identity' has some quite specific connotations. It refers to lived experiences and all the subjective feelings associated with everyday consciousness, but it also suggests that such experiences and feelings are embedded in wider sets of social relations. As Jonathan Rutherford argues, 'identity marks the conjuncture of our past with the social, cultural and economic relations we live within' (1990, p. 19).

Similarly, and without denying the validity of feelings about places, many social scientists would argue that experience is only the starting-point for understanding senses of place. Here is geographer John Eyles:

Experience, everyday life, is not seen as an adequate basis for the construction of knowledge. The existence and importance of structures, mechanisms and forces beyond immediate observation must be accepted.

(Eyles, 1985, pp. 4–5)

Just as Rutherford argues that identity is not simply a question of experience, so Eyles suggests that a sense of place must also be understood in terms of its wider social context. This means that, although senses of place may be very personal, they are not entirely the result of one individual's feelings and meanings; rather, such feelings and meanings are shaped in large part by the social, cultural and economic circumstances in which individuals find themselves. This chapter will emphasize, in particular, how feelings about place are caught up in the power relations which structure all our lives.

Section 3.3 of this chapter will suggest some ways in which it might be possible to think about senses of place more analytically, by considering the social, economic and cultural relations in which identity, and thus also senses of place, are embedded. In particular, that section will explore ways in which senses of place are, like other aspects of geography examined in this series, caught up in processes of power, inequality and resistance. Section 3.4 will offer a case study of the complexity of senses of place, and section 3.5 concludes the chapter.

3.2   How can we relate place to identity?

This section begins the chapter's analysis of senses of place by exploring some of the ways it is possible to feel a sense of place. It tries to describe systematically three different ways in which emotions about places can be connected to the notion of identity. In order to examine these three, I focus on a series of organizations or events which I interpret as articulating the particular senses of place shared by various groups of people. This immediately emphasizes that a sense of place is more than just one person's feelings about a particular place; such feelings are not only individual but also social. All places are interpreted from particular social positions and for particular social reasons. Senses of place are articulated through the processes of *representation* discussed in **Massey (1995)**.   representation

3.2.1   Identifying with a place

One way in which identity is connected to a particular place is by a feeling that you belong to that place. It's a place in which you feel comfortable, or at home, because part of how you define yourself is symbolized by certain qualities of that place. The geographer Relph, for example, has even gone so far as to claim that 'to be human is to live in a world that is filled with significant places: to be human is to have to know your place' (1976, p. 1).

Many intense feelings of belonging focus on domestic places: a room, a house, a garden. Such places can offer a feeling of safety and refuge, although this is by no means always the case. For many women, for example, the home is a site of hard work and perhaps physical and sexual abuse; for some, only by leaving such homes can they find a place in which to belong.

scale However, strong feelings of identifying with a place may also focus on other kinds of places, at a range of different *scales*. A sense of belonging to a place may occur at the local scale. One example of its expression is the brass bands, based in small industrial towns and villages, which boomed in the second half of the nineteenth century. Some of these bands were associated with the workplace, supported by benevolent employers who believed in the morally uplifting qualities of good music, and some were associated with trade union branches; but they were also often established by subscription among the local inhabitants. They played in the local bandstand and during all sorts of civic events: Sunday school processions; trade union galas; Whitsunday walks in the West Riding of Yorkshire; the opening of public buildings. They also competed in music competitions, and in these events the importance of the band to the identity of these towns and villages became very evident. Local people came to support their band, often wearing the band's colours. The musical performances of these bands brought together the local community, and their music was part of the sense of place of the inhabitants of villages and towns.

It is also possible to locate a sense of belonging at the regional scale. The case of the Midwest of the United States of America is a good example of this. As settlers moved westwards across the continent throughout the eighteenth and nineteenth centuries, they built their houses and farmed the land, as far as possible, in accordance with their values so they felt they belonged to that place. J.B. Jackson has evoked their landscape thus:

Towns grew on a grid pattern in a matter of months, only to vanish in weeks when a railroad line was built elsewhere. The closest neighbour left without warning for Oregon, six months away ... Writing in 1850, an English traveller described the American landscape as 'ugly and formal' – ugly in its stumps and dead trees, in the litter-strewn yards, the waste everywhere in evidence; formal in its long straight roads or roadways, its large rectangular fields; its bleak, rectangular little houses, its hilltop churches painted a blinding white, its classical placenames, its endless worn fences.

(Jackson, 1979, p. 160)

landscape Jackson argues that this *landscape* in part reflects two of the basic beliefs of the people settling in the Midwest: Newtonian physics and revivalist Christianity. He says that the religious fervour of many ordinary settlers gave them an intense sense of the transience of their life on earth, and so they had little interest in building grand edifices or permanent houses, or in adapting to the local environment. They also had a sense of themselves as individuals in a large and undifferentiated space through which they could move, and move on when the soil became too exhausted. Thus, like the itinerant preachers who travelled all over the region interrupting the settled hierarchies of the more traditional churches, theirs was a mobile individualism. Jackson also suggests that when these restless settlers did make their temporary halts, they built and ploughed in rational and mathematical ways, creating grid patterns of roads, streets and fields. Their combination of beliefs produced the 'ugly' formality of the Midwest landscape and its sense of place. And both, suggests Jackson, were aspects of the identity of its

European settlers. (Of course, Native Americans have a different relationship to the grasslands from the settlers. Section 3.4 of this chapter will return in more detail to the question of differing understandings of the same place.)

A third scale at which a sense of belonging to a place may be especially marked is the scale of the nation. Many nations imagine themselves through particular places which appear to embody the values that the particular nation prizes:

National identities are co-ordinated, often largely defined, by 'legends and landscapes'; by stories of golden ages, enduring traditions, heroic deeds and dramatic destinies located in ancient or promised home-lands with hallowed sites and scenery ... Landscapes, whether focusing on single monuments or framing stretches of scenery, provide visible shape; they picture the nation.

(Daniels, 1993, p. 5)

An example is the way in which the West of Ireland – the western seaboard and the counties of Connaught – came to symbolize the whole of Ireland to some Irish nationalists in the early twentieth century (Nash, 1993). This was a complex process, but a key aspect of it was certain novels being written at the time. Nationalist Irish writers initially developed a great interest in the region towards the end of the nineteenth century, partly because it was seen as the area least affected by the processes of Anglicization, but also because its bare and rugged landscape seemed to contrast so breathtakingly with the more pastoral landscapes through which contemporary England was imagined (English landscape images will be examined in more detail in section 3.4 of this chapter). Nationalist writers turned to the West of Ireland as a landscape which could regenerate a sense of national identity: being Irish meant being able to identify with the West. Indeed, in some writing being Irish meant being created by the demands of the western environment. The bleak but splendid West demanded strength and a determination to survive, and invited a sensitivity to the sublime too. Because of what nationalist writers saw as the closeness of the people of the West to this wild landscape, westerners came to embody all the virtues of Irishness. They were steadfast, dignified and strong, their relationship to the land a source of stability and calm determination. This characterization was a deliberate challenge to the stereotype of the shiftless, feckless and primitive Irish which many English commentators assumed in their writings on Ireland. Although now challenged by other versions of Irish identity, the West of Ireland remains an important symbol of, and location for, Irishness.

It is also possible to feel a sense of place at the supranational scale. *Europe,* for example, gradually developed as a place with which educated people could identify during the medieval period. Equated with Christendom by the fifteenth century, the region was praised by contemporary writers as having the best climate, the most fertile lands and the most resourceful and skilled populations. By the eighteenth century, Europe was a geographical region which claimed to be the heartland of the civilized world. Even now, Europe is still characterized as a repository of cultural values: Judaeo-Christian religion, Roman law, Greek ideas on politics, philosophy, science and art, and the importance of the Renaissance and the Enlightenment are taken for granted as the most valuable cultural contributions to study and emulate. Generations of students backpack around the European capitals to savour the museums and galleries, and education curricula centre on the same achievements.

Europe

Finally, a sense of place may be experienced at the global scale. Some commentators have argued that recent trends in the global economy are producing a new, global sense of place for some people. They focus in particular on new information and communication technologies. Many of us in the developed world watch satellite television, make phone calls across the globe, watch movies no longer made in Hollywood but by international consortia; some of us fax our colleagues, others use electronic mail, and most of us watch news bulletins from around the world (see **Leyshon, 1995**). Some writers have argued that in these ways we may be caught up in a dizzying electronic geography, seduced by screens and networks, made giddy by the instantaneous transmission of information. Perhaps the most famous author to articulate this contemporary giddiness is Jean Baudrillard. He elaborates what he calls 'the ecstasy of communication': 'I pick up my telephone receiver and it's all there; the whole marginal network catches and harasses me with the insupportable good faith of everything that wants and claims to communicate.' And for Baudrillard this means that people's identities are now pure surface, 'a pure screen, a switching centre for all the networks of influence' (Baudrillard, 1985, pp. 131, 133). Baudrillard is suggesting here that to participate in electronic communications systems is to feel part of the whole global electronic network; it is to develop a sense of place which spans the whole world.

Of course, senses of place may combine these different geographical scales. Images of the West of Ireland, as we have seen, have represented not only that particular region but also a whole nation. Similarly, the image of the American Midwest is central not only to the identity of that region but also to the identity of the United States of America as a whole; its values of individualism, independence, mobility and property ownership are often cited as the epitome of what the USA expects of, and offers, all its inhabitants. Another example of different geographical scales of reference combining to form a particular sense of place is the discussion in the previous chapter of the diverse ways in which the inhabitants of the high-tech villages surrounding Cambridge are connected to other places around the world. This suggests that the geographic references of a sense of place can be globally extensive; senses of place are not necessarily bounded by the local.

3.2.2   Identifying against a place

The idea that identity and place are connected because people feel they belong to a place is certainly not the only connection between identity and place, however. People also establish their sense of place and of who they are by contrasting themselves with somewhere they feel is very different from them.

In thinking about this process of establishing a sense of identity by rejecting an alien place, the work of Edward Said is very helpful. In his book *Orientalism*
Orientalism *(1978)*, Said looks at European (and, to a lesser extent, North American) perceptions of the Near East and Muslim North Africa. Said points out that the Orient has been an object of fascination to the West for centuries, even from before the time of the Crusades. He argues that, over a long historical period, many Western European and North American visitors the Orient have painted the landscapes of what they called *the Orient*, photographed its people, translated its languages, interpreted its cultural practices, and written

about the area in academic texts, novels, poems and travelogues. This accumulated body of knowledge about the place gradually developed a series of assumptions about how to approach 'the East', and it is this vast number of texts about the Orient, with their shared assumptions about the area, that Said calls *Orientalism*. But he argues that all this attention was very far from being an objective study of distant lands. Instead, it propagated a series of myths about the place and its peoples which then influenced how westerners experienced the Orient when they visited.

In the nineteenth century, there was a fashion in Europe for paintings of the Orient, and these paintings visualized many of these myths in popular form. Most of these western images oscillated between two visions of the Orient, and both these are evident in Orientalist paintings of the desert. On the one hand, and more unusually, the desert was shown as a mysterious repository of spiritual revelation, peopled by dignified and pious nomads. The desert was imagined as a vast, challenging space in which spiritual strength could be won. This was a romantic view of the Orient, which tended to obscure indigenous Islamic beliefs with a Christian interpretation of the desert. On the other hand, the collapsed and abandoned ruins of former civilizations which were scattered in the desert were taken as evidence of the inability of the Orient to follow the standard set by the Romans in its past; the Orient somehow could not sustain civilization. Many other images affirmed this understanding of the Orient as a corrupt and depraved place, its rulers tyrants, its peoples barbaric, violence the only law. The so-called 'harem' was seen as evidence of the laziness, decadence and primitive lusts of Oriental men and women, for example. The sense of place these assumptions created about the Orient was quite complex, then, emphasizing both spirituality and barbarism.

Said argues that these images of the Orient clearly influenced the way in which visitors interpreted what they saw in the region. But he also argues that these images helped to shape how visitors understood their home countries too. Said suggests that Orientalism in fact says far more about the fears and desires of the West which produced it than it does about any reality of life in the Near East. This is easy to accept in the case of images of the harem, for example; the many photographs and paintings of harem life that were so popular in the nineteenth century were often entirely the products of the imaginations of western men, and speak eloquently of their sexual fantasies. But Said insists that this is the case for all the knowledges produced about the Orient. The maps, the travel accounts, the landscape paintings, the photographs, all produced what he calls an 'imagined geography' of the area. In the very effort and act of describing, cataloguing, and interpreting, westerners were asserting that the Orient was so exotic that it needed describing, cataloguing and interpreting. And the Orient was 'exotic', not on its own terms, but in terms of an implicit comparison to the West. The Orient was defined as exotic, decadent and corrupt, but these verdicts were passed in relation to a West which implicitly situated itself as civilized and moral in contrast. Thus, while paintings of Roman ruins spoke of Oriental barbarity, they also asserted the need for the more civilized West to rescue those ruins and take them somewhere they would be appreciated: the museums of Western Europe. What were seen as Oriental vices were made to define Western European virtues. Conversely, the notion of a spiritual Orient made sense only in relation to European anxieties about the development of an increasingly

Two 'Oriental' paintings: (top) Léon Belly, Pilgrims Going to Mecca, *1861; (bottom) David Roberts,* Portico of the Temple of Bacchus, Baalbeck, *1841*

alienated and secular kind of urban life in rapidly expanding western cities; here, Oriental virtues were made to define Western European vices. Said thus concludes that Orientalism expressed the values of the cultures producing it. Hence, it is possible to suggest that the 'sense of place' produced by Orientalism, and through which western visitors to that area interpreted what they saw, did not offer a sense of the Orient on its own terms but rather established the Orient as an exotic place against which a European 'home' was defined, usually as all the more favourable. The meaning of (Christian) Europe thus depended on its image of an (Islamic) Orient against which it could identify itself.

These processes are at work today. Many writers have noted a contemporary resurgence of European identity which is reasserting the exclusions of Orientalism. Although, in the imperialist era of the nineteenth and first half of the twentieth century, European nations could put their conviction of their superiority into often violent practice, in the post-Second World War period European confidence in its own hegemony has been threatened. Senses of place are often heightened when perceived to be under threat, and in the case of Europe the threats were seen to be several. The United States emerged from the Second World War an economic and political power far stronger than Europe; most of the colonies of Europe won their independence, formally at least; more recently, Japan has become economically superior; the cultural and political challenges launched in 1968 have forced social change; and the end of the Cold War and the revolutions of 1989 have made Europe's eastern borders far less clear than once they were. In the face of this uncertainty, efforts have been made to reassert a European identity, in large part by insisting on the difference between Europe and other places. The US is thus often perceived as the purveyor of mass, cheap, culture, which, from *Dallas* to Rambo to Madonna, is seen as quite inferior to European civilization. More often, however, Europe and the US are represented as 'the West' against the rest, and a new version of Orientalism is projected. Sometimes this Orientalism focuses on what is described as Islamic fundamentalism, and represents this as a threat to the liberal traditions of Europe. Sometimes Islam is associated with a terrorism represented as irrational and totally antithetical to western democracy. Local racisms and the rise of organized political parties on the far right have fed this affirmation of a bounded and 'pure' European identity. The immigration policies of the European Union are also an example of this reassertion of European identity. These policies were discussed in Chapter 1, section 1.4.2, and they suggest that, while migration from the former Eastern bloc is a challenge to be risen to, immigration into Europe from Turkey, Morocco, Algeria and Tunisia is a threat which must be halted by rigorous border controls and immigration policies. Read and Simpson describe these policies as encouraging 'the recreation of Christendom' (1991, p. 33), and a Turkish writer, Sefyi Tashan, has said of Turkish people that 'in Europe, many people see us as a new version of the Ottoman empire, attacking this time in the form of guest workers and terrorists' (quoted in Morley and Robins, 1990, p. 16). In the light of these perceptions, it is hardly surprising that the European Union has been reluctant to grant membership to Turkey (although Turkey's human rights record is also a contributory factor).

Activity 2   Many of these themes are discussed in Reading A by David Morley and Kevin Robins, entitled 'Techno-Orientalism: futures, phobias and foreigners', which you will find at the end of this chapter. This essay on 'techno-Orientalism' examines yet another aspect of contemporary Orientalism: a fear of Japan. Read sections I and II only at this point, and make a list of the qualities attributed to the Japanese by western commentators. In particular, note how these attributes are contrasted unfavourably with those given to Europe and North America: Japanese homogeneity, for example, in contrast to western pluralism.

From this discussion, we can see that a sense of place may be even more complicated than the previous sub-section suggested. It may explicitly refer to one place, but at the same time implicitly also be making arguments about another place. This leads to an important consideration which will be pursued in more detail in section 3.3 of this chapter: identity and place are not only articulated positively as a list of elements with which to identify; they are also structured in relation to perceptions of other groups and places as different.

3.2.3   Not identifying

It is important to recognize that a particular sense of place may be felt to be irrelevant to identity. For example, the strength of one sense of place may make it difficult to feel concerned for another place. It is often argued that this is the case for most people in relation to Europe: feeling 'European' is argued to be subordinate to feeling 'English' or 'French' or 'Spanish' and so on.

Another reason for feeling little about a place is because you are a stranger there. This is a feeling often experienced by migrants. Chapter 1 of this book emphasized what a large diverse group migrants are. The decision to migrate to a particular location may be motivated by a strong sense of what that place is: the USA as the 'land of the free', for example. But if that decision to move is not taken freely, migrants may feel little attachment to their new home. Not belonging is perhaps felt especially acutely by refugees and exiles who did not leave their homes voluntarily. Moreover, migrants may not be made to feel welcome in their new homes, and this may be a reason for developing a feeling of hostility towards a place. Dislike or fear of a place may create what Zonabend calls 'memory blanks' (1993, p. 123). Aspects of a place may be evaded or forgotten; its sense of place may not evoke belonging at all.

Activity 3   Read Françoise Zonabend's account of people talking about la Hague in Reading B, 'The nuclear peninsula'. La Hague is the site of two nuclear reprocessing plants on the western tip of the Cotentin Peninsula in Normandy. List the ways in which people there evade thinking about the risks of working in that place.

For a variety of reasons, then, identity and a particular place may have little relation to each other.

The various examples of senses of place in this section have been deliberately diverse. They emphasized how complex senses of place can be. A sense of place can be articulated through many different media: novels, paintings, foreign and domestic policy, music, films, advertisements, the built and farmed landscape, everyday conversation, and many more that this section has not mentioned. Senses of place can draw on one or more geographical scale: a sense of place may be intensely local, or it may refer both to the local and the global. A sense of place may also make sense in relation to more than one place: thus, Orientalism offers both a complex series of interpretations of 'the Orient' and also a series of ideas about Western European identity in contrast. A sense of place may work by inviting people to articulate their identity in terms of belonging to a particular place; or a sense of what one place is may be established through a contrast with another place represented as alien; or a sense of place may be contradictory; or a sense of place may have little to do with the articulation of identity. Senses of place may become more intense when those who feel they belong there feel threatened.

Finally, this section has also suggested that senses of place involve different groups of people in different ways. The same location may become meaningful to different people through different senses of place. For example, it is very doubtful that Bedouins or Native Americans shared the same sense of place (of 'the Orient', or the Midwest) as those who came from elsewhere to visit or to settle. Another example of different senses of place is the different perceptions of the globe held by jet-setting executives of multinational corporations and by international green organizations like Friends of the Earth. The former may, as Baudrillard suggests, see the world as a series of information flows with giddying possibilities; the latter, though they use those same information networks, are more likely to emphasize the constraints of a finite globe of finite resources. Indeed, these different senses of place contradict each other and may become the source of conflict. The next section looks at the different ways in which it has been argued that senses of place should be related to these questions of social difference and unequal power relations.

Summary of section 3.2

o   Senses of place can be expressed through a diversity of media.

o   Senses of place can be established at different geographical scales, and these can intersect.

o   Senses of place relate to identity in different ways: they may invite identification with a place; they may establish identity by offering a contrast between the place that is 'home' and the place that is 'away'; or the meaning of a sense of place may be irrelevant to how people identify themselves.

o   Senses of place may become more intense when they are perceived as being under threat.

o   The same location may be interpreted through different senses of place.

Activity 4

o   Return to the description you made of a place that is particularly important to you (for Activity 1 at the beginning of this chapter). At which scale of those discussed in section 3.2.1 do you feel it belongs? Does it belong to another scale not listed there? Or does it invoke several spatial scales?

o   This section has shown that senses of place can be articulated through many different media: music, landscape painting, advertisements, corporate policy documents, letters, to name but a few. In which form was your description? Why did you choose that and not another form?

o   Was it a place you identify with or against? Or was it a place quite unconnected to who you feel you are? Or is your relationship to it quite different from the three possibilities this section has described?

3.3   Explanations for a sense of place

Many geographers, sociologists and anthropologists, among others, have argued about explanations for the social meaning of place and for different senses of place. Their arguments about senses of place can be grouped into three kinds. They all assume, however, that places have no inherent meaning, only the meanings humans give to them.

3.3.1   A sense of place is natural

It has been argued that wanting to have a place where you feel you belong is a natural human attribute. Sometimes it is suggested that this desire is a territorial instinct. More often, it is argued that the need for place is more a kind of survival strategy. Smith has commented that:

The occupation of territory is fundamental to human existence. To survive even at the most 'primitive' level of social organization and technology requires access to natural resources of the land, sometimes supplemented by the sea but never wholly independent of terra firma. Whether perpetually on the move, as hunters and gatherers, or in fixed and permanent settlements, access to particular territory or to the product thereof is a necessary condition of life. And this may require exclusive access if the means of subsistence are to be assured: a place of their own may become their own place.

(Smith, 1990, p. 1)

Other writers, however, are sceptical about such arguments which naturalize a 'need' to belong to a particular place. They argue that such generalizations across the extraordinary diversity of human cultures are extremely difficult to make with any confidence. Accordingly, many social scientists use other explanations for senses of place.

3.3.2   A sense of place is constructed by underlying structures of power

Many commentators have argued that, far from being natural, a sense of place is related to what distinguishes humans from nature: their ability to think and reflect. In this argument, a sense of place is seen as a result of the meanings people actively give to their lives. It is part of the systems of meaning through which we make sense of the world. We might describe this as a cultural explanation for sense of place. Following this line of argument, a sense of place can be seen as part of our cultural interpretation of the world around us.

But of course there is not one culture, but many, and some writers have argued that it is an awareness of cultural *difference* which may encourage a sense of place to develop. They argue that different groups in a society may notice their differences from other groups and want to mark that difference, and that one of the ways in which they do that is by claiming that they belong to a particular place to which other groups do not belong. A sense of place can thus be a way of establishing a difference between one group and another.

difference

This process of claiming place can take the form of elaborate rituals – think of the Eisteddfod as an assertion of Welsh identity, for example – but it can also happen in quite everyday, small-scale kinds of ways. Graffiti, for example, can be used by different groups in urban areas to mark out the territory they see as theirs. In 1974, geographer David Ley published the results of his study of street gangs in Philadelphia, and he noted that graffiti were a major means of marking out the turf of competing gangs. In the centre of its territory, graffiti celebrated the gang and its exploits. Towards the boundaries of its territory, graffiti became both more frequent and more aggressive, often taking the form of obscene insults towards other gangs and their members. From this pattern, Ley argued that graffiti were being used to establish the boundaries of each gang's area. At the boundary of the gang's area, where the gang felt most threatened, graffiti were asserting that the place was its own. This territorial sense of place emphasizes an important aspect of many senses of place: they are about establishing social difference by establishing spatial boundaries. And just as senses of place can focus on the whole range of geographical scales, so boundaries between places can be established at different scales.

The importance of *boundaries* to many senses of place begins to raise further questions about how senses of place can be understood as part of wider social processes. For boundaries have a dual role. Firstly, they work to establish insiders: those who belong to that place. We have already seen that 'belonging' can be a central component in senses of place. But belonging to one place means that it may be difficult to feel a sense of belonging for somewhere else; and it may also mean that those who are perceived as belonging elsewhere are excluded from belonging to other places they may want to identify with. Thus, the second function of the boundaries of a place is often to establish outsiders: those who do not belong. To return to the example of European identity, we have seen how the assertion of a particular definition of Europe as Christian involves racist rejections of Islam.

boundary

At this point in the argument, then, it seems necessary to address more directly the relationship between social inequality and senses of place. Whose sense of place is more powerful in a particular situation? Whose sense of place has to fight to be expressed? Why are some senses of place negative for some people? Just as previous chapters have explored geographical flows of people, capital, commodities and information and have argued that these flows are not only uneven but unequal, so too this chapter will now argue that senses of place are not only different but part of unequal social relations. This is certainly the argument made by Said in his discussion of Orientalism. You will recall, from the account in section 3.2.2, that Said argues that Orientalism was an elaborate series of myths of the so-called Orient. But Said also argues that the sense of place they conveyed was central to European colonialism. He argues that the idea that the Orient was less civilized than Europe legitimated European invasions and economic exploitation of that area of the globe. Orientalism, then, justified European imperialism by refusing to recognize the autonomy of the cultures and peoples of the Near East. Senses of place, then, can be seen as a result of underlying structures of power such as colonialism and imperialism.

power

territoriality

Many commentators have linked the claim to belong to a particular place to the dynamics of *power* relations. Robert Sack is quite clear about this: 'territoriality is a primary geographical expression of social power. It is the means by which society and space are related' (1986, p. 5). He argues that *territoriality* is nothing more or less than a claim to control people by controlling an area. Those who belong to a particular place are distinguished from those who do not; and while the latter may be excluded from that place, the former are expected to conform to its conventions. Sack's description of territoriality corresponds to what this chapter has described as the sense of place which involves identifying with somewhere. However, his argument about senses of place and social power is relevant to all kinds of senses of place. Many writers have argued that all senses of place are inextricably bound into social power relations in some way.

economic
restructuring

The most obvious example of the way power relations can structure senses of place is cases where one sense of place becomes so dominant that it obscures other, perhaps more important, understandings about that same place. This process has received much attention lately, particularly in the context of recent patterns of *economic restructuring* in the developed world. You will be familiar with the way in which analyses of economic restructuring processes are now emphasizing the perception of particular places by multinational corporations. In reaction to the discrimination with which those corporations now choose sites for investment, many places are now very concerned about the image they present to the outside world. Local councils and development corporations increasingly spend large sums on presenting an attractive image to the outside world, claiming, for example, that 'Glasgow's miles better' or extolling the virtues of 'Brighter Belfast'.

Since its establishment in 1981, for example, the London Docklands Development Corporation (LDDC) has undertaken a series of advertising campaigns presenting Docklands as a desirable place to be. Between 1981 and 1989 it spent £31 million on such campaigns, and in 1990 another campaign cost £3 million. The earlier campaigns were directed at business investors. Some advertisements emphasized the centrality of London as an industrial and financial centre, and others stressed the communication links between Docklands and both the rest of London and other world cities, particularly New York. These campaigns played on some of the stereotypes of the East End of London already current at the time. Their characters spoke Cockney and one television campaign parodied a TV comedy programme about East End petty criminals. And they were influential in shaping outsiders' perceptions of the area; when the owners of small businesses who had moved into Docklands soon after this campaign were interviewed, they

Differing senses of place: (top) an image from the LDDC Press Office showing the development of East India Dock; (bottom) a protest image produced by the Docklands Community Poster Project

said they found these adverts charming, giving 'character' to the place (Burgess and Wood, 1989). Later campaigns emphasized the glamorous lifestyle the LDDC wanted to argue was possible in Docklands, and advertisements showed cultural events, watersports, fine restaurants and river views. Like many other companies or corporations involved in efforts to regenerate declining inner-city areas, the LDDC was attempting to appeal to the stereotypes held by, and the cultural tastes of, the kind of people with money to invest in either land or business or property in Docklands. It has also funded music festivals, commissioned public sculpture, and sponsored laser and music spectacles. The Design Museum is located on the riverfront just east of Tower Bridge, there have been plans for a branch of the Museum of London to be located in the LDDC area, and efforts have been made to persuade the National Portrait Gallery to relocate there. While many of these events and institutions may appeal to a wide range of people, there is no doubt that the main motive of the LDDC in encouraging them has been to make its area attractive to wealthy outsiders with capital to invest in the area. The LDDC has the money to invest in these campaigns and spends it in order to attract more investment.

However, many of these kinds of efforts to establish a sense of place so that certain groups are tempted to move to an area erase alternative interpretations of those places. Many property development companies trying to sell expensive apartments and houses in inner-city locations produce glossy brochures which do not mention other residents of the area, and indeed often talk about the place as if it was a completely empty space. In many US cities, developers even suggest that such areas are the new frontier awaiting settlement. But of course many of these areas are still home to large working-class communities, who have very different interpretations of the areas. Given its persistent refusal to respond to the demands of these communities in what the communities perceive as an appropriate way, the LDDC has been faced with many angry protests from local people arguing that their needs are being ignored in the LDDC's priorities, and this shows that local people have a different set of priorities from the developers. These protests have taken a variety of forms, and have been organized by many different groups, but a persistent theme is that local people have a right to be heard because, in the words of a poster made for one protest, 'this land is our land'. Local people counterpose their sense of place to that of the LDDC. They argue that their localities are communities in which people care for each other; their sense of belonging to the East End of London involves being part of a collective community which, unlike the LDDC they argue, puts people before profit. Many of their protests focus on landmarks which were once central to thriving communities, and are now demolished or converted into luxury flats encircled by security systems. It is because these alternative understandings of East End places and identities are obscured in the advertisements for capital investment in Docklands that the sense of place created by those adverts must be seen as an aspect of unequal social relations. In these advertisements, the structural power of capital dominates the senses of place through which Docklands is understood.

Activity 5 Do you live in a town or city which has tried to attract inward investment? If so, what kinds of images have been used in its campaigns? What aspects of place do they emphasize and which do they neglect? Why?

3.3.3 A sense of place is part of the politics of identity

You might have felt that the arguments of section 3.3.2 were so concerned with understanding senses of place in terms of their relationship to power relations that they did not pay enough attention to the ways in which senses of place are also very personal. Certainly, the emphasis on emotion and feeling with which this chapter began was rather neglected in the previous sub-section, which addressed the relationship between identity and place at quite a general level. Much writing on senses of place which emphasizes the intersection of place and power tends to offer a structural analysis of the relationship between the two; that is, it looks for the structures of power which underlie a particular sense of place. Remember, for example, the quotation from Eyles at the beginning of this chapter, and his insistence that experience alone was not enough to understand senses of place: 'the existence and importance of structures, mechanisms and forces beyond immediate observation must be accepted', he says. A possible consequence of this argument is that all analytical effort focuses on those structures, mechanisms and forces. This in turn may produce one of two problems: either the experiential aspects of senses of place get neglected; or the analyst may simply assume that he or she knows what the experiential consequences of particular representations of places are. In both cases, the feelings and emotions with which senses of place are infused are not explored.

However, some writers concerned with power relations have also spent some time considering the emotional dynamics involved in the intersection of identity with senses of place. For example, Benedict Anderson (1983), in his analysis of nationalism, reminds us that although its critics may dismiss nationalism as a brutal and myopic form of identity, none the less many people believe in the rights of their nation passionately enough to kill and die for it. Senses of place may be as empassioned and violent as this. In trying to understand how identity is involved in the often intense emotional construction of senses of place, many writers have turned to the importance of boundaries, discussed in section 3.2.2. They too have suggested that boundaries are important because they help to define identity by marking not only what/where it *is*, but also what/where it is *not*. Thus, to return to the discussion of Irish national identity in section 3.2.1, it is possible to see that the positive attributes of Irishness enumerated by Irish nationalists were praised by them in part because they were seen as the opposite of Englishness. This process of establishing an identity through a contrast with what one is not has been analysed by many writers, and they argue that it is central to dominant ways of thinking in the West.

This argument is complex and draws on a range of theoretical debates, but in outline it is fairly clear. It is argued that this way of thinking by defining something in opposition to what it is not is fundamental to the production of knowledge in the West. It is a way of regulating meaning. In particular, it constructs a certain understanding of difference. Difference – different social groups, different cultures – is not seen in its own terms, but is perceived only in relation to the identity of the observer. Said's discussion of Orientalism employs just this argument. As we saw, he says that none of the commentaries on 'the Orient' represented that place or its people in terms of their own cultural values or social mores; instead, the region was understood only as that which the West was not. The notion of the 'uncivilized' Orient works to establish the West as civilized.

Other   Said uses a particular term for this structure of feeling. He describes the Orient as the *Other* of the West. By this he means that the Orient was seen only in terms of an implicit contrast with the West. This process is not a calm and logical one, however; it is full of emotion, fantasies, fears and desires. The Orient was all that the West both feared and wanted in itself; hence the complexity of its simultaneous praise for the spirituality of desert people and its dislike of what it saw as Oriental customs. Rutherford describes the emotionally fraught process of creating an Other thus:

> *the centre expels its anxieties, contradictions and irrationalities onto the subordinate terms [the Other], filling it with the antithesis of its own identity; the Other, in its very alienness, simply mirrors and represents what is deeply familiar to the centre, but projected outside of itself. It is in these processes and representations of marginality that the violence, antagonisms and aversions which are at the core of dominant discourses and identities become manifest – racism, homophobia, misogyny and class contempt are the products of this frontier.*
>
> *(Rutherford, 1990, p. 22)*

Here, Rutherford also emphasizes the power relations through which this process of constructing identity works. He suggests, in effect, that there is a politics of identity. Ideas about difference – about sexual difference, racial difference, class difference, bodily difference – are articulated through the construction of the Other. The Other is the socially marginalized, the less powerful, the working class, black, female, gay, lesbian, disabled, the geographically peripheral. Individuals and communities may be described in one or more of these ways. Often those perceived as Other are jumbled together and rejected in one sweeping gesture. Here is a comment on the perception of non-European Others in recent debates about European migration policy; its author argues that underlying those debates is a racism:

> *which cannot tell one black from another, a citizen from an immigrant, an immigrant from a refugee – and classes all Third World peoples as immigrants and refugees, and all immigrants and refugees as terrorists and drug dealers.*
>
> *(Sivanandan, quoted in Read and Simpson, 1991, p. 2)*

Activity 6   Many of these themes are discussed in Reading A on 'techno-Orientalism'. Read sections III, IV and V now, and note how Morley and Robins describe the process through which Europe is constructing Japan as its Other.

We can thus suggest here that exclusionary accounts about who belongs in a place and who does not are made through the construction of Others. The way in which powerful institutions like developers or development corporations create a sense of place which marginalizes the already-existing interpretations of that same place held by less powerful groups – as described in section 3.3.2 – can also be understood as an example of this process of creating Others through a sense of place; for example, compared to the gleaming new developments, the rest of the area (and its communities) is represented by those developers as a decrepit anachronism.

The responses by those less powerful groups to their definition as Other are diverse. Some groups, especially if they feel threatened by the consequences of this process, may insist on their own alternative sense of place; for example, insisting on an older vision of East End community may be an empowering way to challenge the policies of the LDDC. But here again, exclusions are entailed; that old East End vision relies on a sense of long family tradition, and of generations of families living in the same place, in order to claim that 'this land is our land', and clearly more recent immigrants to the area will not be able to make that same claim. Other groups may simply reject a place if its dominant meaning excludes them. Still others, however, may try to imagine quite different senses of place. One example this chapter has already mentioned briefly is the global network of groups affiliated to Friends of the Earth. This network operates by respecting the opinions and autonomy of its members. Its members try not to treat any other members as their Other but rather, by listening carefully to their views, to respect each other. This network is trying to develop senses of place and identity which are cooperative and consensual.

Section 3.3 has argued that in order to understand the causes of senses of place it is necessary to connect them to wider social relations. Places may become significant only in the context of unequal power relations between different groups. This is particularly evident when the manner in which certain senses of place include some people and exclude others is considered. The passion and the violence of the boundaries between those perceived to belong and those perceived as alien may be understood, in the West at least, in terms of the emotional dynamics of the Other. The notion of the Other allows us to connect senses of place, power and identity in an analytical manner which does not neglect the emotional dynamics of place. Some senses of place can also be understood as efforts to think about place and identity in ways which escape the process of excluding the Other.

Summary of section 3.3

o   There are different explanations for why senses of place develop. They can be divided into three broad types: those that argue a sense of place is natural, those that argue that it is a consequence of underlying structures of power, and those who see it as a way of defining the Other.

o   The idea of the Other emphasizes the emotional dynamics of power relations.

o   Senses of place may develop as a challenge to dominant senses of place.

Activity 7 Before the case study in the next section, consolidate your understanding of the chapter so far. Return to what you have read of Reading A and note how the authors' arguments connect to the summaries of sections 3.2 and 3.3 of this chapter. For me, the most important connections are:

o   their argument that the West defines itself, in part at least, by a contrast with what it perceives it is not;

o   their analysis of Japan as the Other of the West;

o   their emphasis on the power of the West which enables it to construct a particular, influential understanding of Japan;

o   their argument that it is when the West feels particularly threatened by, and vulnerable to, Japanese economic strength that its fantasies about Japan proliferate;

o   their emphasis on the ambivalence of those fantasies;

o   their noting of Japanese commentators' resistance to these western fantasies.

3.4   Case study: Englishness and the rural idyll

If senses of place are an important part of the way in which power relations are reproduced, they are bound to be contested as social power struggles

Englishness   develop. This section asks you to look at a series of images of *Englishness*, and to consider their embeddedness in struggles over relations of class and 'race', in particular.

Recent years have seen a resurgence in English patriotism. Mrs Thatcher successfully appealed to this patriotism to win support for the waging of the Falklands/Malvinas War and for the government's attitude towards the miners' strike. However, it could also be argued that these are examples of a sense of place being heightened during times of perceived threat. For, in recent years, Englishness has also been challenged from a variety of sources: immigration from abroad has continued; Scotland and Wales have campaigned for devolution and independence; Northern Ireland continues to trouble the unity of the British state; and economic change produced a popular perception of 'two nations' during the second half of the 1980s. Thus, Englishness was very much a contested identity during the 1980s, and continues so today. And one of the key ways in which that contest has been articulated is through a particular sense of place of England.

Images of place are central to ideas of Englishness. Lowenthal argues that: 'nowhere else is landscape so freighted as legacy. Nowhere else does the very term suggest not simply scenery and *genres de vie,* but quintessential national virtues' (1991, p. 213). The way in which the land has been imagined as England has varied historically, but, as the nineteenth century progressed, England was more and more often being pictured in terms of a landscape still symbolically resonant today: a landscape of green rolling hills, shady nooks, copses, winding lanes and nestling thatched villages. This was the landscape Constable painted, and it was towards the end of the nineteenth century that his canvases became popular; it was at this time that the *Haywain* and Willy Lott's cottage came to symbolize all that was worthy and decent about England.

There are several reasons why this particular landscape came to represent Englishness (Howkins, 1986; Potts, 1989). By the end of the nineteenth century, the industrial north of England was losing its position as the workshop of the world, and the economic centre of Britain was increasingly London; London was also the centre of an Empire. It seemed, then, that the economic and political heart of the nation had shifted south. But London itself did not appear appropriate as a symbol of the nation, for many contemporary commentators could see only too clearly the deleterious effects of rapid urbanization and industrialization on city life. Large cities seemed environmentally polluted, socially chaotic and morally degenerate; the slum was seen as a canker at the heart of the Empire. The search for a symbol of the nation thus turned to the countryside of the south of England. The soft hills, small villages around a green, winding lanes and church steeples of the English southern counties came to represent England and all the qualities the culturally dominant classes desired.

Lowenthal (1991) suggests that there were three qualities which this 'south country' landscape was meant to convey: consensus, continuity, and the nation itself. By consensus he means that this landscape was represented as one where social life was harmonious and free of conflict. Social hierarchies were shown to exist, but it was suggested that the squire and the villager each knew their place and were content with it. This social structure was legitimated as part of a long tradition in which many generations had participated. As well as this imagined human continuity, Lowenthal comments on the continuity of human modification of the physical environment which this image of the south country was meant to invoke. This sense of place suggested that the relationship between humans and nature had reached a balance through the centuries; it was shown as a deeply historical landscape. Finally, this landscape was argued to stand for all England. It was this image which stood for the country as a whole.

This was obviously a very particular vision of the English countryside, which ignored certain regions and ignored processes of rural change and conflict. Nevertheless, English men and women were asked to identify with this landscape and this sense of national identity, and seemed to a large extent to have done so. It was propagated in all sorts of media: in paintings, like Constable's, but also in novels and poems. Architecture and garden design by the end of the nineteenth century were turning to vernacular rural traditions for inspiration too. Classical music invoking England – like Elgar's work – was praised, and there was a revival of interest in English folksong. The magazine *Country Life* started publication in 1897, and its accounts of leisured and harmonious English rural life made it very popular. Howkins (1986) points out that this sense of place became especially acute during the First World War; it was used to symbolize all the qualities for which the troops were fighting. And it also seems to have provided some kind of comfort to those trapped in the trenches; *Country Life* was avidly read there, a reminder of the better life that was somewhere possible. All these aspects of Englishness were reiterated in the inter-war period, so that in 1939 soldiers once again marched to war singing:

> There'll always be an England
> While there's a country lane,
> As long as there's a cottage small
> Beside a field of grain.

Although this was by no means the only song that was sung, and although other songs mentioned other places, this song in particular exemplifies a certain sense of Englishness as a place worth defending. And this 'south country' was a sense of place fostered by dominant groups in order to encourage social harmony and loyalty to the nation and to the state.

This sense of belonging to England's green and pleasant land was heightened in both the nineteenth and twentieth centuries by contrasts with other places. The aesthetic and social idyll represented by the southern English countryside was made all the more eloquent by comparisons with the landscapes of the Other. The barbarity of the exotic Orient (and Africa) was one Other landscape, as section 3.2.2. showed. Another was the Arctic

The aesthetic and social idyll of the southern English countryside as depicted in John Linnell's painting The Last Glean Before the Storm, *c.1846/7*

The harsh polar landscape of Edwin Landseer's painting Man Proposes, God Disposes, *1864, enhances, by implicit contrast, the sense of belonging to England's green and pleasant land*

(Pringle, 1991). A key image here is Edwin Landseer's canvas, *Man Proposes, God Disposes*. This was exhibited in 1864 and caused great controversy. It was thought to refer to the loss of John Franklin's expedition in search of the Northwest Passage. That expedition set sail in 1845, and nothing was known of its fate until 1854, when a report reached England that the bodies of the crews had been found with evidence of cannibalism. In 1858, the deaths of all those on the expedition when it reached the Artic were confirmed. The polar bears ripping the Union Jack and gnawing at a human ribcage in Landseer's painting were seen as a reference to the possible cannibalism. This inference was made in the light of Darwin's arguments about evolution – the bears were seen as representing the animal instincts remaining in humans, forced into the open in extreme circumstances. This fear was especially sharp at the time Landseer exhibited *Man Proposes, God Disposes*, since the middle-class viewers of his paintings were worried at the same time about the physical and moral degeneration of poor urban populations, and the threat to social order this perceived degeneration of the Other posed. The ice and the bears were thus metaphors for the social fears of the Victorian middle-class.

The dominant sense of England, then, can be interpreted in terms of a particular landscape image which contains only one particular version of English place and its social relations. Any hint of social conflict has been removed. It is also constructed through a contrast with Others: Other landscapes which also represent Other social groups.

Activity 8   Look at this painting. Note down how it conveys the ideas of Englishness discussed above. What kinds of identity are being displayed in these images? Do they represent a particular class? How, exactly? Note down any other connotations the image brings to mind.

Mr and Mrs Andrews, 1748, by Thomas Gainsborough (The National Gallery, London)

The portrait of Mr and Mrs Andrews seems to me to exemplify many of these arguments about Englishness, even though it was painted some time before the period in which the 'south country' became the dominant landscape of English senses of place. The landscape is that gently rolling one, and offers an orderly scene of sensitive land management: the neat fields, the rich harvest, the improved breeds of sheep. The two figures are sheltered by an English oak, which frames this idyllic scene. Implicit is a contrast to less civilized places. However, the specificity of the social relations represented by this image and its sense of place can also be detected. The absence of the people who work the fields is noticeable, for example. Indeed, this is a painting which celebrates not the working of the land, but its ownership. Ownership of land is celebrated in the substantiality of the oil paints used to represent it, and in the vista opening up beyond Mr and Mrs Andrews which echoes in visual form the freedom to move over property which only landowners could enjoy. Berger insists that the fact that this couple owned the fields and trees about them is central to its meaning: 'they are landowners and their proprietary attitude towards what surrounds them is visible in their stance and their expressions' (1972, p. 107).

Activity 9 Now take a look at this cartoon by Steve Bell. In what ways is he using the English landscape? How do his figures function?

Cartoon by Steve Bell: after Mr and Mrs Andrews *by Thomas Gainsborough (Leeds Postcards and Steve Bell)*

The kind of landscape which has come to represent a quintessentially English scene is not inevitably conservative. It can be used to argue for what in the 1980s were seen as radical policies, like nuclear disarmament.

This image was drawn by Steve Bell for the Campaign for Nuclear Disarmament. He has turned to *Mr and Mrs Andrews* in order to emphasize the long tradition of an English landscape owned in common. The impact of his cartoon derives from a strong sense that the English landscape painted by Gainsborough is part of common heritage, a heritage being denied 'us', ordinary folk, by the imposition of nuclear weapons on that landscape. The impression is of that landscape defiled, and defiled moreover by the United States. This is a further reminder of the ways in which one sense of place is defined by contrast to an Other; and English landscape is here being betrayed by what Bell represents as a grotesque transatlantic alliance between Margaret Thatcher and Ronald Reagan.

So far, the images in this discussion have been contesting the meaning of this 'English' landscape: does its sense of place, for all its inclusive pretensions, actually belong only to the élite, the property owners, the politicians, or does it belong to ordinary people too?

Challenges to the Englishness of these images are not difficult to find, however. One is offered by an advertisement for a car.

Activity 10   How does the advertisement reproduced on pages 112–13 hope to sell you a car by showing you a reproduction of Gainsborough's painting? What does the advertisement imply is shared between the car and the image?

The car is French, a Renault. Other paintings used in this advertising campaign were French and North American. All were used to represent, not national identity, but international taste. Here the argument returns to earlier discussions about global senses of place. Advertising consultants Saatchi and Saatchi have suggested that there is a greater social gulf between Manhattan and the Bronx than between Manhattan and the seventh arrondissement in Paris, and the advertisement for Renault can be seen in these terms; it replaces the invocation of national place with an international place, an international class of the wealthy. This international class may feel little allegiance to any particular nation even as it buys commodities clearly associated with particular nations: German cars; Japanese CD equipment; French *haute couture*; ski holidays in Aspen, Colorado; summer vacations in Tuscany; and English antiques. In this advertisement, then, the class connotations of Gainsborough's canvas are not referring to the English social hierarchy, but to an international hierarchy in which national identity means less and less.

A second challenge to established visions of the English landscape comes from Ingrid Pollard, a member of the Black Environment Network.

Activity 11   Look at the two photographs and captions by Ingrid Pollard on pages 114–15. What relationship to the English countryside is Pollard articulating here?

An advertisement for the Renault Safrane range of executive cars

'... feeling I don't belong. Walks through leafy glades with a baseball bat by my side ...'

' ... a lot of what made ENGLAND GREAT is founded on the blood of slavery, the sweat of working people ... an Industrial REVOLUTION without the Atlantic Triangle? ...'

The Black Environment Network has pointed out that the numbers of black people who are members of organizations such as the National Trust, Ramblers' Association or Youth Hostel Association are very small. They suggest that one reason for this may be that the vision of Englishness which rural images of England convey is a white Englishness. The English sense of place discourages black membership of rural organizations because the countryside is not seen as an appropriate location for black people. In her photographs, Pollard is hoping to rework the meaning of the English rural landscape so that it speaks of black identities too. She is challenging the exclusion of black identities from a particular sense of place of England. She is demanding that they no longer be the Other of white Englishness.

This section has explored one dominant sense of Englishness: a particular image of the English countryside. It has also looked at various reactions to that sense of place which challenge its dominant meaning. Like all senses of place, then, the particular ways in which this English sense of place represents only particular social identities mean that other identities have contested its validity.

Activity 12 In the light of the discussion in this section, go back to the description you made of a place that is particularly important to you (for Activity 1 at the beginning of this chapter). Can you now place it in terms of a wider social context? Are there elements of it that might be explained by what you perceive of as your class position? Might you feel the same way about it if your gender was different, or if you were black instead of white, or white instead of black?

3.5   Conclusions: place, resistance and the politics of identity

This chapter has developed a discussion about 'a sense of place' which emphasizes that senses of place often work to establish differences between one group of people and another. These differences are complex and can be based on class, gender, 'race' and many other aspects of identity. These definitions are bound into social power relations. The politics of claiming to be an insider are also often the politics of claiming power. This chapter has focused in particular on those processes of claiming power through particular senses of place. Very often they are made emotionally resonant through the process of Othering. But the chapter has also argued that senses of place are very complex and that particular definitions of place can be contested. This process of contestation is perhaps more evident now than ever before. Increasing flows of ideas, commodities, information and people are constantly challenging senses of place and identity which perceive themselves as stable and fixed. The increasing interdependence between places means that, for many academics at least, places must be seen as having permeable boundaries across which things are always moving. Identities, too, more and more often involve experiences of migration and cultural changing and mixing. This means perhaps that the process of Othering – of defining where you belong through a contrast with other places, or who you are through a contrast with Other people – is more and more difficult to sustain. Perhaps ways of establishing senses of place and identity are emerging which do not invoke Others, but instead handle difference in more respectful kinds of ways. It is possible to think of difference without thinking in terms of an Other; as the previous chapter argued, it is possible to think about interrelations between people and places with tolerance and humility. Identities can be established through positive interrelations. Perhaps the terms of co-existence are being renegotiated, and new ways of thinking about place and identity are developing.

Activity 13 Read section VI of Reading A by Morley and Robins. How far do you think that the 'terms of co-existence' between Japan and the West have changed since Morley and Robins wrote (i.e. 1992)? Are more positive interrelations developing? And if you think not, why not? You might also want to consider whether Morley and Robins themselves perpetuate the representation of Japan as the West's Other.

References

ANDERSON, B. (1983) *Imagined Communities: Reflections on the Origin and Spread of Nationalisms,* London, Verso.

BAUDRILLARD, J. (1985) 'The ecstasy of communication' in Foster, H. (ed.) *Postmodern Culture,* London, Pluto Press.

BERGER, J. (1972) *Ways of Seeing,* London, British Broadcasting Corporation.

BURGESS, J. and WOOD, P. (1989) 'Decoding Docklands: place advertising and the decision-making strategies of the small firm' in Eyles, J. and Smith, D.M. (eds) *Qualitative Methods in Human Geography,* Cambridge, Polity Press.

DANIELS, S. (1993) *Fields of Vision: Landscape Imagery and National Identity in England and the United States,* Cambridge, Polity Press.

EYLES, J. (1985) *Sense of Place,* Warrington, Silverbrook Press.

HOWKINS, A. (1986) 'The discovery of rural England' in Colls, R. and Dodd, P. (eds) *Englishness: Politics and Culture 1880–1920,* Beckenham, Croom Helm.

JACKSON, J. B. (1979) 'The order of a landscape: reason and religion in Newtonian America' in Meining, D. W. (ed.) *The Interpretation of Ordinary Landscapes,* Oxford, Oxford University Press.

LEY, D. (1974) *The Black Inner City as Frontier Outpost: Images and Behaviour of a Philadelphia Neighbourhood,* Washington, DC, Association of American Geographers.

LEYSHON, A (1995) 'Annihilating space?: the speed-up of communications' in Allen, J. and Hamnett, C. (eds) *A Shrinking World: Global Unevenness and Inequality,* Oxford, Oxford University Press/The Open University (Volume 2 in this series).

LOWENTHAL, D. (1991) 'British national identity and the English landscape', *Rural History,* Vol. 2, pp. 205–30.

MASSEY, D. (1995) 'Imagining the world' in Allen, J. and Massey, D. (eds) *Geographical Worlds,* Oxford, Oxford University Press/The Open University (Volume 1 in this series).

MORLEY, D. and ROBINS, K. (1990) 'No place like heimat', *New Formations*, Vol. 12, pp. 1–23.

MORLEY, D. and ROBINS, K. (1992) 'Techno-Orientalism: futures, phobias and foreigners', *New Formations*, Vol. 16, pp. 136–56.

NASH, C. (1993) '"Embodying the nation": the West of Ireland landscape and national identity' in Cronin, M. and O'Connor, B. (eds) *Tourism and Ireland: A Critical Analysis*, Cork, Cork University Press.

POTTS, A. (1989) '"Constable country" between the wars' in Samuel, R. (ed.) *Patriotism: The Making and Unmaking of British National Identity, Volume III: National Fictions*, London, Routledge.

PRINGLE, T. (1991) 'Cold comfort: the polar landscapes in English and American popular culture 1845–1990', *Landscape Research*, Vol. 16, pp. 43–8.

READ, M. and SIMPSON, A. (1991) *Against a Rising Tide: Racism, Europe and 1992*, Nottingham, Spokesman.

RELPH, E. (1976) *Place and Placelessness*, London, Pion.

RUTHERFORD, J. (1990) 'A place called home: identity and the cultural politics of difference' in Rutherford, J. (ed.) *Identity: Community, Culture, Difference*, London, Lawrence and Wishart.

SACK, R. (1986) *Human Territoriality*, Cambridge, Cambridge University Press.

SAID, E. (1978) *Orientalism*, London, Routledge.

SMITH, D. M. (1990) 'Introduction: the sharing and dividing of geographical space' in Chisholm, M. and Smith, D. M. (eds) *Shared Space, Divided Space*, London, Unwin Hyman.

ZONABEND, F. (1993) *The Nuclear Peninsula* (trans by J. A. Underwood), Cambridge, Cambridge University Press.

Reading A: *David Morley and Kevin Robins, 'Techno-Orientalism: futures, phobias and foreigners'*

[I]

What Sony and Matsushita have both recognized is that [...] the industry is becoming a global one, and that economies of scale and increasing corporate integration are necessary to control world markets. Sony describes its strategy now as one of 'global localization', meaning that while it operates across the globe it aims to gain 'insider' status within regional and local markets [Robins, 1989]. They are set to conquer the world.

Europe and the United States have been put on the defensive. Herbert Schiller points to the irony of the situation:

The buyout of MCA/Universal – one of the Hollywood 'majors' – by the Japanese superelectronics corporation Matsushita has already had one beneficial effect. It has caused the American news media, along with the government foreign-policy makers, to recognize a problem whose existence they have steadfastly denied for the past twenty-five years – cultural domination by an external power.

[Schiller, 1990, p. 828]

Suddenly there is an anxiety about exposure to, and penetration by, Japanese culture. The fear is that Japanese investors are 'buying into America's soul'. There is a fear that, in contrast to western openness, Japan is characterized by a culture of self-censorship: 'It is not that any overt censorship takes place, but rather that the norms of a society well attuned to subtle signals make unnecessary rigid rules about what is acceptable discourse' [Sanger, 1990]. Would Sony or Matsushita be prepared to make a movie about a taboo subject such as the war-time role of the late Emperor Hirohito? There is also a fear that Japan might turn 'cocacolonization' into 'sake imperialism'. What is apparent, too, is the sense that Japanese culture is incompatible with the Hollywood ethos. Whereas America is characterized by 'ethnic democracy' and pluralism, Japan is seen as a culture of 'ethnic purity' and homogeneity [J. Fallows quoted in Tran, 1990]. Japan is seen as a consensus and conformist society, the obverse of the individualistic and creative ethos that made Hollywood a world culture. Most vocal of all is Jeffrey Katzenberg, chairman of Disney Studios. 'Film-making at its essence,' he asserts, 'is about the conveyancing of emotion.' And what is clear about the Japanese is that they are lacking in emotion. The Japanese

culturally err on the side of withholding emotion. In saying this, I am not simply offering an American perspective. The Japanese are the first to tell you this about themselves.

This sense of discipline and self-control has no doubt been a major factor in achieving the Japanese economic miracle that has turned a small island nation into one of the world's pre-eminent industrial powers.

But it is also why I firmly believe that the recent marriages between Japanese hardware makers and American moviemakers may not be ones made in entertainment heaven.

There will be a chasm in the fundamental understanding of the movie business that will likely prove exceedingly frustrating for Japanese and Americans alike.

['The teachings of Chairman Jeff', *Variety*, 4 February 1991, p. 26]

If the Japanese are investing in western popular culture it is, according to a vice-president of Disney, because 'they respect us for our ability to create magic – I think they admire something about the American spirit of ingenuity – almost a wildness or recklessness, a sense of fun – that the more conservative cultures aren't capable of' [J. Myers quoted in Huey, 1990, p. 54]. Respect – respect from an inferior culture – is one thing. The 'invasion of Hollywood' and the loss of a 'national heritage' are quite another.

At one level, the response is obvious, and it is made forcefully by Ishihara: 'The sentimental attachment to a Hollywood institution like Columbia Pictures and a New York landmark like Radio City Music Hall is understandable. But the American public ... should realize that it takes two to make a deal: Americans put these properties on the market' [Ishihara, 1991, p. 89]. What is made clear is that Japan is not in the business of making movies, but in the business of making money. Within the United States, too, there has been criticism of cultural and economic protectionism. 'Bruce Springsteen doesn't lose his value because he's working for Sony Chairman Akio Morita instead of CBS Chairman Larry Tisch', says economist Robert Reich [quoted in Tran, 1990, p. 53]. According to Reich, this kind of defensive cultural chauvinism and techno-nationalism is no longer appropriate to an era in which frontiers and borders are being eroded. In the context of rapid globalization, the question 'who is "us"?' is increasingly problematical and perhaps even irrelevant [Reich, 1987, 1990; Ishihara, 1991, p. 69].

At one level, perhaps, this is true. But at another level America still believes it has a 'soul', a national soul, and to see Japan as the enemy now is one way to bring the identity of that soul back into focus. Despite the apparent logic of both Ishihara and Reich, what seems clear is that the West both needs and wants its Japan problem. The idea of 'the coming war with Japan' seems to meet a desire of some kind.

[II]

[...]

At the psychic level, the question 'who is "us"?' arouses profound disquiet. That the Japanese are unlikely to hijack Bruce

Springsteen or Michael Jackson is beside the point. What is so disturbing is the manner in which Japanese interests appear to work behind the scenes, remotely manipulating western concerns, operating through the chameleon-like strategy of global localization.

Japanese economic strategies appear to be unfair and adversarial. Rather than buying American or European products, they prefer to buy raw materials or even whole businesses. And they operate with an unnerving dedication to this cause. James Fallows sees this in terms of 'Japan's lack of emotional connection to the rest of the world', in terms of a kind of asceticism and dedication that is almost inhuman [Fallows, 1989a]. In *You Only Live Twice*, Bond's police contact, Tiger Tanaka (who had hoped to be a kamikaze pilot during the war), describes the martial art of *ninjutsu*:

My agents are trained in one of the arts most dreaded in Japan – ninjutsu, which is, literally, the art of stealth or invisibility. All the men you will see have already graduated in at least ten of the eighteen martial arts of bushido, or 'way of the warrior', and they are now learning to be ninja, or 'stealers-in', which has for centuries been part of the basic training of spies and assassins and saboteurs.

[quoted in Johnson, 1988, p. 108]

More recently, Shredder, in *Teenage Mutant Ninja Turtles*, hidden away in the darkness of the sewer system, operates by the same ninja principles to erode and undermine American civilization. What these popular cultural expressions reflect is an anxiety about the 'stealth' of Japanese corporations. The Japanese stealers-in are perceived as having a robot-like dedication to achieving world hegemony and to undermining the principles of western modernity.

These anxieties must be seen in the context of an increasing sense of insecurity about European and American modernity. [...] The modernization project was cumulative, future-orientated, based upon the logic of technological progression and progress. Its various elements were also designed to be exported and to transcend their European origins and exclusiveness. Modernization

and modernity, with their claims to universalism, could be transposed to other host cultures. In Japan this project found a fertile environment. The technological and futurological imagination has now come to be centered here; the abstract and universalizing force of modernization has passed from Europe to America to Japan. 'In the future,' Jean Baudrillard writes, 'power will belong to those peoples with no origins and no authenticity, who know how to exploit that situation to the full': 'Look at Japan, which to a certain extent has pulled off this trick better than the US itself, managing, in what seems to us an unintelligible paradox, to transform the power of territoriality and feudalism into that of deterritoriality and weightlessness' [Baudrillard, 1988, p. 76]. Japan has now become modern to the degree of seeming postmodern, and it is its future that now seems to be the measure for all cultures. And, thereby, the basis of western identity is called into question.

From 1846 to 1914 Great Britain was the leading creditor nation in the world. Then the United States assumed that role for the next seventy years. In 1985, it became the turn of Japan. It is the largest creditor and the largest net investor in the world, and its surplus on current and capital accounts is the highest ever recorded. Half the world's goods and services and half its population now come from the fifty countries that rim the Pacific – and the world's economic centre of gravity has begun to shift, from the Atlantic to the Pacific – from the Greenwich Meridian to the International Date Line [Wilkinson, 1983; Shibusawa *et al.*, 1991; Zich, 1991].

The roles have been reversed in other spheres, too. In the nineteenth century, Europeans and Americans regarded Japan as an exotic playground, while the Japanese regarded Europe and the United States as disciplined, group-orientated societies possessing the secrets of efficient industrial production. Today, it is the Japanese who flock to the United States and to Europe for exotic tourism, and it is the Americans and Europeans who regard Japan as an austere and disciplined society with frighteningly efficient industries. In a reversal of the traditional asetheticized image of Japan, its people are now increasingly seen as workaholics, as 'economic animals' under the governance of a 'Japan Inc.' pursuing GNP growth at the expense of everything else, spreading pollution, and spawning intimidating futuristic megalopolises [Williams, 1991].

If the 'Pacific era' is finally coming into being, then it has been long and anxiously anticipated. In 1903, its imminence was announced by President Roosevelt: 'The Mediterranean era died with the discovery of America; the Atlantic era is now at the height of its development and must soon exhaust the resources at its command; the Pacific era, destined to be the greatest of all, is just at its dawn' [quoted in Knightley, 1991]. This geo-economic and geo-political ascendancy of Japan has always seemed an awesome prospect. The (potential) rise of Japan has always threatened to put 'us' in danger. From the late nineteenth century onwards, fears of the 'Yellow Threat' have constantly resurfaced in the popular imagination. At its most fantastic, there is an image in which 'Japanese and Chinese hordes spread out all over Europe, crushing under their feet the ruins of our capital cities and destroying our civilizations, grown anaemic due to the enjoyment of luxuries and corrupted by vanity of spirit' [R. Pinon quoted in Wilkinson, 1983, p. 59].

The early years of the twentieth century saw the growing popularity of Fu Manchu and Yellow Peril-type literature in Europe and the United States. The basic fear has long been of a Japan that is seen as being engaged in an inexorable struggle with the West, whether by military means, or, more recently, through trade wars (cheap, 'shoddy' goods from Japan have been a persistent source of anger and anxiety). The image of 'Japan Inc.' can readily be seen as an echo of the West's age-old fear of 'Oriental Despotism' – a phrase first used by the ancient Greeks to describe the Persians, but one which still provides the inherited script according to which the West now imagines (post)modern Japan.

[III]

[…]

Edward Said's premise in *Orientalism* was that:

as both geographical and cultural entities – to say nothing of historical entities – such locales, regions, geographical sectors as the 'Orient' and the 'Occident' are man-made … Therefore as much as the West itself, the Orient is an idea that has a history and a tradition of thought, imagery and vocabulary that have given it reality and presence in and for the West.

[Said, 1985, pp. 4–5]

Naoki Sakai develops the point further:

the Orient does not connote any internal commonality among the names subsumed under it, it ranges from regions in the Middle East to those in the Far East. One can hardly find anything religious, linguistic or cultural that is common among these varied areas. The Orient is neither a cultural, religious or linguistic unity. The principle of its identity lies outside itself: what endows it with some vague sense of unity is that the Orient is that which is excluded and objectified by the West, in the services of its historical progress. From the outset the Orient is a shadow of the West. If the West did not exist, the Orient would not exist either.

[Sakai, 1988, p. 499]

The 'Orient' exists because the West needs it; because it brings the project of the West into focus.

Up until the Renaissance, Europe belonged to a 'regional tributary system' that included Europeans and Arabs, Christians and Muslims. Until then, the countries of Western Europe only occupied the north-western edge of a geographical complex whose centre was at the eastern end of the Mediterranean basin. Subsequently, however, a 'North-South split, running through the Mediterranean – which only replaced the East-West division at a late date – [was] falsely projected backward' and was 'presented as permanent, self-evident and inscribed in geography (and therefore – by implicit false deduction – in history)' [Amin, 1989, p. 93]. In this transition, northern Europe became redefined as the centre of the system, and all other regions were relegated to the status of its peripheries. In all of this, history is rewritten: Christianity is annexed arbitrarily to Europe, and becomes one of the central terms by which Europe understands itself (despite the fact that Christianity is middle-eastern in origin). A further crucial step involves the arbitrary annexation of Hellenic culture to Europe. As Samir Amin emphasizes, the history of 'Western thought' is conventionally traced back to Ancient Greece, and it is generally considered to come of age with the Renaissance (re)appropriation of Greek culture and philosophy [*ibid.*, pp. 90, 94].

It has become a commonplace to observe that, from the time of the Crusades, and then, more dramatically even, from the moment of the Ottoman army's arrival at the gates of Vienna in 1683, it has been the 'threat from the East' which has produced attempts at European unification, both as a defensive response and as a rationalization for aggressive policies of expansion and the consolidation of white, Christian, 'civilized' Europe against its Other. However, the 'East' is not always or necessarily 'outside'. It can also designate the 'Other within'. German writers referred to Jews as 'Asiastics' or 'Orientals' right up to the present century, and both Samir Amin and Edward Said stress the way in which the category 'Europe' – through the category 'Aryan' – has, at least since the time of Renan, been defined by contrast with the category 'Semitic' (a category which includes both Jew and Arab). We are, as Robert Young argues, forced to consider the relation of anti-Islamic and anti-Arab feeling to its 'dark shadow', anti-Semitism: 'In this context the Jews came to represent the Orient within, uncannily appearing inside when they should have remained hidden, outside Europe: thus the logic of their expulsion, or extermination, becomes inextricably linked with Orientalism itself' [Young, 1990, p. 139]. Within the terms of European racism, both Arab and Jew are subsumed together in the figure of the Orient, against which the western world struggles to differentiate itself. [...] A number of commentators have recently shown that it is the Japanese who are now coming to occupy that space in the imagination of the West. [...]

[...]

In 1989, the Japanese overtook the Russians in opinion polls as the nation which Americans fear most. The 'official' explanation of this is in economic terms. As McKenzie Wark says, this scenario reflects the loss of American mastery: a scenario in which 'manifest destiny' turns out to lead 'from Fordism to Sonyism', and thereby to the premature end of the American century [Wark, 1991]. It is, however, not simply a matter of economic hegemony. More significant is the racism and paranoia evoked when the Japanese are seen to be buying up things – Hollywood studios, record companies, the Rockefeller Centre and so on – that are somehow felt to be properly or quintessentially 'American'. It is a question of strangers 'stealing in' on the American Dream. And the Japanese are, as Waldemar Januszczak says, now the 'ultimate twentieth century strangers'. As he observes:

If the Canadians (rather than the Japanese) had bought Columbia Pictures or Mickey Mouse or the Rockefeller there would have been no point in an outcry. Canadians, after all, are just like Americans, only less so. The Japanese, according to the occidental popular imagination, are aliens from the East who are probably trying to take over the West.

[...] This, as Januszczak goes on to argue, is 'a position in the Caucasian imagination that has hitherto been occupied by Freemasons and foreign agents and Rosicrucians and little green men from outer space cunningly disguised as humans; and, of course, Jews. Like the Jews, the whole Japanese nation seems to add up to one huge secret society, bent on making money out of Christians' [Januszczak, 1990].

Contemporary expressions of anti-Japanese feeling incorporate a long tradition of racist fascination and fear, one whose language and imagery is being reforged in contemporary political and cultural rhetoric. As Judith Williamson notes, by way of example, at the centre of Ridley Scott's highly successful film *Black Rain*, there is the antagonistic interplay of American cultural imperialism and Japanese 'economic' expansion. Michael Douglas complains: 'You Japanese sit on what you've got so tight I can't even pull it out of your arse.' His Japanese co-star, Ken Takakura, dismissively retorts: 'Music and movies are all your culture is good for ... We make the machines' [Williamson, 1990]. There is, of course, a specificity to American–Japanese relations. When *The Japan That Can Say No* was officially published in English in 1991, one of the most contentious (and most often cited) passages was that in which Ishihara claims that there was a 'virulent racism' in the American decision to drop nuclear bombs on Hiroshima and Nagasaki [Ishihara, 1991, p. 28]. It is hardly incidental, in this context, that the motive for *Black Rain*'s chief villain swamping America with counterfeit dollars is revenge for the 'black rain' which fell on Hiroshima.

[IV]

[...]

We must recognize how abruptly and dramatically the histories and geographies of the dominated were fissured by their encounter with the West. National and regional geographies were disrupted by this contact, and histories and stories of the past had to be retold in a new light:

It is as if the pre-contact time had been wrenched off and replaced by an unfamiliar temporal system that would efficiently dissolve the residual old. Peoples were also displaced from their sundry geographic centralities to the peripheral positions assigned by the Western metropolis: thus appellations like the Middle East and the Far East ... A new history and [a] new geography combined to produce the magical peripheries of the primitive.

[Miyoshi and Harootunian, 1988, p. 388]

Naoki Sakai stresses the involuntary nature of modernity for the non-West: modernity for the 'Orient' was primarily about subjugation to the West's political, economic and military control. The modern Orient was born only when it was invaded, defeated and exploited by the West; only when the Orient became an object for the West did it enter 'modern times'. [...] What is clear is that the 'West' is not simply and straightforwardly a geographical category: 'It is, evidently, a name always associating itself with those regions, communities and peoples that appear politically or economically superior to other regions, communities and peoples' [Sakai, 1988, pp. 476–7]. Onto the geography of 'East' and 'West' is directly mapped the distinction between the 'pre-modern' and the 'modern'. The category 'West' has always signified the positional superiority of Europe, and then also of the United States, in relation to the 'East' or 'Orient'.

It is on this basis that we can begin to understand the contemporary hysteria and panic about Japan. Japan has come to exist within the western political and cultural unconscious as a figure of danger, and it has done so because it has destabilized the neat correlation between West/East and modern/pre-modern. If the West is modern, Japan should be pre-modern, or at least non-modern. That is the case if it is to fit the terms of the established scheme by which 'we' order our sense of space and time and allocate their place in it to 'them'. The fact that Japan no longer fits throws the established historico-geographical schema into confusion, creating a panic of disorientation (if not yet, to be sure, of dis-orientalism).

Western social science has understood 'modernization' as a unilinear process of economic and social transformation, stretching from the cultural and intellectual world of seventeenth-century Europe to the post-1945 United States. It finds the emergence of Japan as an economic superpower hard to reconcile with this model (based as it is on a Euro-American definition of modernity). The scandalous and unthinkable possibility is raised that the West may now have to 'learn from Japan' – that is, to 'orientalize' itself in order to become economically competitive with the emerging economies of a 'Confucian zone' in the twenty-first century. The unpalatable reality is that Japan, that most Oriental of Oriental cultures, as it increasingly outperforms the economies of the West, may now have become the most (post)modern of all societies.

What Japan has done is to call into question the supposed centrality of the West as a cultural and geographical locus for the project of modernity. It has also confounded the assumption that modernity can only be articulated through the forms the West has constructed. Indeed, what it has made clear are the racist foundations of western modernity. If it is possible for modernity to find a home in the Orient, then any essential, and essentializing, distinction between East and West is problematized. Japan can no longer be stereotyped as the 'Orient'; it is not possible to marginalize or dismiss Japanese modernity as some kind of anomaly. Its distinctiveness insists that we take it seriously. And, at the same time, it insists that we seriously consider the implications of this for the West's own sense of privilege and security.

[V]

[...]

In his book, *White Mythologies*, Robert Young emphasizes 'the relation of the Enlightenment, its grand projects and universal truth-claims to the history of European colonialism'. 'The appropriation of the Other as a form of knowledge within a totalizing system,' he argues, 'can thus be set alongside the history (if not the project) of European imperialism, and the constitution of the Other as "Other" alongside racism and sexism' [Young, 1990, pp. 9, 4]. [...] In the deconstruction of this Europeanization of culture and knowledge, the work of Edward Said has clearly been of particular importance. *Orientalism* offers a cogent analysis of the process through which the 'Orient' has been produced as an object, not only of knowledge, but also of power, inscribed in both the discourses and the institutions of imperialism and colonialism.

Said's work on the 'Middle East' is clearly of relevance in looking at the West's construction of a 'Far East', but as Richard Minear rightly stresses, 'the historical relation between "the West" and Japan was very different from that which obtained between "the West" and Said's Orient' [Minear, 1980, p. 508]. Thus, whilst it did succumb to western

force in the nineteenth century, and also in the middle of the twentieth, 'Japan did not become a colony.' 'Nor,' Minear adds, 'did the abiding cultural ties which bound the West to the Orient exist between Japan and the West. Japan held no special interest.' This meant that the particular relation between Orientalist knowledge and imperial and military power, which has been so important in the case of the Middle East, did not hold in the case of Japan: Japanese studies 'never experienced the naked "authority over the Orient" which Said sees as an integral part of Orientalism'. 'Nor,' Minear adds again, 'did Japan wait for the West to discover its own past, its history, its identity.' Japan was always a sophisticated and literate culture, and, indeed, some of the most widely read books on Japan in western languages were written by Japanese. What is clear is that 'the West had very little to teach Japan about itself' [*ibid.*, pp. 514–5]. This apparent hermetic integrity of Japanese culture has been crucial to the way it has functioned within the Orientalist *imaginaire*.

Its irreducible difference has been the source of both fascination and anxiety. Thus Far Orientalism – from Lafcadio Hearn's *Glimpses of Unfamiliar Japan* through to Roland Barthes' *The Empire of Signs* – has been seduced by the elaborate and arcane rituals of Japanese culture; this Orientalism has been one in which Japan functions as a locus of self-estrangement and cultural transcendence. In his account of *The Japanese Tradition in British and American Literature*, Earl Miner suggests that 'Japan, a civilization as highly refined as the West, is familiar and congenial in its modern conveniences, in addition to having the additional grace for a world-weary Westerner of new and idealized forms of behaviour and art' [Miner, 1958, p. 270; see also Melot, 1987/88]. In contact with this refined exoticism, the world-weary Westerner has indulged in unashamed aestheticism, eroticization and idealization. Japan has been the 'proper meeting-ground of East and West', where western rationalism might seek fulfilment through its 'marriage' (Fenollosa) with eastern mysticism [Miner, 1958, p. 271].

Yet this uniqueness of Japanese culture, which makes it exceptionally seductive, may also provoke fear and anxiety. There is a fear of what lies behind the enigmatic facade of Japanese aestheticism and spiritualism. There is a fear that Japan's irreducible difference will remain aloof from, and impenetrable to, western reason and universalism. A fear, too, that western culture might itself be overwhelmed by the oriental Other. This is now a fundamental issue in discussions of the 'Japan problem'. A recent leader article in the *Financial Times* symptomatically suggests that 'Britain, though not Britain alone, fears some emasculation' ['Learning more about Japan', *Financial Times*, 19 September, 1991]. Bruce Cumings reveals the existence of an unpublished report, commissioned from Rochester Institute of Technology by no less than the CIA, which tries to address the question of how different the Japanese are from 'us':

The report deems the Japanese 'creatures of an ageless, amoral, manipulative and controlling culture ... suited only to this race, in this place'. Which 'creature' do they most resemble, you might ask. Well, the Japanese get along 'as does the lamprey eel living on the strength of others'. The lamprey eel will not stop sucking the lifeblood of the rest of us, this 'treatise' implies, until it has devoured the entire world.

> *[Cumings, 1991, p. 367]*

It may be ludicrous, even comical, but it is racist. It may be extreme, but it reflects a prevailing attitude towards the Japanese 'Other'.

'The most consistently interesting questions caused by Japan,' according to James Fallows, 'involve its differentness' [Fallows, 1991, p. 7]. If difference can be seductive, it is always disturbing, dangerous, and ultimately intolerable. The 'Other' must be assimilated or excluded: within 'our' universe there is no place for difference as such. 'What is at issue,' writes Cornelius Castoriadis, 'is the apparent incapacity to constitute oneself as oneself without excluding the Other – *and* the apparent inability to exclude the Other without devaluing and, ultimately, hating them.'

It is almost always the case in the encounter between cultures, Castoriadis argues, that the Other is constituted as inferior:

The simplest mode in which subjects value their institutions evidently comes in the form of the affirmation – which need not be explicit – that these institutions are the only 'true' ones – and that therefore the goods, beliefs, customs, etc., of the others are false. [...]

The sole foundation of the institution of ('our') society 'being belief in it and, more specifically, its claim to render the world and life coherent, it finds itself in mortal danger as soon as proof is given that other ways of rendering life and the world coherent and sensible exist' [Castoriadis, forthcoming]. Difference is not easy to live with. But what if another culture were to seem, and to claim itself, 'equivalent' or even superior to 'ours'? What if it will not be excluded or converted? What if, as is the case with the Japanese, it seems to flaunt its differentness?

[...]

Japanese culture has developed a kind of reverse Orientalism, what Roland Robertson describes as 'Occidentalism', based on claims about the selfish individualism, materialism, decadence and arrogance of westerners (particularly Americans), and also on an explicit pride in Japanese racial purity, which has been contrasted with the allegedly debilitating consequences of American racial and ethnic heterogeneity [Robertson, 1991, p. 192]. This kind of Japanese self-projection and self-assertion can assume highly provocative and confrontational forms. When, in the context of the Gulf War, one Japanese commentator described the Americans as 'our white mercenaries' [quoted in Buruma, 1991, p. 26], it was difficult for the western forces to take. When Ishihara throws out a warning to 'the Caucasians' that their creative energies are becoming exhausted and their civilization is in its terminal phase, this can be decidedly unnerving and destabilizing. To be warned that the future belongs to those who are 'in and of the Orient' exposes a raw nerve.

There have been two kinds of western response to these 'Occidentalist' challenges. The first has been defensive, reflecting a certain disorientation and loss of self-confidence. Perhaps Japan *has* become Number One? The 1980s saw a quite significant shift in American perspectives on Japan, especially following the publication of Ezra Vogel's widely read *Japan as Number One*, and the emergence of the question about what America could 'learn from Japan'. This has also translated itself into attempts to reassert national self-image and self-esteem by recovering the essence of American difference. Indeed, what one sees is '[...] much debate about the ways in which American national culture could be enhanced and protected from global relativization. In certain respects the idea of American exceptionalism is the equivalent of the idea of Japanese uniqueness' [Robertson, 1991, p. 189]. James Fallows, for instance, has argued that America could be made great again by capitalizing upon the 'American talent' for disorder and openness and by rejection of the 'Confucianism' which he says has taken hold of American society in the form of credentialism, reliance upon educational testing, and so on [Fallows, 1989b].

But if there have been such responses of adjustment, there has also been a more aggressive retaliation against what is seen as Japanese provocation. An outburst of 'Japan bashing' flared up around 1987, and it did so as an immediate consequence of the thawing relations between the West and the Soviet bloc. It is the transformation to the so-called New World Order that is now changing American and European attitudes to Japan. Now there is a growing hostility to what is seen as its ruthless and dedicated economic expansionism, anger at a corresponding insensitivity to global concerns (the environment, famine) and resentment about its lack of political solidarity (the Gulf War). Two recent Japan-bashers, Michael Silva and Bertil Sjögren, suggest that we have to cast our minds back to the wartime period if we want to gain insights into 'the Japanese mindset'. In trying to understand Japanese economic strategy, these authors

explicitly use Pearl Harbor as a reference point, one that 'more than vaguely parallels today's economic confrontations' [Silva and Sjögren, 1990, p. 156]. And, in a much cited article, James Fallows points to 'Japan's ever-present fears that the rest of the world is about to gang up on it and exclude it'. The last time Japan felt like this, Fallows goes on, was the moment of Pearl Harbor, when the country's military leadership 'was convinced that the West had decided to choke Japan to death, with boycotts, so Japan might as well strike' [Fallows, 1989a, p. 40]. Japanese 'narcissism', a 'weakness of universal principles', and a 'lack of emotional connection to the rest of the world', all add up to make Japan seem a powerful figure of danger. Japan is different – a natural enemy. The western mood is resentful and belligerent. The talk is of 'the coming war with Japan' [Friedman and Le Bard, 1991].

[VI]

Orientalism and Occidentalism head to head – cultures in contestation. Who is to be the 'unmarked' (the natural) point of universal reference? Who is to occupy the 'centre' in relation to which the 'Other' must define its particularity and marginality? 'West' against 'East'. We could say that it should not, need not, be like this. In the words of Ihab Hassan, Occident and Orient 'have "contaminated" one another, and this is, mainly, to the good'. These interactions, we might say, 'hint at the possibilities of human understanding, an understanding neither universal nor stubbornly local' [Hassan, 1990a, pp. 74, 83; see also Hassan, 1990b]. And yet what we have is mutual paranoia: 'This idea that the others are quite simply others, which in words is so simple and so true, is a historical creation that goes against the "spontaneous" tendencies of the institution of society' [Castoriadis, forthcoming]. There are powerful psychic investments in the desire to exclude the other.

[...]

In one sense, then, the West's 'Japan problem' is about the confrontation between cultural narcissisms. But to leave it at that would be too easy. There is something that is even reassuring about the possibility that Japan's phenomenal economic and technological success is attributable to 'the Japanese mind'. To invoke oriental conformity, stealth and ruthless dedication is to suggest that Japan does not play by the rules. The comparative lack of success of the European and North American economies must then be a consequence of abiding by universal principles and moral codes. Through such reasoning, it is possible, even in the face of competitive failure, to reaffirm the essential (that is, civilizational) supremacy of western culture.

Differentness is functional: it cannot be willingly or easily relinquished. Through the manic assertion of difference, the identity of western culture and identity can be sustained. And if the encounter with difference is painful, what it averts — what it represses, denies or disavows — is something that is more painful still. What it defers is the encounter with western self-identity and self-interest, as well as the recognition of what is common in both the Japanese and western experiences of modernity.

[...]

There is something profoundly disturbing in this Techno-Orientalism. Following Castoriadis, we have suggested that western xenophobia and racism are motivated by the apparent incapacity of a culture to constitute itself without excluding, devaluing and then hating the Other. That the Others must be instituted as inferior, Castoriadis describes as the 'natural inclination' of human societies. This is the logic of a kind of self-love that constructs itself in terms of a cultural and national narcissism. But there is something more, something deeper, something we might even describe as 'unnatural' in this logic of Techno-Orientalism. As Castoriadis goes on to suggest, hatred of the Other can also be seen as the 'other side of an unconscious self-hatred' — a hatred that is 'usually for obvious reasons intolerable under its overt form, that nourishes the most driven forms of the hatred of the Other' [Castoriadis, forthcoming; Zizek, 1990, pp. 56–7]. To explore this

possibility speculatively, and perhaps only metaphorically, we might suggest that the resentment expressed against Japanese technology (rationality, development, progress) reflects an unconscious and primal hatred of this aspect of western maturity. There is perhaps a (delirious) refusal, rejection, detestation of that modernity into which our own culture has been transformed; of that (totalitarian) element of modernity that threatens some deep-seated aspect [...] in western society.

Perhaps Japan is just a mirror of our own modernity and of its discontents. Maybe Japan simply reflects back to us the 'deformities' in our own culture. As it asserts its claims on modernity, and as it refuses the investment of western Orientalist fantasies, there might just be the real possibility to 'learn from Japan'. We shall increasingly be compelled to take seriously this Japan that can say no. Perhaps we should be less concerned with what we think it reveals about 'them', and more attentive to what it could help us to learn about ourselves and our own culture. Japanese no-saying is important because of the radical challenge it now presents to our understanding of modernity and of the cultural and ethnic conditions of its existence until now. Japan is significant because of its complexity: it is non-western, yet refuses any longer to be our Orient; it insists on being modern, yet calls our kind of modernity into question. Because of this Japan offers possibilities. It potentially suggests to us a way beyond that simple binary logic that first differentiates the modern and the traditional, and then superimposes this distinction on West and Orient. In so far as Japan complicates and confuses this impoverished kind of categorization it challenges us to rethink our white modernity.

This kind of intellectual and imaginative challenge cannot, and will not, obviate conflicts between Europe and America and Japan, but it could make it possible to handle real differences of interest in more complex ways. What Japan tells us is that we have to move beyond a worldview that confronts western modernity with its (pre-modern) Other. Contrary to Ishihara's argument, the modern era has not entered its terminal phase with the displacement of 'Caucasian' modernity. Modernity is now, more than ever, the condition of all cultures in this world. The issue is on what terms they are inserted into that modernity, and on what terms they will co-exist. Japan's achievement is that it is now no different from Europe or the United States in terms of its modernity. What is significant about Japan is its ethnicity, and the fact that it is the first non-white country to have interpolated itself into modernity on its own terms. In so doing it has exposed the racist foundations of modernity as it has been constructed until now.

References

AMIN, S. (1989) *Eurocentrism*, London, Zed Books.

BAUDRILLARD, J. (1988) *America*, London, Verso.

BURUMA, I. (1991) 'The pax axis', *New York Review of Books*, 25 April.

CASTORIADIS, C. (forthcoming) 'Reflections on racism', *Thesis Eleven*.

CUMINGS, B. (1991) 'CIA's Japan 2000 caper', *The Nation*, 30 September.

FALLOWS, J. (1989a) 'Containing Japan', *Atlantic Monthly*, May.

FALLOWS, J. (1989b) *More Like Us*, Boston, Houghton Mifflin.

FALLOWS, J. (1991) 'The crucial difference', *Times Literary Supplement*, 27 September.

FRIEDMAN, G. and LEBARD, M. (1991) *The Coming War With Japan*, New York, St Martin's Press.

HASSAN, I. (1990a) 'The burden of mutual perceptions – Japan and the United States', *Salmagundi*, No. 85–6, Winter/Spring.

HASSAN, I. (1990b) 'Alterity? Three Japanese examples', *Meanjin*, Vol. 49, No. 3, Spring.

HUEY, J. (1990) 'America's hottest export: pop culture', *Fortune*, 31 December.

ISHIHARA, S. (1991) *The Japan That Can Say No*, London, Simon and Schuster.

JANUSZCZAK, W. (1990) 'The new Jews', *The Guardian*, 29 December.

JOHNSON, S. K. (1988) *The Japanese Through American Eyes*, Stanford, CA, Stanford University Press.

KNIGHTLEY, P. (1991) 'Spider's web across the ocean', *The Guardian Weekly*, 17 March.

MELOT, M. (1987/88) 'Questioning Japanism', *Block*, No. 13.

MINEAR, R. H. (1980) 'Orientalism and the study of Japan', *Journal of Asian Studies*, Vol. 39, No. 3.

MINER, E. (1958) *The Japanese Tradition in British and American Literature*, Princeton, NJ, Princeton Universty Press.

MIYOSHI, M. and HAROOTUNIAN, H.D. (1988) 'Introduction', *South Atlantic Quarterly*, Vol. 87, No. 3.

REICH, R. (1987) 'The rise of techno-nationalism', *Atlantic Monthly*, May.

REICH, R. (1990) 'Who is us?', *Harvard Business Review*, January/February.

ROBERTSON, R. (1991) 'Japan and the USA – the interpenetration of national identities and the debate about Orientalism', in Abercrombie, N. *et al.* (eds) *Dominant Ideologies*, London, Unwin Hyman.

ROBINS, K. (1989) 'Global times', *Marxism Today*, December.

SAID, E. (1985) *Orientalism*, Harmondsworth, Penguin.

SAKAI, N. (1988) 'Modernity and its critique', *South Atlantic Quarterly*, Vol. 87, No. 3.

SANGER, D.E. (1990) 'Politics and multinational movies', *New York Times*, 27 November.

SCHILLER, H. (1990) 'Sayonara MCA', *The Nation*, 31 December.

SHIBUSAWA, M., AHMAD, H. and BRIDGES, B. (1991) *Pacific Asia in the 1990s*, London, Routledge.

SILVA, M. and SJÖGREN, B. (1990) *Europe 1992 and the New World Power Game*, New York, John Wiley.

TRAN, M. (1990) 'Hollywood rides into Rising Sun', *The Guardian*, 30 November.

WARK, M. (1991) 'The tyranny of difference: from Fordism to Sonyism', *New Formations*, No. 15.

WILKINSON, E. (1983) *Japan Versus the West: A History of Misunderstanding*, Harmondsworth, Penguin.

WILLIAMS, F. (1991) 'All work and no play taking its toll of the Japanese', *The Independent*, 31 August.

WILLIAMSON, J. (1990) 'Butch Ridley and the Sunrise Kids', *The Guardian*, 1 March.

YOUNG, R. (1990) *White Mythologies: Writing History and the West*, London, Routledge.

ZICH, A. (1991) 'Japan's sun rises over the Pacific', *National Geographic*, Vol. 180, No. 5, November.

ZIZEK, S. (1990) 'Eastern Europe's Republics of Gilead', *New Left Review*, No. 183, September/October.

Source: Morley and Robins, 1992, pp. 139–152, 155–6

Reading B: *Françoise Zonabend, 'The nuclear peninsula'*

It stands to reason, perhaps, that if a person is to live in conditions of tolerable moral comfort he [*sic*] does not wish to keep reminding himself or being reminded of the fact that he inhabits a special sort of place and works in a dangerous establishment. Naturally, no one wants to subject himself to questions on the subject. If he lives there, if he works there, it is because the risk to him is nil. Consequently, any question about danger incurred or risks run will be rejected, denied, or parried in some way. People who interview populations living in the vicinity of nuclear power stations are well aware of this phenomenon: every poll ever published shows that, the nearer the people live to a nuclear power station, the more they will swear by its reliability [Ansel *et al.*, 1987, pp. 451–9]. Similarly, those who observe workers in high-risk industries are familiar with the way in which they refuse to acknowledge the dangers of their job to the point where it is hard to get them to admit to taking essential safety precautions [Dejours, 1980; Duclos, 1988, pp. 37–54].

In the nuclear industry there is no question of anyone refusing to accept the dangers of radioactivity or of working in a radioactive environment. The effects of nuclear energy are too well-known for that. If the risk is denied or defied, it is because in this place every precaution is taken.

[…]

At la Hague a close watch is kept on the air, the rain, the sea water, the fauna and flora, the ground water, the cow's milk, and the flesh of shellfish in the area around the plant. Samples are taken and measures implemented by the plant's own Radioprotection Department and by the Central Department for Protection Against Ionizing Radiation (*Service central de protection contre les rayonnements ionisants* or SCPRI), which comes under the Ministry of Health, and the results are sent annually to the mayors of all the municipalities (*communes*) of the canton.

Staff at nuclear establishments undergo medical examinations at more or less frequent intervals, depending on the section of the plant they work in. No one is exempt. The results of those examinations and analyses are sent to the people concerned.

So, if every precaution has been taken, how shall a person *admit* or even *think* that he is still in any danger, and why, in any case, should he wrestle, whether actually or psychologically, with a risk that is improbable in the extreme? Certainly far less probable, at all events, than such everyday risks as driving a car, which everyone takes and thinks nothing of. This is why every question about danger incurred elicits the response that it is safer working at the plant or living nearby than getting the car out each morning.

The spoken word, in this context, becomes a vehicle for any number of ruses designed to obscure the ostensible, purported meaning of the narrative heard. Language may tell or leave untold, guide or mislead, shed light or spread confusion. Many times in such accounts what is really being said hides itself away behind words intended to mask it. A whole set of stratagems is deployed with the single aim of creating opacity and ambiguity. The end-result is that what finds expression in a roundabout way is a buried request, symptomatic of an inexpressible distress.

Let us look at some examples. If you ask technicians directly about the jobs they do in the plant and about the risks to which they are exposed when entering radioactive areas or handling ionizing products, they reply readily enough, it is true, but they do so in a wholly remote, impersonal way, using technical terminology in an ostensibly 'scientific' type of utterance very like that found in current publications dealing with this type of work. It is unusual for them to talk spontaneously about their own experience, or their apprenticeship, or any incidents in which they may have been involved. In other words, the everyday reality of their jobs seems to be something they cannot talk about, and perhaps it is. They have, as it were, a ready-made discourse for answering questions. In fact, it sometimes struck me as pointless noting down what they said, since they always handed out the same old thing. What, indeed, is the point of taking down a lesson that somebody reels off without a single mistake, that is identical to the one you can read in the official scientific brochures, and that in the circumstances merely confirmed that the people I was interviewing *knew* what they could expect?

However, if, as was invariably the case, all questions bearing directly on incidents that might have happened to the interviewee were parried or obscured in this way by a scientific discourse, it is reasonable to suppose that what is involved here is a way of the speaker not saying or not hearing himself say something he wishes to conceal.

Throughout this study it was as if none of the technicians I met had ever been the victim of an incident involving radioactivity. Incidents occur daily, in fact, but 'trouble' occurred only to others, never to those I was speaking to, as if for one reason or another they were unable to tell me about the *histoires* that

had concerned them. Never did their words convey anything of the personal, private side of their experiences. By means of enunciative tactics of this kind the field of anxiety was continually being manipulated and reshaped.

However, in such accounts of lives spent entirely in the service of le *nucléaire,* there will sometimes be a moment of hesitation, often towards the end of the interview when the talk is more relaxed, more familiar. I am on my feet, about to leave, the tape-recorder is switched off, when the interviewee, extricating himself from his militant role or dropping his guard of scientific language, voices or rather murmurs (as if I were not there) one or two thoughts that offer a glimpse of the fear and moral anguish he keeps constantly suppressed. For instance, I recall a conversation with one technician who had worked at the plant for fifteen years, a militant trade unionist who spent more than two hours telling me about the reliability of the equipment at *his* plant and maintaining that he worked there in complete safety. Then, at the very end of our conversation, as if to redress the balance in some way after all the rationalizations, he abruptly treated me to certain confidences, as it were, about cancer, about how he might be threatened by it, and about how, should he ever contract the disease, it would prevent him from enjoying his retirement. This made him wonder whether, in the circumstances, it was necessary to spend one's entire life in the service of an industry in which worker safety could never be totally guaranteed.

Exactly the same oscillations in speech, swinging from peremptory affirmation regarding the safety of nuclear establishments to anxious questions about the risks to which those same establishments expose whole populations, are found among the people of la Hague. Take the mayor of one municipality, so fervent a supporter of the nuclear industry that the management of the plant once sent him to Japan to persuade the inhabitants of a region soon to have its own French-built reprocessing plant that living in the vicinity of such an establishment is a cinch. Nevertheless, at the end of our conversation (which he had not wanted me to record on tape), having extolled the benefits that the village communally and he personally derived from the presence of the plant, he broke off and was silent for a moment before resuming:

I want the truth ... The truth means knowing which is right: are small doses dangerous, or are they not? You have those on the one hand who would eat limpets that had been living in the pipe [discharging liquid effluent from the plant into the sea] for six months and others who wouldn't eat them for anything in the world. Who's right? Who's telling the truth? It's incredible! No one can give me an answer ... You ... Do you know what the truth is?

[...]

So it was the act of speech rather than direct observation (or any other method, for that matter; they are all more or less inappropriate in this kind of industrial context) that struck me as capable of providing information about this particular individual and collective experience. Speech, or perhaps I should say oral expression, with its digressions, censorships, intonations, and metaphorical substitutions (in a word, rhetoric), affords the possibility of exposing the processes of deletion, spotting defensive tactics, and generally identifying the thousand and one ways in which people seek to confound anxiety. Speech needs to be interpreted, of course, and in this case the business of interpretation consisted essentially in an attempt to take the words spoken at their face value. But it was also, on occasion, a matter of seeking an understanding beyond the words or by stopping short of the words in order to flush out the implicit meaning behind the ostensible content.

It was in fact in their changes of direction, in the flaws in their arguments, and in the interstices of their speech that our interviewees did, willy-nilly, reveal something of themselves and allow a latent anxiety to show through. To an even greater extent it was in slips, puns, and instances of misappropriation of vocabulary as well as in metaphor and in the workings of the imagination that one glimpsed a real anxiety that was being denied by these people in their preoccupation with going on living and working in this place without suffering too much discomfort and self-questioning.

There are of course many other areas and many other manifestations in which this suppressed anxiety may be read.

I could, for example, have directed my attention towards the frantic consumption of organized sporting or leisure activities to the point where the free time of plant employees is always full, as if they were incapable of even a few moments' relaxation, alone with themselves. Granted, the general works council of the plant has a large budget at its disposal and has been able to mount a massive cultural and sporting programme.

'You can do twenty-six different sports here ... On top of that, the plant is building a whole sports complex just for us in one of the villages nearby!' The speaker, a young technician who had recently been taken on, was citing one of the reasons why he had moved to la Hague.

Recently the management and the various works councils have set about creating a veritable works culture that will guarantee social harmony on the shop floor and peace of mind at home.

Then, too, there is the silence in which people who work at the plant bury the jobs they do on the site and the minor incidents that sometimes occur. Husbands or fathers will never talk about what they do there, and their wives and children all say they know nothing of what happens 'up there'. Moreover, no one dares to ask, neither the men's families, nor their friends, nor their relations. It is as if everyone respected the pact of silence that those who work at the plant have unwittingly imposed. The doctors and medical auxiliaries whom I met insisted that patients of theirs from the plant never ask them about the possibility of a link between what is currently wrong with them and the work they are required to do. It is just as if, on the one side as on the other, nobody wants to know. In this context of doubt and suppressed anxiety, but also of impotence in the face of a risk that no one can put his finger on, the only realistic stance is one of silence.

The researcher also needs to be attentive to the hundred and one rumours flying about on the subject of workers at the plant or what fate has in store for those who live on the threshold of this dangerous complex, wrapping the place in a web of muttered incantations and conjurations.

I might, with the same object in view, have tried to reach a better understanding of the language of looks, the unspoken dialogue that takes place between people when a siren goes off unexpectedly or an unfamiliar bang is heard from the direction of the plant. Or perhaps to grasp the significance of the absence of disaster dreams. Of the people I interviewed, all but two assured me that they never had such dreams, as if everyone here unconsciously forbids him or herself to dream about a nuclear apocalypse. It would have meant, of course, finding out about the sorts of screening dreams that were blocking them out. But that would have been an enormous undertaking.

I observed, rubbed shoulders with, and analysed all these manifestations, whether collective or solitary, tiny or substantial, as well as others that were sometimes silent, sometimes obtrusive. They constitute as it were parallel languages that have the effect of enriching the utterances made in direct exchanges, like so many anonymous words adding their bit to those overtly uttered, omitted, or distorted, balancing them, qualifying them, directing their drift.

All these languages, be they silent or expressed, mumbled under the breath or articulated out loud, speak with one voice of a pain that cannot be denied, a buried anguish, a happiness lost for ever.

References

ANSEL, P., BARNY, M. H. and PAGES, J. P. (1987) 'Débat nucléaire et théorie de l'opinion: l'approche de l'opinion publique en France', *Revue Générale Nucléaire*, 5, 1987, pp. 451–9.

DEJOURS, C. (1980) *Travail: Usure Mentale*, Paris, Le Centurion.

DUCLOS, D. (1988) 'La construction sociale des risques majeurs', in Fabiani, J. L. and Theys, J. (eds) *La Société Vulnérable*, Paris, Presses de l'Ecole Normale Supérieure, pp. 37–54.

Source: Zonabend, 1993, pp. 2–7

The contestation of place

by Pat Jess and Doreen Massey

4.1   Introduction

In this chapter we want you to become more actively involved with some of the issues which have been raised in this book so far. One message of the book is that *the identities of places are a product of social actions and of the ways in which people construct their own representations of particular places*. It is people themselves who make places, but not always in circumstances of their own choosing. Chapter 1 explored how migration as a form of globalization immediately raises questions of rights to place – 'whose place is it?' On the one hand there are those who claim to be settled, but on the other lies the fact that few places, if any, can claim to have been isolated from migrations and cultural hybridity. Chapters 2 and 3 have referred to the fact that issues of place and of the right to control the character and future of particular areas have, in this era of globalization, become both more salient and more fraught. Identities of place are frequently disputed – sometimes by groups living in 'the same' place, sometimes between 'insiders' and 'outsiders', sometimes in ways which open to question all of these categories.

contestation
cultural identity

In this chapter we use ideas of *contestation* and *cultural identity* to interrogate these issues in specific cases. Each of the cases involves some kind of conflict over place. What are at issue, we suggest, are *rival claims to define the meaning of places and, thereby, rights to control their use or future*. Thus, for example, in the first two of these cases the dispute is about what should happen in a particular place, what kind of development should be allowed and what not. However, in arguing their positions the different sides in each dispute describe the places differently: they see the place from different points of view and they emphasize different (even opposing) characteristics. The argument about the future of the place thus rests very much on whose interpretation of the place wins out. In a sense each side is laying a claim to how the place should be thought of, how it should be represented – in other words, how it fits into our *geographical imagination*. This clearly recalls the

geographical
imagination

discussion in **Massey** (**1995**) about the power which is involved in naming places – who gets to put what on the map and how. In the third and fourth cases, although the immediate issues are not about 'development', exactly the same kind of contest over the representation of place – the cultural meaning of a particular area – is going on to support the argument. All, then, are good examples of how our geographical imaginations matter and how they are the subject of contestation.

Moreover such claims are, as we shall see, frequently based on interpretations not just of the present character of a place but also – and often more importantly – of its past. The implication is that the character of this history (or, more precisely, this particular interpretation of the history) should be used as a guide for, indeed is the justification for, what should happen in the future. In this sense, what is being named, or interpreted, is not just a space or place, but a place as it has existed through time: what one might think of

envelope of space–time

as an *envelope of space–time*.

The cases we draw on are quite different from one another but are linked by a particular issue which is highlighted in the commentary which follows each case and introduces the next one. These commentaries are not intended to be exhaustive. We have not attempted to extract every shred of geographic or social interest, so if you note points which we do not make, they may equally be valid. The cases themselves are quite tricky and there are rarely simple 'solutions' in such situations. We are not asking you to take sides – though you may well find that you do! – but we are asking you to analyse these conflicts in a way which will enable you to critically assess other cases which you may find in news media, in books or in your own locality. What we are actually asking you to do is to read a series of case studies, mainly newspaper reports, with particular questions in mind. We really do want you to engage actively with the material and, to help you to do this, we have added commentaries which contain specific questions and also some specific responses from us. We would like you to treat these questions as Activities, that is, to take time to think through the answers as well as reading our discussion. In short, we want you to read, question and critically assess. The Activities are 'progressive' in the sense that initially, for the first two case studies, we spell out in some detail the kinds of questions which are needed to interrogate the cases in such a way as to reach some understanding of the important issues involved. In the third case study we add a further dimension for you to think about. When you reach the final one we expect that you will feel quite familiar with the approach we are taking and we leave you to consider some quite difficult and complex issues without placing directions or constraints upon your thinking.

We collected the case studies around three sets of key questions which link this chapter to the volume as a whole. These questions reflect on issues of representation, identity and place, and on the theme of local–global relations. You have met these ideas already in the previous chapters of this book and, to some extent, in the previous volumes in this series. In working through the case studies you should keep these questions firmly in mind:

o   *questions of definition and representation of place:* who are the protagonists and how do they define and represent place; what language do they use; what values and interests do they represent?

o   *questions of cultural identity and place:* what kinds of relationships appear to exist between culture, identity and place?

o   *questions about local–global relations:* how do local characteristics and the workings of global processes interact in particular places to produce unique outcomes?

The articles which you will read are taken from newspapers and this raises a number of points. Material of this kind dates, but really this does not matter because it is the issues rather than the cases in themselves that are important. You will be able to find similar issues and particular cases in national and local press, and in magazines or journals, and be able to interrogate these in a similar way to those in this chapter. But do remember that no source is likely to be 'neutral'. You should always be aware that the reporting of situations is affected by attitudes and values: editorial policies and what reporters and feature-writers notice and choose to highlight or champion will affect your perceptions of the case. Always ask yourself, who says so and why are they saying it? In other words, be critical of sources of information and comment – even of us!

There are four case studies for you to consider. The first concerns part of the area known as the Wye Valley. In this case we are particularly interested in issues of local development and change, and in different notions of 'place'. How do definitions of place affect attitudes to change and how do we construct and represent our ideas? The point to grasp lies in the complexity of the concept of place and how it is expressed. In this case it is, perhaps unexpectedly, the newest arrivals in the area who are objecting to a proposed development. In our second case, however, there is the rather more frequent situation of local people resisting the incursion and activities of other groups. This case takes us to Honduras and analyses further a situation introduced in **Massey** (1995). It raises complex questions of exactly who are 'the locals' and what should be their rights over the area in which they live.

Issues of local–global relations and of cultural identity and place provide the link to our third case study which focuses on the village of Elveden in Suffolk. Here, these issues are translated into notions of boundedness and exclusivity, of who belongs and who does not. We also draw attention to the way in which language is used in representing place. Note that this case is at the very local level.

Ideas of boundedness and exclusivity are raised to a different level of social power in our fourth case where we consider the use of territorial boundaries for social control. The case is European immigration and the notion of Fortress Europe, involving issues of constructions of place and contested images. If we all live on one planet, why do we have to divide it up, draw boundaries and then defend them?

Figure 4.1 Location of the Wye Valley

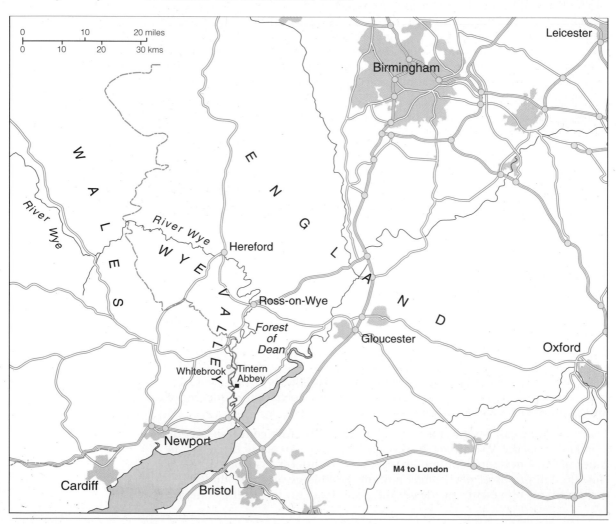

4.2 Changes in the Valley: claims to the nature of place

Keep in mind the key questions outlined above concerning definition, representation and relationships as you read the first case study about proposed development in the Wye Valley (see Figure 4.1).

VALLEY FOLK DIVIDED OVER 'FARM FOR TOURISTS'

By PETER DUNN

Bob and Cilla Greenland looking round outbuildings at Pilstone farm in the Wye Valley, which they plan to turn into a tourist attraction

Plans for a 'traditional' farm to attract tourists have set a group of writers and artists in the Wye Valley against their longer-established neighbours.

The 'incomers' were confident of victory after a skilfully orchestrated media campaign against the scheme, but Monmouth council planning committee approved it by 19 votes to 10. Councillors went against the advice of their own planning officers, who considered it inappropriate for an Area of Outstanding Natural Beauty.

The name of Tom Sharpe, author of *Blott on the Landscape*, featured in the campaign, and the headlines virtually wrote themselves. 'A real-life battle for

Mr Blott-On-The-Landscape', the *Western Daily Press* called it. 'Author Tom Sharpe's hit black comedy turned to reality yesterday when he began a battle against a Blott on the Landscape,' the *Daily Express* said.

The Wye Valley is home to a colony of artists, writers and musicians, many of whom have been crusading eloquently to stop the 15th century Pilstone Farm being converted into a centre for tourists.

Bob and Cilla Greenland's plan is to turn the semi-derelict 47-acre property near the village of Whitebrook into a traditional farm, selling locally raised lamb and pork, with a restaurant, craft shop and 85-space car park screened by trees. The

Greenlands, who run a similar business at Wolvesnewton, eight miles away, found a willing vendor in Major-General John Hopkinson, whose family has owned the farm since the 16th century.

Opponents called the scheme a 'virtual reality whimsy', quoting Wordsworth's 'Lines Composed a Few Miles Above Tintern Abbey' where nature 'never did betray the heart that loved her'. They included Vernon Handley, conductor, Julian Mitchell, a writer of *Inspector Morse* scripts, Martha Gellhorn, 84, war correspondent, and Julia Gregson, formerly a writer on the *Times*.

Julian Mitchell summed up their mood. He said: 'I'm not opposed to rural development. What I am opposed to is inappropriate development in an area which for centuries has been sought for its seclusion.'

Some local people became irritated by the incomers' tactics for three reasons.

Firstly, Tom Sharpe does not live in the area, as a press release suggested, and has had nothing to do with the campaign. 'I don't even know where this development is or what it is,' he said at his home in Cambridge yesterday. 'Someone's got it terribly wrong.'

Secondly, one of the most prominent campaigners, Maggie Biss, whose 18th-century home adjoins the property, had her own designs on it as a tourist attraction when it came on the market two years ago. Mrs Biss, who does part-time public relations work, says she considered buying it as a bee farm or holiday lets but changed her mind.

Thirdly, two other protesters, Charles and Anne Hawes – who moved from Hackney, London, six years ago –

caused hilarity among farmers with a scheme to prevent tractors and noisy machines being used on two days each week.

Julia Gregson, author of the press release announcing Tom Sharpe's support, said: 'That was embarrassing. It was a mistake which was corrected as quickly as possible. These campaigns are put together by incredibly busy people and it was an error of judgement not to check with him.'

Bob Greenland, who spent the early part of last week lobbying councillors to counteract the media campaign, found an ally in Don Spencer, Monmouth councillor, dairy farmer and member of the valley's Area of Natural Beauty advisory committee.

He said: 'The problem with Pilstone itself is it's only 40-odd acres of land surrounded by forest. If a neighbouring farmer took it over it means the buildings go derelict. With the development Greenland's proposing, at least you'll see stock back on the fields and he's going to repair the buildings and put slates where there's only rusty tin at present.'

Mr Greenland is apprehensive about the campaign breaking out again. He says: 'some of the people complaining hadn't even seen the place or contacted us at any time. They described it as an unspoiled 15th-century farmhouse when half of it's a rather hideous modern building which we want to improve.

'They quoted Wordsworth when once the Wye Valley was highly-industrialised with iron works, charcoal works, all sorts of things. It's now a major tourist area, which is why we need to move here.'

Source: *The Independent*, 7 August 1993

This is a wonderfully ironic case. The proposed new development aims to be a 'traditional' one and the group which is doing the protesting consists of the newest arrivals.

Activity 1 What are the objections raised against the proposal to turn the derelict farm into a tourist farm?

Look at the terms which are used and try to relate the argument back to the discussion in previous chapters. For instance, what does 'inappropriate' mean (it's used twice)? This is the kind of terminology which raises, or is meant to raise, feelings that things would be 'out of place'. But that in itself implies both that the place should not change and that there is agreement on what is the character of the place to begin with. What is the vision of this place which the protestors have in mind when they wield this term in their argument?

And what about the term 'seclusion'? Could it be that it carries within it just a hint of that process of establishing differences, the process of 'Othering' which is discussed in Chapter 3, section 3.3.3? What is it the protestors wish the area to be secluded from?

So, what is the idea of this place which is being defended here? The protestors have a vision of 'the real Wye Valley'; what is it? And how valid do you think it is?

Is there *any* valid notion of 'the real Wye Valley'?

There are plainly contrasting and opposed views here of the character of this place; and these views seem to reflect the interests of those who hold them. The 'colony of artists, writers and musicians' is the centre of opposition. From what is said in this article, these relatively recent arrivals have come to the Wye Valley with two main ideas of its character in mind: they are hoping to find some kind of Wordsworthian experience of nature and they are looking for 'seclusion'. It is these characteristics of the place which are most important to them. It is perhaps worthy of note that this group does not earn its livelihood directly in or from the Valley itself. Their 'longer-established neighbours', however, do seem to earn their livings locally, either in tourist-orientated businesses or through farming, and the ones we hear from in the article both are cynical of the incomers' tactics and have a more down-to-earth, less romantic, view of the place.

The view of the place asserted by the incomers is interesting for two other reasons. First, it pays little heed to the present 'locals' and their economy – the example of them causing 'hilarity' by their scheme to prohibit tractors and noisy machines for two days a week is a high point of this. It put us in mind of the portrait of Mr and Mrs Andrews, by Gainsborough, which was discussed by Gillian Rose in the last chapter (section 3.4). There, the absence of the people who work the fields is noticeable: this is a painting which celebrates not the working of the land but its ownership. It celebrates *a sense of place from one particular point of view, excluding others*. It is not landowners and workers that are at issue in the Wye Valley story but the form of debate is similar. The artists and writers love the place for its tranquillity and apparent nearness to nature. This is quite different from the view expressed by local farmers. It is an image of the place – a construction of it – which has, in fact, been developed elsewhere, in the objectors' previous homes maybe, perhaps while reading Wordsworth. Indeed, the perspective of the artists involves *erasing* that of the farmers – even attempting to reduce the intrusive noise they make. The very attitude to nature is different between the two groups: the incomers' definition and appreciation of nature is infused with a Wordsworthian romanticism; the farmers work the land. Perhaps all this reflects a more widespread difference in attitude to the countryside – in our imaginary rural geographies – between urbanites and rural workers in the UK?

Second, the protestors' position claims to be a view of the place which is validated by history. Thus Julian Mitchell, a writer of *Inspector Morse* scripts, is cited as describing it as 'an area which for centuries has been sought for its seclusion'. There is undoubtedly one reading of the history of the Valley which would agree with this. Seclusion was presumably one of the characteristics of the place which attracted the Cistercians to found Tintern Abbey in the early twelfth century (though today it is regularly surrounded by thousands of tourists) and in the late eighteenth century the Wye Valley became a fashionable Mecca for those in search of the 'picturesque'. It is this version of the past (of which they were not a part) to which the objectors are now laying claim. They are effectively arguing that the history of the place should be seen in this particular way. But there are other elements also to the history of the place. From the fifteenth century the Valley was the location for iron, wire and brass works. Mr Greenland contrasts the quotations from Wordsworth with the fact that 'once the Wye Valley was highly-industrialized with iron works, charcoal works, all sorts of things' (though he, too, may be exaggerating his case somewhat!). And today's farmers in the Valley are presumably not there primarily for the 'seclusion' either.

What the opponents of the development are doing here is adopting a strategy which is very common in battles of this sort. This is to define 'the essential nature' of the place in terms which are appropriate to your case, then claim for that essential nature a historical validity – it's been like this 'for centuries'. The unspoken assumption is that it should stay that way. A claim is being made for what should be the nature of this envelope of space–time. The especial irony in this particular case is that the view of this local area as quiet, secluded, contemplation of nature is constructed and claimed by *non*-locals out of their own very present reasons for being there and (perhaps) an intermittent, or a selective, interpretation of history. The fact that the current locals see the place as a mixture of tourism and farming is bracketed off and forgotten.

This is a local case, but the issues it raises are by no means parochial: that is, they are not confined to this one place alone. Such issues arise all the time, in one form or another, in confrontations all over the world.

4.3 Rights to land in Honduras: power relations and social space

One such example is the next case study, that of land rights in Mosquitia, the Caribbean coastal area of Honduras: see Figure 4.2.

Land use map presented in congress seeks to affirm Indian rights in the Mosquitia

By PETER DUNN

Representatives of the four indigenous groups and native ladinos pose for a photograph during the First Congress on Indigenous Lands of the Mosquitia held this week in the capital. From left to right are Nathan Pravia, a Miskito and project supervisor; Hernán Martínez, a Pech Indian; Jorge Salaverri, representing native ladinos; Ricardo Ramírez, a Garífuna and one of the 21 interviewers; Elmer Waldemar, a Miskito and interviewer; and Isidoro Sánchez, a Tawahka Indian (Photo by Eric Schwimmer)

With the 500th anniversary of Christopher Columbus' discovery of the New World less than three weeks away, the indigenous peoples of the Honduran Mosquitia have reaffirmed their rights to exist, to own their ancestral lands and to use this remote region's natural resources through a unique land use map, which was presented at the First Congress on Indigenous Lands of the Mosquitia held Tuesday and Wednesday in Tegucigalpa.

During two days of lectures, slide shows, presentations and a sampling of the Mosquitia's cultural heritage, the region's four indigenous groups – Miskito, Tawahka-Sumu, Pech/Paya and the Garífuna – and "native" ladinos showed the nation and world that Gracias a Dios department is not an uninhabited region just waiting to be parceled out to all comers, but is extensively used by the Indians to eke out a living, much in the same fashion as their forefathers did prior to the arrival of "Colón."

Moreover, the gathering was used by the Indians to draw up a list of proposals to resolve such delicate questions as land tenure, socio-economic development, conservation, and the rational use of the Mosquitia's natural resources. And taking advantage of the presence of high-level government officials during the congress, the Indians demanded greater social assistance and an end to human rights abuses by omnipotent military authorities based in the region.

BIG SUCCESS

According to Andrew Leake, who together with cultural geographer Peter H. Herlihy of Southeastern Louisiana University headed the project, the congress was a "tremendous success, beyond what I expected."

Leake explained, "I was going to take a few chairs out the night before because I didn't expect that many people to come. We sent out approximately 400 invitations; we started out with 300 then calculated maybe half would come, so then we sent out a further 100 and for both days we've had a full hall.

"And the other factor is people have stayed, and usually in these events they come and then leave very early on." Moreover, he added, "I think the preparations that the Indians have made in terms of what they're going to present resulted in very good short and varied presentations which have kept people's attention."

This latter aspect, he said, was important in creating an "environment within which the politically delicate issue of Indian lands" could be presented objectively.

Leake, whose contract with MOPAWI (Mosquitia Pawisa or Development of the Mosquitia, a non-profit Honduran development organization) expires Dec. 15, described the government's assistance and support for the map project as unprecedented, saying that "every door's opened, everybody has done more than what they should have" including the military, which had representatives present at all times during the two-day meeting.

IMPACT

The map, the central issue of the congress, has already begun to have an impact on the way the government thinks in terms of the Mosquitia's development, said Leake.

"It's already moving people high up in government to rethink their strategies in terms of reserve delimitation, they've copped on to the idea of Indian land use as related to vegetation cover and we're already seeing, just within these two days, people coming up to us to ask us for this information … It's probably the most transcendental event in the Mosquitia's development history which dates back to like 20 or 30 years. It's the first time that … people have been really put on the map."

Another indication of the project's success, he added, is the fact that they have received invitations from Nicaragua, Panama and Paraguay to carry out similar land use mapping projects in those countries – even though the final version of the map still hasn't been published.

This response, he said in modesty, is not just due to their work, but to the "idea that Indians can provide the information which in conjunction with professional, geographic interpretations can generate legitimate maps of Indian land use and the location of Indians."

THE MAP

According to Leake, the idea of preparing a social land use map for the region grew out of the Indians' constant problems with land tenure, and their concern over the destruction of the Mosquitia's natural resources by cattle ranchers, coffee growers and campesinos who assume it has no owners. In addition, Indians had also expressed concern over the granting – by the government – of concessions to foreign firms to exploit wood resources (Stone Container Corp., for example) and to conduct oil exploration.

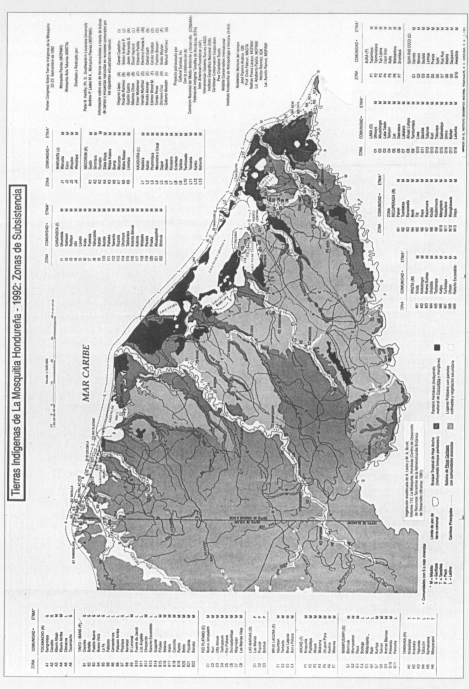

Indigenous lands of the Honduran Mosquitia 1992: zones of subsistence. This is the final version of a preliminary map included in the original newspaper article, which was presented at the First Congress on Indigenous Lands of the Mosquitia, in Honduras, in 1992. The delimination of the zones of subsistence is based on field data collected by native Indian surveyors through the administration of questionnaires in community meetings held in each village in the Mosquitia. The authors of the map then worked with each surveyor, interpreting their information on to 1:50,000 scale maps of the region. At a scale of 1:500,000, this map incorporates only a small fraction of the total information collected (Source: courtesy of the map authors Peter H. Herlihy, University of Kansas and Andrew P. Leake, University of Hertfordshire; Oswaldo Munguia, Executive Direction of Mosquitia Pawisa (MOPAWI); and Cirilo Fleman, President of Mosquitia Asla Takanka (MASTA). Map published by the Instituto Nacional Geografico, Honduras)

143

Briefly, the project – conducted by MOPAWI and MASTA (a Mosquito advocacy group) and financed by Cultural Survival and the Interamerican Foundation – consisted of the gathering of information in 22 population centers of the Mosquitia by 21 "interviewers" or "surveyors" who were selected by MOPAWI or democratically chosen by their respective communities and then trained in Puerto Lempira. (One sector, the proposed Tawahka reserve, had already been mapped by Herlihy.)

Traveling on foot, in dug-out canoes or on horse, the interviewers then left for their assigned areas to ask people such questions as where they fish and hunt, where they get the wood to build their homes, and the names of streams, creeks, mountains, lagoons and other geographic landmarks.

After 20 days in the field, the interviewers returned with the preliminary information, which was studied by Leake, Herlihy and others and given to a cartographers of the Instituto Nacional de Geografía to represent it (the information) in the form of a map. Following the preparation of the initial map, the interviewers returned to the field for another 13 days to verify the facts and information obtained from their first visit, and to add anything that was left out.

The result of their work is a map that Leake described as "highly accurate, particularly with place names. The Indians knowledge of place names, particularly on the 1:50,000 map … is very, very precise, and a lot of the points have been cross-checked between two or three different surveyors. We would say it is accurate to 95 percent," he added.

ECOLOGICAL PRESSURES

Aside from presenting the map, the gathering allowed the Indians to express their concern to the public over the continuing deforestation and destruction of the region's varied ecosystems – from pine covered savannahs to tropical broadleaf forest – by "outsiders," local and foreign alike.

Ricardo Ramírez, a Garífuna and one of the 21 surveyors, described the situation in the Río Plátano Biosphere Reserve – a 525,100-hectare protected area covering parts of the departments of Gracias a Dios, Colón and Olancho – as critical.

Due to deforestation, said Ramírez, rivers are drying up and their is heavy erosion, in addition to decreased rainfall.

Other problems, Ramírez said, include the use of explosives to fish by ladinos in the southern part of the Plátano River, and a wanton lack of respect by military authorities – namely the Public Security Force (FSP) – to indigenous peoples.

Police officials, he added, take advantage of the Indians humility and ignorance by levying heavy fines for minor offenses. For example, he said, once a slightly drunk man cried out, for which reason he was arrested by the FSP and then told he must pay a several hundred lempira fine in order to be released.

Moreover, he criticized Bay Islands fishermen, saying they are depleting the region's marine resources by overfishing, without the Mosquitia communities receiving any benefits.

During the information gathering for the map project, he said, some surveyors received death threats from economically powerful persons and large landholders. All that they were offered were "bullets," not "love" and understanding, he concluded.

DEFORESTATION

Speaking for the upper Patuca River region, Soriano Cardona, a Tawahka Indian, blamed cattle ranchers, coffee growers, merchants, campesinos and large landholders for the destruction of that sector's forests, and stressed the importance of land for his people's subsistence.

Moisés Alemán, a Miskito, expressed concern over oil exploration around Ahuas, which could bring further deforestation and, in the event petroleum is discovered, the possibility of oil spills. Moreover, Alemán rapped the quincentenial celebrations, saying that Columbus' discovery of the New

World has only brought indigenous peoples "misery, poverty and contempt."

Describing the Mocorón sector as the "supermarket of wood," Miskito Simón Greham said the inhabitants of the area still feel the effects of the 26,000 Nicaraguan Miskito refugees that received shelter there in the early 1980's during the Nicaraguan Resistance's armed struggle against the Sandinista regime. The refugees, he said, caused extensive damage to the environment, principally deforestation and the destruction of its flora and fauna.

Moreover, Greham said that the zone is being invaded by cattle ranchers who are adding to the deforestation. And equally worrisome, he added, is the intention of the foreign firm Wellington Hall to exploit forest resources along the Warunta River.

With respect to the coastal region, Duval Haylock said fishing boats – which pay no taxes to the department's municipalities – employ large drift nets, taking in enormous quantities of the Mosquitia's marine resources, of which they use only 40 percent.

OFFICIALS PRESENT

Listening to the Indians problems, proposals and demands were high-level government officials, including Vice President Jacobo Hernández Cruz, Defense Minister Flavio Laínez and CONAMA (the National Commission on the Environment) Chairman Dr. Carlos Medina. And attending Wednesday's sessions were President Rafael Leonardo Callejas' sister Melissa and Liberal Party presidential candidate Carlos Roberto Reina, who described the Indians proposals (with respect to the development of the Mosquitia, etc.) as "just" and "logical."

Representatives of the Lencas, an eastern indigenous group, and Nicaraguan Miskitos also attended the congress.

During the latter part of the congress, the participants discussed, drew up and reworded a series of strategies with respect to land tenure, conservation, use of resources and the socio-economic development of the Mosquitia – a document which they will present to the public and press this week.

Among some of the more important resolutions approved at the congress were:

- Allow for greater participation of indigenous peoples in the region's development, from the elaboration of proposals for projects to their planning and execution.
- Require that all projects take into account the region's ethnic diversity.
- Give women increased participation in development.
- Require environmental impact studies for all projects.
- Implement bilingual and bicultural education programs.
- Take steps to resolve the problem of legalization of Indian lands.
- Undertake inventories of the region's flora and fauna, of indigenous peoples in this task.
- Require that oil exploration in the Mosquitia meet with the approval of the Indians.
- Prohibit the use of the Mosquitia as a toxic waste dump.
- Ask the government and military to enforce laws against the persons responsible for deforestation and the destruction of animal life (through hunting and commercialization.)
- Prohibit the colonization of the region by non-indigenous peoples, and relocate colonists in the Río Plátano reserve and the proposed Patuca reserve.

Only time will tell if the Indians achieve their goals, and begin the next 500 years knowing they have the support and understanding of the government and their fellow countrymen, who will hopefully rectify the damage done by Spanish colonizers and their descendents that lead to the extermination of hundreds of thousands of Central American Indians and extensive deforestation – a loss felt by all mankind.

Source: *Honduras This Week*, 26 September 1992, pp. 1, 4, 19

145

Figure 4.2   Location of Honduras

500 years later, indian groups claim their place on map

By WENDY MURRAY ZOBA

The verdict is not yet in as to whether or not the arrival of Cristobal Colón on the shores of the Americas was the boon or bane of these nations. And during this year, the quincentennial "celebration" of his famous or infamous discovery, some native American peoples have decided that it is time to take destiny by the throat.

The four remaining indigenous tribes of Honduras – The Pesch (also known as Paya), the Tawahka-Sumu, the Garífuna (though not "indigenous" in the true sense of the word), and the Miskito – gathered this week for what they hope will be a historic step in indigenous development. The First Congress of Indigenous Peoples of the Mosquitia assembled at the Hotel San Martín on Sept. 22-23 for the purpose of introducing themselves to the nation and to one another, and to unveil the map which they, themselves, have researched and compiled. They hope, as a result, that their motherland and those who orchestrate her business, will get to know them better. Also, that they will remember them in the course of time, when seemingly lucrative business proposals drop into their laps, or when legislation regarding land use and delimitation must fall to the verdict of the powers that be.

These people represent the last vestiges of cultural authenticity, as it existed ante-Columbus. And, though in some cases their Spanish may be broken or their concepts of distance and space somewhat obscure, these are the last of what can be considered truly "Honduran." The First Congress was their moment to speak, explain, and hopefully, be heard regarding who they are and what they are doing with the land and legacy that has been left to them.

HAVE YOU MET ...?
THE MISKITOS

The Miskito Indians have dominated eastern Honduras for centuries and are considered the only true native aborigines of the Mosquitia. They inhabit three zones there, including the savannahs, the coastal plains, and the tropical forests. Descendents of the "Chibcha" are Miskitos who mixed with black slaves along the northern coast during the colonial period when they also came into contact with English and German pirates. They introduced "modern" weapons into the culture of these native peoples, who later used them in pressuring and subduing other smaller Indian groups in the region.

Most Miskitos are bilingual, speaking their native tongue in their homes and villages, and Spanish at school. Depending upon which part of the Mosquitia they inhabit, the Miskitos are known to be excellent horticulturalists, cultivating yuca, bananas, beans, rice and corn. They also breed chickens and depend upon hunting and fishing for daily sustenance.

Numbering between 30,000 and 40,000, their society is well developed and they have expanded into an economically diverse social force. Their coastal lobster industry sometimes brings in as much as Lps. 5 - 10 million a year.

THE GARÍFUNAS

The Garífunas, along with the Miskitos, enjoy a thriving population of some 60,000 to 70,000 scattered along the northern coast of Honduras (with over 2,000 living in the Mosquitia). This group is not truly indigenous, as they were deported to the Bay Islands in 1796 by the British, from the island of Saint Vincent. It seems that these "belligerent" black African slaves were threatening a revolt so the British packed them off to the coastal Islands of Honduras. They soon migrated to the mainland, where they continue to preserve their African culture. The black African slaves mingled with the Island, or Carib, blacks from which has emerged the hybrid culture of the Garífunas.

Fishing in their hand-sewn dug-out canoes continues to provide the main

Garífuna youth may enjoy tropical life [...], but the future of Honduras' Indians hangs in the balance (Photo by Suyapa Carias. A different photograph appeared in the original newspaper article)

source of income and sustenance for this group. But they enjoy an assortment of fresh tropical fruits in their diet, and embellish their cultural history through the preservation of their well known "punta" dancing.

They have been able to maintain a strong ethnic identity and have kept their native language intact (though they speak Spanish as well). Their African heritage is clearly evident in their villages, as their dwellings consist of bamboo and thatched roofing, which sets apart these transplanted members of Honduras' indigenous community.

THE TAWAHKA-SUMU

Neither time nor land space has fared well for this small struggling group located on the lower river banks in the Mosquitia. A generous estimate would put their numbers around 900. However, before Columbus, they flourished along Honduras' eastern border with Nicaragua and probably numbered between 9,000-10,000.

This group felt intense persecution from the Miskitos who were aided by the British in pushing the Tawahka-Sumu inland and westward.

Their native tongue and cultural heritage have been nearly lost, as they have been forced to inter-marry with "mestizos" (mixture of Indians and "ladinos"). They survive today at a subsistence level, hunting and fishing for food on a hand-to-mouth basis, while at the same time living under the constant threat of uncontrolled land penetration and colonization by peasants and cattle ranchers.

THE PESCH (PAYA)

This group once occupied a quarter of the land space in Honduras in pre-Columbian days. However, a population study undertaken in 1982 reflected that the number of Pesch surviving in the Mosquitia at that time was a mere handful.

Today, their numbers are estimated to reach near 2,000. However, only a portion of those could be considered "pure." The Pesch have mixed with both the "ladinos" and the Miskitos, which has resulted in a marked erosion of their ethnic identity and their language.

These people have adopted small scale mining operations – washing gold – as a source of income. Nevertheless, they depend on hand-to-mouth subsistence, harvesting yuca and corn while hunting and fishing. They, along with the Tawahka-Sumu, live under the continual threat of land invasion by ranchers and campesinos.

Source: *Honduras this week*, 26 September 1992, p. 5

Miskito musician gives congress 'upbeat note'

By ERIC SCHWIMMER

For Elmer Waldemar, a native of the village of Río Plátano and one of the map project's surveyors, the First Congress of Indigenous Lands of the Mosquitia wasn't just giving lectures or explaining the region's problems to participants. It was also an opportunity to show the public the cultural richness of his people through Miskito music and song – a pastime he thoroughly enjoys.

During the few breaks between presentations, Waldemar and fellow Miskitos could often be heard performing songs in their native tongue while strumming guitars and beating tortoise shells, providing an upbeat atmosphere to the event.

Describing his people as humble and fond of their lands and nature, the 27-year old musician said he believes the social land use map will help to show that his people "have a right to our land."

He added, "We are humble, and love our land but we don't like seeing the destruction of so many acres of the (Río Plátano) biosphere's forest. We protect it ... We are agriculturalists, but we are not persons who farm many acres of land, only a little. And with the little we use we are able to feed ourselves."

Waldemar said he interviewed people in seven communities in the Río Plátanodistrict, traveling from one village or hamlet to another on foot or in a dug-out canoe. Wherever he went, he obtained such information as the names of places where Indians hunted, where they fished, the hills where deer roam and how many hours it takes to walk to these places.

Waldemar said his worst experience during the field assignment was a run-in with insects. "I was traveling up river and planned to sleep in a house that didn't have an owner. It was night so I went inside the house, and there were so many mosquitoes there that I couldn't sleep at all and the roof was in ruins," he said laughing.

With respect to the upcoming quincentennial of the New World's discovery by Columbus, Waldeman said his people are neither in favor nor against its celebrations. "For the moment, we only want our lands to be permanent, that is, we love our land, we are fond of the land ... moreover, we are celebrating it (the arrival of Columbus), with this congress," which was "organized to reaffirm our rights to indigenous lands in the Mosquitia."

Source: *Honduras This Week*, 26 September 1992, p. 4

(Note: Typographical errors which appeared in the original versions of these articles have not been corrected here.)

This case of battles over land in the Caribbean coastal area of Honduras was introduced by **Massey (1995)**. It is a situation where the different ways in which the place is thought about are made more concrete through their representation in alternative maps; there are very clearly different representations of the same area. It is a case parallel to that discussed in Chapter 3, section 3.3.2, where local people counterposed their sense of place to that of the London Docklands Development Corporation as a means of resisting LDDC plans. They are both cases of relatively marginalized groups insisting on their own, alternative, sense of place. In this Honduran case the differences in view cover many issues – from how the place is named, to how it is evaluated in terms of natural resources, to what should be its economic and social future. Let us examine three aspects of this conflict.

First, on the face of it, this is a straightforward confrontation between locals and incomers, insiders and outsiders, the locals resisting the developments proposed by the latter. But *the case raises the important question of how we define 'locals'.*

Activity 2 As Chapter 3, section 3.3.2 asks, who defines insiders and outsiders, and who controls those processes of *inclusion* and *exclusion*? What do the articles tell us about this in the case of Honduran Mosquitia: what groups are involved; do they have a concept of insiders and outsiders; what rights do they see as stemming from such definitions?

In this case there are four groups in the local alliance of 'insiders'. Of these, the Garífuna are clearly not 'indigenous': they hail from a complex and international history, arriving in the area through the mechanisms of British-controlled slavery and maintaining still today a clearly African inflection in their culture. But even the group which the articles term 'the most indigenous' is not in any sense composed of purely local influences. The Miskito have certainly lived in the area for centuries but over those centuries they have absorbed contacts with many another 'external' culture – from English pirates to Spanish colonizers. There have, in other words, already been influxes of outsiders and outside influences. These have been absorbed in the past – they are indeed now part of the very character of the insiders – so why prevent more outside influences now? One of the claims currently being made is for *exclusivity*, by prohibiting 'the colonization of the region by non-indigenous peoples' and for the relocation of existing colonists. Not only does this raise acutely the question above of how exactly one defines (and who is to define) who is indigenous, but it also poses very starkly the issue of what rights such 'locals', presuming they can be so defined, should have over an area. It is clear that in the past the Miskito have been none too respectful of the localities of others – they seem to have persecuted the Tawahka-Suma for instance, pushing them, with British help, into new areas. As earlier chapters have argued, replacing one exclusionary sense of place with another which is equally exclusionary may not represent a great advance. It raises again the issue of 'purified' spaces discussed in Chapter 2, section 2.5.

These are tough questions. Certainly it is possible to argue that the mistakes of the past are no justification for continuing the same kinds of behaviour into the future. Perhaps it is possible to learn from history and to recognize rights which have been unrecognized in the past. Perhaps these days we should pay more respect to the rights of local people?

But agreement with that position raises two further issues.

Activity 3 What rights are we talking about – does this include rights to total exclusivity and control, as claimed here? And further, if your answer in this case veers towards support for the local people, is this a position you would generalize? For example, would you equally support those white working-class people of the Isle of Dogs against the allocation of council housing to people of Bangladeshi inheritance (Chapter 2, section 2.1.1), or middle-class people in an expensive suburb (the kind which is precisely defined as 'exclusive') resisting, say, a community hostel or cheaper housing for rent?

Take a few minutes to *think* about this, and make a short note of your reaction.

Perhaps what the counterposition of these examples makes clear is that there are no abstract, generalizable, answers. It is difficult *always* to defend the locals, or *always* to defend 'mixing'. And that is because *in each case what is at issue is a different set of relations to place and to the power relations which construct social space.* And as has been argued (in **Allen and Hamnett (eds, 1995)**, and in Chapter 2 of this volume), these 'social relations stretched over space' are

power relations

often unequal. All these cases of contests over place are set in a wider context of social and geographical uneven development. As Chapter 2, section 2.4.3, argued, each form of 'mixing' will have its own geography of power. Remember what the Native American chief replied, in the 1850s, when asked by his braves what was the biggest mistake of the past generation's leaders? He said: 'We failed to control immigration' (Chapter 1, section 1.2.2). As was pointed out there, you may have sympathy with that view while perhaps feeling more circumspect about some of the fiercely anti-immigration speeches made in today's relatively rich first world countries. Whatever your views, it is clear that the two attitudes are set within very different power relations. The mobility of the white immigrants to the New World was the mobility of the powerful: and their culture and their deliberate military exploits were to destroy altogether the places of the Native American way of life. In the case of today's first world, those who would like to immigrate (or, certainly, the ones against whom the barriers are raised) are in a relatively powerless position, seeking escape either from the downside of world uneven development or from persecution of some sort. Moreover, while their entry will certainly produce effects (there will be cultural influences and intermixing, maybe also conflict), it will not completely eradicate the places where they settle.

In the case of Honduras, it is the local groups – the indigenous peoples – who are the less powerful. In relation to social *space*, in terms of the spatiality of power, it is certainly here the local groups who feel themselves to be the powerless ones, defending their patch against globalized operators who can roam the world in search of the best locations and resources. Yet things are always complicated: 'the locals' are also defending the area against *campesinos* (peasants) whose mobility may only be forced upon them by a desperate search to find a place to farm. One way the local people fight back is by arguing for the significance of their own representation of *place*, which is precisely the significance of their alternative map. Part of the argument made by the local alliance is that their lives are very much bound up with and dependent upon the land itself and that the incursion of the ranchers and prospectors would actively destroy their lifestyle. They are claiming, in the terms of Chapter 3, section 3.3.2, a very strong relationship between their sense of place and their cultural identity. It is this aspect of their relationship to place which they are claiming as crucial.

This leads on to a *second* issue: *the nature of the distinction between, and the intersection of, what we might call the local and the global.* There are a number of aspects to this.

Activity 4 To begin with, jot down some of the ways in which 'the global' has been part of the construction of the character of this local area of Honduras.

What is now the established character of this local area, this small piece of land on the eastern coast of central America, in its formation has included contacts with the Caribbean islands, with Africa, with Britain and with Spain (and these are just the connections we know of from the newspaper articles). Even in an area such as this, then, not a major port city nor a cosmopolitan centre but what might be thought of as a relatively quiet and peripheral backwater in the world's historical geography, the 'local culture' which is to be defended is already a mixture of influences from inside the place and beyond. It is an example of the general case made in Chapter 2, section 2.2.3 (and of which we shall read more in Chapter 5), a case of *the global constitution of the local*. It is also a good example of the very early

the global constitution of the local

interpenetration of cultures on the world's 'periphery': issues of the meaning of place and of the invasion of place are not new in many parts of the world.

The relation between the local and the global is also being questioned by the locals themselves. As well as arguing for their own representation of the place, another way they are fighting back is by trying to *change* the relationship between the local and the global alignment of forces.

Activity 5 There are two questions to think about here:

o What are they doing? *How* are the local people attempting to alter the relationship between local and global forces? How are they trying to expand their cause beyond being a local 'place-bound' one?

o Why is it important to them to try to do this?

The local people are actively allying their case with others beyond the local area, not to all local struggles but to those where similarly indigenous peoples find their places threatened. There are links established with Nicaragua, Panama and Paraguay. (The same exercise has now been undertaken with one of the Panamanian groups with whom contact was established and a map has been drawn of an area in the Darien Gap region of that country.) Such attempts to extend the geographical reach of what may begin as purely local struggles are one indication of the way in which spatial form may not only reflect power but be an important element in constituting it. 'Senses of place', as was argued in Chapter 3, section 3.3.2, may be an important part of the way in which power relations are both reproduced and challenged.

This issue of 'local–global' links into the *third* thread of argument: that of *how the region is interpreted in terms of resources and how they should be exploited.* The local groups are essentially arguing to withhold at least some of their local resources from the world market: they are attempting to prevent access to them by the world market. One question immediately raised is whether local groups have the right to refuse access to resources which are in global demand or, alternatively, whether global forces have the right to enter local areas in search of resources. However, it is not just the local/global distinction which is in play here but the way in which that is related to the interpretation of the natural environment of the area.

As **Massey** (**1995**) indicates, the indigenous people emphasize the varied nature of the local resource base and of the way in which they use it. The variety of the produce which they derive from it is quite remarkable. The incomers seem more likely to emphasize large-scale and more monocultural developments. Moreover, the locals object to one area being used as 'a supermarket of wood'. This is a telling term. What it seems to refer to is the habit of other people seeing the trees as simply available for consumption, but available in the form of commodities – turned into things which are simply bought and sold. The locals would argue, presumably, that their attitude is different – smaller scale and less commoditized. Yet, in what we read in these articles, both groups are primarily interpreting the natural environment in terms of resources. There is some mention of the indigenous peoples' close relation to their land but it is not a major theme. We are not finding here, say, a more spiritual attitude to nature or an appreciation of 'wilderness'. Indeed, the assumption behind the statement that 'Gracias a Dios department is not an uninhabited region just waiting to be parcelled out to all comers', is that *were* it uninhabited, it *would* be universally acceptable to 'parcel it out'. As **Sarre (1995)** shows, this is by no means the case. And in terms of this book, we are back to issues of power relations – of who has the power to draw the lines and to decide what will happen.

4.4 Elveden: place, culture and conflict

For the next case study we move to Elveden in Suffolk: see Figure 4.3. We want you to continue to think about 'whose place is it?' because one of the issues which the case illustrates is that of *cultural identity and place*. As we have already stressed in this book, the links between ideas of culture and place are very complex and can often be understood best through an awareness of the *local–global* relations which have influenced that place. Individual places are a unique blend or *combination* of local characteristics and wider ('global') social processes; it is a uniqueness which is constructed and reconstructed over time.

Now that you have worked through two of the four case studies in this chapter you will be accustomed to the way in which Activities are being used. We still want you to use the key questions (from the Introduction) as your framework for tackling the articles but, as below, we will feed in some specific questions for you to work with.

Activity 6   While you are reading the article on Elveden, take notice of the way in which *language* is used to *represent* people, places and views. Also, think about *what* is being defended and what is being promoted, and by whom.

To deal with this question you will need to identify:
(a) the two, main, contrasting views of (the) place, and
(b) who holds these views, who are the 'actors';
(c) how the arguments are presented by each 'side', and
(d) whether you can construct 'counter-arguments'.

Figure 4.3   Location of Elveden

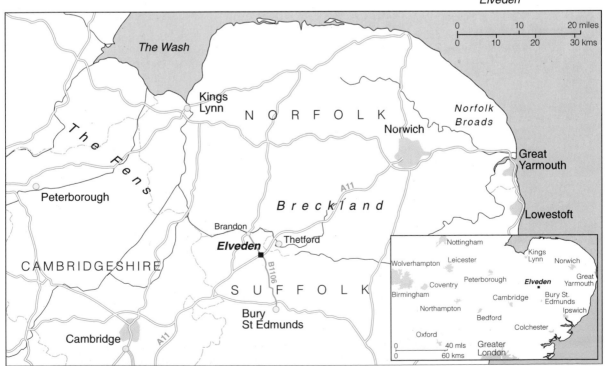

In pursuit of the Suffolk maharajah

By MADELEINE BUNTING

The last maharajah: Duleep Singh stunned the English with his exotic costumes and princely manner

Elveden is easy to overlook – nothing more than a few cottages strung along the A11 London-to-Norwich road. With a speed limit of 50mph, as the landlady of the Elveden Inn says, blink and you'll miss it. The village has an unenviable reputation as an accident black-spot for pedestrians. Otherwise, buried in what locals claim to be the biggest forest in England, Elveden enjoys its obscurity. As does the Guinness family, which owns the school, the pub, virtually all the houses, about 22,000 acres of surrounding countryside and a Blenheim-sized pile of masonry which is slowly crumbling into an ornamental lake behind a screen of trees a few hundred yards from the main road.

To the chagrin of Elveden residents, their village has already been on the front pages of national newspapers and before the year is out, it will have graced many other pages of newsprint if 30,000 members of Britain's Sikh community have their way.

Incongruous though it may seem, this chocolate-box remnant of 19th century

England is a place of pilgrimage for Sikhs. Since the sixties, they have travelled in coaches and packed cars on summer weekends from Birmingham, Wolverhampton, Bradford and London to pay homage to the last Sikh Maharajah, Duleep Singh, who is buried in Elveden's parish church. The three nondescript graves of the Maharajah, his wife and son, stand among the moss-covered, topsy-turvy gravestones. Bits of plastic children's swords left by pilgrims are scattered about, symbolic of the traditional dagger which Sikhs carry.

This year is the centenary of the Maharajah's death and the recently built Nanaksar Tath Isher Darbarl Sikh temple in Wolverhampton is spearheading a plan to raise a quarter of a million pounds to put Duleep Singh – and Elveden – firmly on the map.

The Maharajah is an unlikely Sikh hero. He converted to Christianity at the age of 12. Having signed away his kingdom – and the famous KohiNoor diamond – to Britain, he became a favourite of Queen Victoria before settling down as a larger-than-life huntin', shootin', gamblin' and whorin' English squire at Elveden Hall.

Villagers learned from the local newspaper of plans for rallies, canopies for the graves of Duleep and his family, plaques, portraits and 'cultural exchanges'. The village was horrified, the Elveden Estate Office unenthusiastic in the extreme. Into the controversy stepped the new young rector.

It's a tale for our times – two bits of England representing two nations as disparate as anything Benjamin Disraeli ever considered. Only this time, it's not wealth that divides. A multicultural urban Britain schooled in racial tolerance meets the quintessential rural England – an area on the Norfolk-Suffolk border where landed gentry still hold sway over their estates. The local

Duleep Singh's grave in Elveden churchyard

rector, Paul Ensor, holds a tenuous line between the two.

Everyone at the estate office is in a meeting. This is the hub of the village with the four-wheel drives and tractors coming and going as befits what is reputed to be the largest lowland arable farm in Britain. A curt estate manager, Ed Boyt, says on the telephone that the executors of the estate – Earl Iveagh died last year – are still considering the requests of the Sikhs, but he insists that the hall and its grounds where the Maharajah lived are private. Some villagers will only say that they are waiting to see what line the estate takes – almost everyone works or used to work for the estate.

But the more outspoken over the years have not minced their words. When a Sikh was discovered praying in the church in 1961, there was uproar as the villagers demanded to know whether the church would have to be reconsecrated. The grievance has changed but not the sentiment; now they complain of anything they can think of – litter, noise and trespassing in the hall grounds.

"I have to say the Sikhs are a bit of a nightmare," sighs one villager dressed in headscarf and tweed skirt. "They knock on my door asking the way to the hall and they're not allowed in the hall – it's closed. But they don't always take no for an answer. Besides, sometimes they look, well, er, rather strange. I suppose we're not used to people like that round here."

Mabel Schofield's mother, father and husband are buried in the Elveden graveyard, and she grumbles: "They walk over other graves and leave plastic swords about. They don't think of others. They take too much on themselves, but they probably think I'm prejudiced. It's not worth bothering putting up a plaque, but it's their prerogative. I've lived here for 40 years. It won't bother me. If they have celebrations here, I won't go."

Liam Flack, aged 22, says he's just worried about the numbers: "They'll spoil the peace and quiet. There's carloads that come every weekend.. They don't bother me, but they're always asking directions. I'm not interested in learning about Sikhism."

Ethnic relations were the last thing the rector, Paul Ensor, thought he would have to deal with when he took the parish just over a year ago. After being brought up in Birmingham, and having worked in south London and Croydon with West Indians, Asians and Syrian Orthodox Christians, the most pressing task in his new parish after 'matching and dispatching' was to learn the difference between a sugar beet and a carrot.

Elveden is the grandest and the quietest of the five churches he runs. Elaborate carving of the roof, the pews, the stalls and an immense marble altar-piece are all testimony to estate patronage. Duleep Singh himself donated the church silver and there's a stained glass window given by his children in his memory. Today the congregation numbers little more than a dozen and swells significantly only on Remembrance Day.

Racism has never been much of an issue in this neck of the Suffolk woods.

Racism has never been much of an issue in this neck of the Suffolk woods. But by a curious coincidence, this month's diocesan magazine contains an article written by another Suffolk vicar, Christopher Idle, on rural racism. "After 20 years in London and three in East Anglia, the ugliest racism I have met was at the garden gate of a Suffolk cottage, without a single black face in sight," he writes.

Mr Ensor is as nervous as everyone else about offending the all-powerful estate. "The last thing I want is for this thing to drive a wedge between me and the estate."

He admits that he feels like 'a piggy in the middle'. He is in the unenviable position of having to reconcile the expectations of two entirely separate constituencies – his traditional parish members and a wider world quick to charge the Church of England with not its responsibilities to combat racism. But he is the only possible mediator. While the Church still has some authority in the village, the local council is too distant from village affairs. The parish council chairman.

Duleep Singh, portrayed in English garb by the contemporary cartoonist, Spy

Ian Robertson, takes a gloomy view. "I can understand the Sikhs, or whatever they call themselves, may wish to celebrate the centenary," he says. "I've seen the date on the gravestone." But he adds: "I know very little about Sikhs."

Things are now calming down, Mr Ensor says cheerfully after discussions with his diocese. Of the four requests made by the Sikhs, two have been rejected, one queried and one partially accepted. It's a very English solution.

No, the bishop could not sanction an "inter-faith service" – the Church must preserve the integrity of Christianity. No, canopies over the graves would not be allowed under graveyard law. But a plaque to Duleep Singh's memory on the outside of the church is acceptable and perhaps the bishop will unveil it. Some members of the Sikh community would be invited; it would be a Christian service. The estate has agreed to allow the use of its car park.

That's not quite the celebration of the 150-year-old Anglo-Sikh ties which the Wolverhampton-based Maharajah Duleep Singh Centenary Committee had envisaged. What it wants is a 'festival, carnival atmosphere' in Elveden next August with musicians, poets and performers and 'prominent UK figures including MPs, religious dignitaries and academics' invited. The committee wants a service at Duleep Singh's graveside on the anniversary of his death on October 23. And to win over a few villagers, it has offered to donate money to a local charity and to endow a chair in local history at the University of East Anglia. The meeting tomorrow between members of the Centenary Committee and local government officials will finalise the details.

The Centenary Committee is planning an exhibition on the life and times of Duleep Singh to travel around the country. It has commissioned portraits of him and a researcher to look into his life. The committee sees the centenary as a good opportunity to educate the British that Sikhs have not just landed on their doorsteps but have a long

A shooting weekend at Elveden: Prince of Wales seated centre in front of door, with Lord Rendlesham (sitting next right), Maharajah Duleep Singh (next right), Lord Frederick Fitzroy (standing at rear), Lord Ripon and Lord Walsingham (sitting on ground, front left)

history as allies under the Raj and as stalwart soldiers in the British Army. It is this aspect of the history, rather than Britain's brutal conquest of the great Sikh kingdom of Lahore and the robbing of the Maharajah's family jewels, that the Sikhs wish to remember.

Harbinder Singh, a member of the centenary committee, explained: "We want to take away this veil of anonymity about our history and get people to realise that the link between the British and Sikhs is not just as immigrants but as equal partners. We've now found an historical link – all Commonwealth immigrants have the link of empire – but we have found a special link. We're trying to strengthen Anglo-Sikhism. The rise of racism concerns Sikhs because they are such a visible minority with the turban they wear."

The Maharajah – as the first British Sikh – is a potent symbol in the community because he achieved an accommodation between his own culture and that of Victorian England with remarkable aplomb. From the day he arrived in England as a teenager, Duleep Singh was treated as foreign royalty by the British aristocracy. The 35-year-old Queen

Victoria fell for his dark eyes and invited him regularly to Osborne and Buckingham Palace. She wrote that Duleep was "extremely handsome and has a pretty, graceful and dignified manner. He was beautifully dressed and covered with diamonds ... I always feel so much for these poor deposed Indian Princes." Several of the Maharajah's children were baptised at Windsor with such 'civilised' names as Victor, Frederick and Edward.

The Maharajah rebuilt Elveden Hall fit to entertain royalty. In later years, the Prince of Wales regularly attended the shooting parties at Elveden, reputed to be one of the finest shooting estates in the country.

Yet all the while the Maharajah remained distinctively Indian. He wore gorgeously embroidered, jewelled clothing and turbans. During his lease of Mulgrave Castle on the Yorkshire Moors he and his manservants rode along the beach to Whitby on elephants and stunned locals by their brilliant costume for grouse shooting on the moors. At huge cost, he modelled theinterior of Elveden Hall on his memories of the Indian palaces of his childhood.

More importantly, the Sikhs maintain that he abandoned Christianity in his later life and after protracted disputes with the British government to increase his annual allowance of £25,000, embraced Sikhism and attempted to return to the Punjab. The British feared he could prove a focus for rebellion and he was arrested at Aden. He died in Paris.

Duleep Singh may not fit very neatly into the role of religious folk hero – there was a Covent Garden flat and a chorus girl mistress. Even more awkwardly, Elveden tradition has it that the Maharajah called for Christian scriptures on his death bed.

But Dr Roger Ballard, of the anthropology department of Manchester University, points out that while ethnic groups are jostling for greater recognition from Britain, it is understandable that they look around for heroes. "Duleep Singh is a good candidate; Sikhs can celebrate his distinctiveness and his connections with or a fundamentalist so they steer clear of the Royal Family. There's not too much on the downside. He wasn't a fanatic or a fundamentalist so they steer clear of squabbles with Muslims and Hindus. He's an excellent folk hero,

providing you can overlook the exotic pet role he played."

The beauty of Duleep Singh as a symbol is that at different times in his life he was accepted by the British establishment as an equal *and* victimised by it for his championing of the Sikh cause.

The coach-loads of Sikh children from Wolverhampton who went to Elveden last summer were thrilled. It's the very Englishness of Elveden which makes the story so potent. The wrought iron gates, the empty mansion and the romantic sweep of parklands exert a snobbish fascination. All this once belonged to their co-religionist.

Harbinder Singh is undaunted by the villagers' frostiness; he says he is more determined than ever. The centenary scheme has the support of 30,000 of Britain's 250,000 Sikhs and money is pouring in.

But the Sikhs are up against a passive, stubborn, rural brand of British racism. Since the villagers' main complaint is that the Sikhs ask for directions, perhaps a few signposts wouldn't go amiss ... to ease racial tension.

Source: *The Guardian*, 3 March 1993

This article provides two very distinctive views of place – 'quintessential rural England' and a shrine, a place of pilgrimage. These views are held by two sharply contrasted groups of people, one represented by 'head scarf and tweed skirt' and the other by the fact of wearing turbans. If a person from elsewhere were to wonder about what really is the difference between head scarves and turbans, we would probably identify a difference based on *culture*. The cultural identity of the villagers is assumed in 'the very Englishness of Elveden', although Liam Flack sounds as though he might come from County Armagh. Perhaps this apparent or possible exception serves to make the point that even 'Englishness' is far from being a single, homogeneous type. As we have seen in Chapter 3, section 3.4, such labels belie a complexity wrought by centuries and decades of mixing. The fact of complexity is perhaps more striking when we turn to the cultural identity of Duleep Singh, which is quite problematic. On the one hand, Duleep is described as a stereotypical English squire who 'was treated as foreign royalty by the British aristocracy'; but on the other, Sikhs maintain that in later life Duleep 'embraced Sikhism and attempted to return to the Punjab'. There is reference to 'his championing the Sikh cause' and being 'victimized for it', and to his remaining 'distinctively Indian'; yet his 'children were baptised at Windsor with ... such names as Victor, Frederick and Edward'. Whether this is ambivalence or hybridity is something which you might recall when you come to read Chapter 5.

The villagers of Elveden are represented as resisting the idea of the village becoming a place of Sikh pilgrimage, defending what they see as their own place. They complained about things like litter and noise but their comments clearly express a sense of difference and an attitude of exclusion. Perhaps you picked out elements of language which expressed this? They view this as cultural incursion which they seem determined to resist. The language of Harbinder Singh is reportedly very different and his views are apparently 'inclusive' rather than exclusive: that is to say, he is trying to promote the idea of mixing and openness rather than of putting up barriers and refusing to communicate. He speaks of 'trying to strengthen Anglo-Sikhism' (although there is no definition of what he means by that) and he also invokes facts of history. This is where aspects of local–global relations really become quite interesting. It is clear that there are aspects of global history which are very important, even to this small place in rural England, but which 'the locals' in this case would prefer to ignore, denying their global links with Sikhs in India, Wolverhampton or anywhere else. The proposal by the Sikh committee to endow a Chair of local history at the University of East Anglia begs an interesting question of 'whose history?'

Underlying the different views expressed here, and hidden to some extent in the language used or reported, is the issue of *racism*, 'a passive, stubborn, rural brand of British racism' which emerges from what the villagers say and to an extent also, from what they do not say or do. If they honestly are annoyed by requests for directions, why not put up signposts? The attitude seems to be that the Sikhs do not belong. They are 'others', 'out of place' here. And if Duleep Singh did live there, he did so as an English gentleman, endowing the Church with silver and entertaining royalty. It is a classic case of a struggle over the definition of insiders and the exclusion of those thereby defined as outsiders (even though the latter may *want* to identify with the place, as was argued in Chapter 3, section 3.3.3) and in the context of a vision of a 'classic English village'. In this vision there is no place for 'others'.

We have pointed here to the importance of noting language in the context of representations – what people say and how they describe things. It is also useful to identify the sources of our information in terms of 'who says what people say' and who has reported it. In this case our article comes from *The Guardian* and the writer may or may not have views on the issue or on those involved which the use of language may underline.

You may, like us, have wondered what actually happened in August 1993 or on 23 October 1993, in which case you may like to know that the celebrations focused on the nearby town of Thetford, as the following articles from a local newspaper show.

Sikhs make Norfolk pilgrimage

Four thousand Sikhs are expected to attend an international open-air festival in Thetford tomorrow after a nearby village closed its doors on the centenary celebrations.

The festival marks the death of the last Sikh Maharajah, Duleep Singh, who lived in the village of Elveden and is buried in the local churchyard.

The Maharajah Duleep Singh Centenary Trust said it would have been more appropriate to hold the festival at the Maharajah's former home – Elveden Hall – rather than the Breckland Leisure Centre, Thetford.

"It's a bit like the Queen without Buckingham Palace but Elveden's loss is Thetford's gain," said trust director Harbinder Singh.

Mr Singh said the Elveden estate office, which owns most of the village, had given no logical explanation for its resistance to the celebrations.

"They seem to have a phobia about people coming to the village," he said.

"We are not a bunch of illiterates from some banana republic. Most of us were born and educated at university here."

Tony Yates of Breckland Leisure Management said councillors were very interested in the centenary and Mayor Kath Key would be at the festival.

"It is a great honour for us to have the festival here and it's also very good for the future of the centre. We have never had anything as grand as this before," he said.

Because of the crowds expected, police have been in contact with the organisers to make sure the event goes ahead safely.

"We are aware that it is an ethnic event – something which we are not used to in Norfolk let alone Thetford," said Chief Insp. Martin Wynne. "But I am not anticipating any problems."

Programme for the big day

The festival of Indian culture, music and dance at Breckland Leisure Centre, Thetford, is open to the public and entry is free.

Refreshments are available all day and there is a children's play area with bouncy castle.

The programme of events:

- 11am, Sikh ceremony.
- 11am–4pm Exhibition in marquee of portraits and memorabilia of Duleep Singh.
- 12.45pm–1.30pm, Introduction, speeches and presentations by various local VIPs including Thetford Mayor Kath Key.
- 1pm onwards, Punjabi folk dances, musicians and displays.
- 1.30pm–4pm, Various Sikh poets, historians, academics make their addresses.
- 4pm, Closing ceremony with release of helium balloons.

Source: *Eastern Daily Press*, 31 July 1993

PRINCE WHO BRIDGES YEARS, AND CULTURES

Exactly 100 years after his death, Duleep Singh was yesterday hailed as a symbol of unity between two communities.

Sikh and Christian leaders gathered at the last Maharajah's former home, Elveden Hall, near Thetford, for

the unveiling of a plaque by the Bishop of St Edmundsbury and Ipswich.

The grand ceremony was a far cry from the way the Sikh leader died – penniless in France, having frittered away his fortune on extravagances.

The Rev Paul Ensor, whose parish covers Elveden, said it was a contradiction that a Sikh leader was buried in a quiet Suffolk church.

"This demonstrates the heritage between the Sikh and Christian communities and it's an opportunity for us to grow together in sympathy and understanding," he said.

Mr Ensor told the multi-cultural audience of turbaned Sikhs and raincoated local people clutching umbrellas that Duleep himself had been a mixture of contradictions.

Exiled from his Punjabi throne by the British in 1848, he became known as the Black Prince of Elveden and was a favourite of Queen Victoria.

A hunting and shooting man, Duleep Singh was treated like a country gentleman – but he retained his Indian identity.

His exotic costumes and princely manner stunned English people and his Suffolk home was decorated inside like an Indian palace.

A century later, the man who held parties for royalty was still drawing crowds from across the country.

One man had even come from Canada for the celebration. Thomas Hess said he had met a lot of Indians in his work with immigrants in Edmonton.

"I have lots of friends in the Sikh community and I was in Germany for a business trip so I though I would take the opportunity to come here," he said.

The second half of the centenary celebration was held at Breckland House, Thetford, where a portrait of the Maharajah and a model of a memorial to be erected in the town were unveiled.

Town Mayor Kath Key welcomed the guests to Thetford and said she thought the painting, by Ipswich-based artist Anthea du Rose, was wonderful.

Harbinder Singh, of the Duleep Singh Centenary Trust, said the Maharajah had spent 32 of his 55 years in England and was a symbol of the close ties between the Sikh and the Christian communities.

Piara Khabra, the MP for Ealing Southall, and artist Anthea du Rose, with the portrait of Duleep Singh

Source: *Eastern Daily Press*, 23 October 1993

4.5 Europe: boundaries, ethnicity and exclusivity

boundaries

The commentary above implicitly criticizes the villagers of Elveden for trying to create *boundaries* around their place specifically to prevent certain 'outsiders' from coming in. Both Chapter 2, section 2.4.1, and Chapter 3, section 3.3.2, have pointed to the way in which the establishment of boundaries can be crucial in the formation of certain kinds of sense of place. They define not only what a place is, but what it is not. Yet, as all our discussions of space and of globalization have recognized, there are in effect no closed places. Boundaries, in that sense, are always 'artificial'. They are socially constructed lines which inevitably cut across other flows and interconnections which construct the space in which we live.

boundedness

Both racism and an insistence on the *boundedness* of place rest firmly on issues of who belongs and who does not. In these terms they are strongly exclusionary. In Elveden this is shown at an informal and very local level but increasingly it is being seen, in the 1990s, as a European phenomenon. The phrase 'Fortress Europe' is used to express a new boundedness of, essentially, a new place. It is defined very largely in terms of who is *excluded*, less clearly in terms of who might be included. As the internal borders of the EU came down, barriers against immigrants have been reinforced and invented.

The question of 'Europe' – how it is to be defined and what is its character – is a major issue of the 1990s. It raises questions of how we define personal identities in relation to geographical entities: who should be granted citizenship, and who not; how our identities may be built on 'difference' – we know who we are because we know who we are not; and it forces us to face issues of international migration. We shall see here the intimate connections between identity, movement/migration, and the construction of boundaries in space.

Chapter 1, section 1.4.3, asked the question whether international migration should not be a human right, and contrasted the widely accepted arguments that goods and capital investment of all kinds should be allowed to flow freely across boundaries (we call it 'free trade') with the widely practised phenomenon of the erection of barriers to the free movement of people. We begin to address these issues here in the context of Europe and its constituent nation-states.

illegal immigration

We have selected four short articles which deal with issues surrounding the concept of boundedness but without actually mentioning 'boundaries' as such. The four cases are linked around issues to do with immigration and *definition*. In fact they are each about the concept of *illegal immigration* which raises the issue of the distinctions drawn between legal and illegal: what are the criteria; who decides on these criteria; what are the implications of drawing distinctions between 'us' and 'them'? These are the questions which we should like you to keep in mind as you work through the set of articles.

The Activities for this final section are more open-ended, more open to debate than the earlier ones. This is quite deliberate! We want you to think about the issues raised, which are complex, challenging and often quite difficult. You may not be able to reach 'an answer' in the sense of 'yes or no': the important thing is to think the issue through and to be able to recognize, construct and de-construct the arguments.

We begin with Germany and its long-standing population of guestworkers.

WHERE THE LAW OF BLOOD STILL RULES

By ANNA TOMFORDE

How long does it take to become a proper German? Anita, born of a Nigerian father and a German mother 23 years ago, still gets strange looks when she goes to have her German passport extended. "People ask me twice or three times whether I really am German, and how I speak the language so well ... they are fooling themselves if they believe that Germans can only be white," she said, speaking with a distinct Cologne accent.

She is one of 250,000 Germans of Afro-Asian descent who have founded an 'Initiative of Black Germans' which aims to overcome social isolation, resentment and racism.

Under German citizenship law dating from 1913, which was much abused bythe Nazis and which has not been significantly changed since, descent 'by blood' rather than place of birth, defines who is German. This means that access to citizenship is almost impossible for the country's 6.5 million foreigners who make up 8 per cent of the population.

The current debate about changing this state of affairs is therefore also seen in the context of how a future Germany will define itself. "Post-war liberalisation is being tested, and could be overtaken by a new German nationalism," said Prof Claus Leggewie, a sociologist at Giessen university.

I.n the words of Oskar Lafontaine, deputy Social Democrat leader, Germany should like France or the United States, adopt a "truly Republican understanding of nationhood" because history had shown that nationalist radicalism flourished where the 'law of blood' ruled.

"Nowhere has blood dripped so thickly into law," said Cornelia Schmalz-Jacobsen, the Government-appointed Commissioner for Foreigners who is spearheading a campaign for easier citizenship and dual nationality.

"Many of the problems we have with immigrants today would not have arisen if we had allowed people who have long formed an integral part of our population to become Germans."

She has proposed that children of foreigners whose parents live in Germany should have an automatic right to citizenship and that everyone else should be entitled to become German after eight years as well as being able to hold dual nationality.

Her suggestions have been rejected as too radical by Chancellor Kohl's Conservative-led government. But the government has realised that moves towards making citizenship easier to obtain have become unavoidable.

The Christian Democrats have suggested that citizenship should be granted after a period of between 10 and 15 years, but a majority of them, and especially the rightwing Bavarian CSU (Christian Socialist Union), continues to oppose any moves towards dual nationality. They argue that it would lead to legal complications, 'conflicts of loyalty', and problems with military service.

The government will present its own reform of citizenship laws this summer, but experts fear that the sensitive debate will be dragged into the campaign for next year's general election.

According to Mrs Schmalz-Jacobsen it is the requirement that original citizenship would be renounced that prevents most of the 1.8 million Turkish workers and their families from seeking German citizenship. Surveys have found that 83 per cent of Turks want to stay in Germany where many first arrived under the initial *Gastarbeiter* (guest worker) recruitment scheme of the early 1960s.

If automatic citizenship was granted to children of the fourth and fifth generation, there would be 1.5 million foreigners left living in Germany as citizens with restricted rights, she explained. Every year, 30,000 Turkish children are born in Germany.

But only about 1,000 Turks a year manage to go through the immensely complicated process of naturalisation, which is granted as an exception rather than a right. Figures show that 25 per cent of immigrants' children are less than 18 years old, and that two-thirds of them were born in Germany, making up what Mrs Schmalz-Jacobson calls "youths without a German passport".

Some 100,000 foreign students are enrolled at German universities, but nationality laws still prevent non-German doctors from setting up their own surgery and make it impossible for teachers or lawyers to gain civil servant status.

At present, one in 12 jobs is held by a *Gastarbeiter*. The Turks, having moved on from being industrial workers to self-employed business, have created 125,000 jobs, contribute 9 per cent to the GNP, and account for 7 per cent of the total tax revenue. They pay 8 per cent of the money paid into pension funds but, because of their low average age, take out only 2.5 per cent. "We profit from them", said Mrs Schmalz-Jacobsen, "and yet they have no rights."

Heribert Prantl, a commentator on Munich's Süddeutsche Zeitung, says that in 1993, the discussion about who is German seems unreal. It is an anachronism, he argues, which, if the Government does not speed up reform, could be overtaken by European reality.

"In a united Europe there will be one European citizenship after which being German, French or Turkish would be secondary."

Source: *The Guardian*, 2 March 1993

This article is about *definitions*: about who is German and what that means and, just as importantly, who is *not* German and what that means. The issue has already been introduced in Chapter 1, and it might be useful to look back to that for historical background (see section 1.3.1). The very opening paragraph of the article clearly puts on the agenda a crucial issue which runs through many of the debates about the conceptualization of place: what is, or should be, the relation between ethnicity (here talked about in terms of 'blood') and geography? The 1913 law in Germany gave access to 'citizenship', and thus to the whole bundle of rights which go with it, only to those of 'German blood'.

Activity 7 Before we move on, consider what your opinion of this is. What is implied in the phrase 'descent by blood' rather than, for instance, 'place of birth'?

First of all, the article says nothing about how such a criterion is defined or tested, but it does raise visions of examinations for 'racial' purity. Lying behind the law is an assumption of eternal rights to a place by one group. It must therefore be assumed that either this group has 'always' been there or that this is simply a claim on this piece of space, a straightforward powerplay, in which one self-defined group annexes a piece of space and labels it as their own: see Box 4.1. Those who oppose the 'law of blood', according to the article, argue that people gain rights from being in a place, from living there and participating in it. The contribution of Turkish migrants to the German economy – in jobs, output, tax revenue and pension contributions – is referred to: as the Commissioner for Foreigners points out, 'We profit from them and yet they have no rights'. In other words, these people have helped build the very thing that is Germany: the 'global' connections (i.e. Turkish immigration) are, here, literally part of the building of the 'local place'. Many people and parties therefore argue that the law must be changed. Yet there is still disagreement within this group.

Activity 8   Mirroring our earlier question of 'how long do you have to have been in a place to be counted as a "local"?', the issue now raised is how long do you have to have been in Germany to gain German citizenship and the rights which go with it?

o   What are the different positions on this?

o   What do *you* think? Which position would you take?

o   Why might the whole argument be 'an anachronism'?

Box 4.1 Where is Germany?

While many of us may not have known where Mosquitia or Elveden is, most of us would probably never even think about whether we 'know' where Germany is. In fact the space which is now labelled 'Germany' has been peopled over time by many groups of migrants who have moved mainly from the east. Indeed, 'Germany' did not exist as a political entity until 1871 and it provides an example of our concept of 'envelopes of space–time' (see maps overleaf).

The Germany of 1871 was altered after the First World War to become smaller, in response to ideas about Germany which were held by other European states. 'National self-determination' was a much-vaunted principle of the Treaty of Versailles in 1919 and was granted to many so-called nationalities but not to Germans. Plebiscites were used occasionally and inconsistently to determine post-war borders in certain resource-rich areas. This is an example of the use of *power* to define and represent literally what is on the map of Europe.

Germany's geography changed again in the 1940s, firstly with the Nazi vision of unifying the Volk and obtaining *lebensraum* (living-space) by extending territorially, mainly eastwards. History was invoked to support the image of a Great German Empire – the geographical imagination of a space to fit a people. Secondly, German surrender in 1945 produced a spatial division of Germany, again by direction of victorious 'allies' who had clear ideas about what Germany should be like, and power to enforce those ideas.

This political differentiation into two separate Germanies was reversed in 1992, creating the latest version of what is known as 'Germany'. There remains a considerable 'German' cultural and political heritage to the east of the present boundaries, expressed in architecture, place-names, agricultural practices, religious influences and ethnic minorities – for example, in the Ukraine, Rumania and Hungary – and, more recently, in economic investment such as that by Volkswagen in the Czech and Slovak Republics.

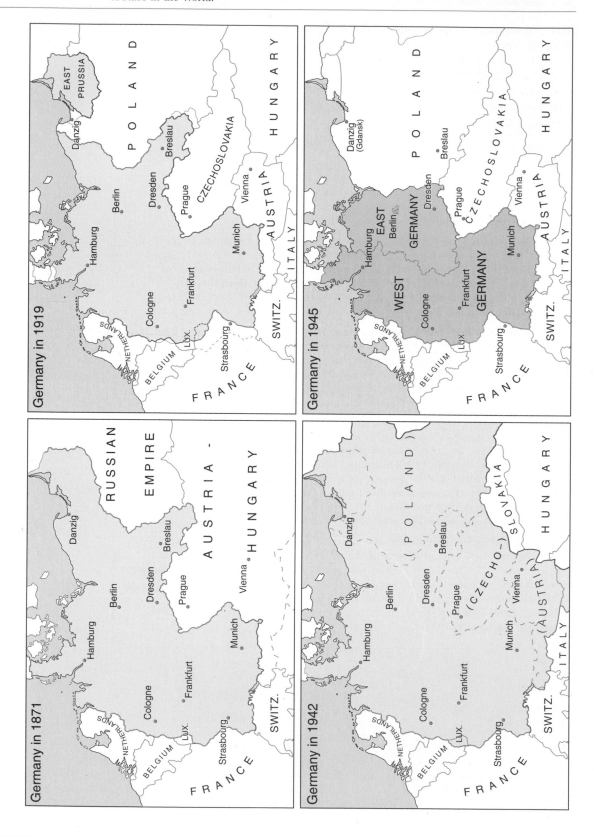

EUROPE TO FORCE VISA LAWS ON UK

By JOHN CARVELL

Britain will be forced within the next three years to scrap preferential arrangements which allow citizens of most Commonwealth countries the right to visit relatives in Britain without the need of a visa, according to documents sent to ministers by the European Commission.

They say that the Treaty of European Union which John Major signed at Maastricht will forbid any member state from running its own visa policy after June 1996 when a common European Union visa policy must come into operation.

The commission's draft list of countries whose nationals would require a visa to enter the EU includes 31 Commonwealth members which are exempted from Britain's current visa requirements. They include most of the African and Caribbean members – but not Jamaica some of whose nationals were subjected to close questioning when they tried to enter Britain before Christmas.

Although the list has not yet been discussed by ministers and can theoretically be negotiated, it will be almost impossible in practice for British ministers to take names off it.

The commission has adopted the list agreed by the Schengen countries – the inner ring of EU members which have been pushing ahead with co-operation on police and immigration matters without Britain, Ireland and Denmark.

Although Britain can veto proposals until the end of next year, decisions will be made by majority voting after January 1996, under the terms Mr Major agreed at Maastricht.

The commission's plans are contained in a draft regulation which it has sent to national capitals over the last few days. It sets out a 'negative list' of 127 countries whose nationals would have to apply for a three-month visa to enter any part of the EU. This list is being described by commission officials as the 'blacklist', partly because most of the people involved are black.

It includes 31 Commonwealth countries which are exempt from current British visa requirements, including Zimbabwe, Zambia, Tanzania, Sierra Leone, Namibia and Barbados. South Africa and Kuwait are among countries with close links to Britain which also appear on the Commission list.

The list contains seven Commonwealth members whose nationals already require visas before entering Britain because ministers deemed there was a special risk of illegal immigration: Bangladesh, Ghana, India, Nigeria, Pakistan, Sri Lanka and Uganda.

Tara Mukherjee, president of the EU Migrants Forum and one of the leaders of the Indian community in Britain, said: "It is a blacklist in the true sense of the term. Not a single white Commonwealth country is included."

Earlier versions of the draft included a 'positive list' of 20 countries whose nationals would be exempted from visa restrictions. They included Canada, Malta and New Zealand.

The other Commonwealth members – including Australia and Jamaica – were consigned to a 'grey list' of countries whose status has not yet been agreed by the Schengen group. The commission said they must all be allocated to either the 'negative' or 'positive' list by June 1996. The published draft only names the proposed negative list.

If the commission's legal interpretation is correct, the Government will be forced before the likely date of the next general election to choose between snubbing the Commonwealth and breaking EU law. Mr Major may have to decide whether Eurosceptics on the Conservative backbenches can be relied on to be more hostile to allowing black Commonwealth citizens into Britain than to edicts from Brussels.

The Home Office said yesterday that the commission document was a proposal which had not yet been discussed by ministers.

Mr Mukherjee said he feared it was almost inevitable that the commission's draft blacklist would become permanent and would be supplemented with other new Commonwealth countries.

"I am afraid that the present British government is only paying lip service to the importance it attaches to the Commonwealth. It cannot see a political value in anything which does not yield an economic return," he said. "Citizens of Commonwealth countries with the Queen as their head have until now been given the privilege of coming into Britain without a visa unless they came from a few places where the Government thought there was an immigration problem.

"Even if ministers wanted to maintain that system, they are now going to be outmanoeuvred by the countries in the Schengen club. This will be the price we pay for the UK stand."

Source: *The Guardian*, 8 January 1994

The question of German citizenship may become an anachronism because of the advent of 'Europe' and European citizenship. One of the things which European Union represents is the coming together of countries which in the past have had their own individual links beyond their boundaries to overseas territories and trading partners. In the UK these special relationships were above all with the countries of the Commonwealth.

Activity 9 Check back again through the article and identify the point that membership of the EU means what we might call *re-drawing the boundaries of connections* and consider what that actually means – the lines, the relationships between Britain and the world, from 'the Commonwealth' to the EU and, with that, a redefinition of identities. Being a member of the Commonwealth and a citizen of a Commonwealth country will no longer mean the same kind of relationship with Britain.

o   How will this affect patterns of rights to travel and migrate?

o   How might this affect the process of 'Othering'?

o   How does this 're-define' certain groups?

This raises the issue of *legal* definitions. The law defines who gets in and who must stay out. So who makes the laws? And what might be the objectives of this law-making?

o   What notion of a general European identity might underlie these changes in rules?

What is at issue here is an attempt to suppress individual countries' histories of international links, and the administrative arrangements which reflect them, such as exemption from the need to acquire visas. It is measures such as these which have led to accusations that what we are building is a 'Fortress Europe' and establishing a sense of place by creating 'others' – the 'new version of Orientalism' discussed in Chapter 3, section 3.2.2.

If this is so, what is the Fortress being built to defend against? One thing, during the 1990s, is the potential arrival of people from the countries of the ex-Soviet Union and Eastern Europe. Many of them are refugees from wars and collapsing societies. And many of these people arrive at the eastern borders of the European Union.

Greece taxed by refugee influx

By HELEN SMITH

Christina, a shy and pretty teenager, came to the brothel about three weeks ago. "She's yours for 2,000 drachmas [£6]," says her pimp.

"We will never tell our children how we started out, but there was nothing else to do," he whispers in halting Greek.

Christina and the young boy are Albanians. But in the seedy red-light district of Athens she could be a Bulgar or an Iraqi, a Russian or a Romanian – all immigrant groups who have in desperation taken to the trade.

From the Middle East and Africa, the Balkans and eastern Europe, refugees are pouring across Greece's borders at a rate described by officials as 'terrifying'.

Virginia Tsouderou, the deputy foreign minister, sighs: "They are now close to half a million, which means they comprise some 6 per cent of Greece's workforce and are an enormous strain on our already crippled economy. A lot are a security risk and have been caught with arms."

The influx of immigrants began in 1989 with the collapse of communism. Since then about 300,000 Albanians alone have trekked across the mountains and over the frontier.

Only a fraction, including about 40,000 ethnic Greeks from the Soviet republics and 50,000 political refugees – Turks, Kurds, Iraqis, Iranians, Ethiopians and Somalis – are legal. Many of the immigrants are brought to Greece by organised gangs of traffickers.

"The most serious threat comes from the east, where huge numbers are being ferried from Turkey to our islands," says Mrs Tsouderou.

In the past year more than 2,000 Iraqis have been dumped on Greece's outlying islands in the eastern Aegean after paying Turkish fishermen as much as £2,500 to transport them.

Last October, Athens and Ankara were at loggerheads when 68 Iraqis trying to enter Greece illegally from Turkey were stranded for 18 days at sea.

Now the conservative government is bracing itself for a mass influx of refugees from former Yugoslavia in the event of civil war spreading south.

Yasmina Chourfi, acting representative of the United Nations High Commissioner for Refugees in Athens said: "We've heard that it [the government] is already creating reception centres along the northern frontier."

She added that Greece's 37,000 miles of coastline were impossible to control. "With the tightening of visa requirements across Europe, Greece will become the flank for an influx."

The majority are economic migrants. Although hundreds have been forced to resort to prostitution, the flow has meant cheap labour and bigger profit margins for employers. But to the Greeks at large, their arrival has been unwelcome.

Source: *The Guardian*, 27 January 1993

This article also highlights the importance of legal definitions: in this case, who gets in and who does not? The answer raises the issue of ethnicity. The 'legal' immigrants are 'ethnic Greeks from (former) Soviet republics and ... political refugees'. However, since these are quoted as being 'only a fraction', it begs the question about the other refugees, described as an 'influx' which began 'with the collapse of communism'. This situation produces a real irony out of a history of interdependence: how can European Union governments close their boundaries to people fleeing developments which the countries of Western Europe themselves did so much to encourage? One of the criticisms most frequently made by western governments about the former societies of the Soviet Union and Eastern Europe was that these societies did not allow their citizens freedom of movement. Yet, now that they *are* allowed to leave their countries the response of the 'West' is to hide defensively behind its borders!

Not all the migrants referred to in the article about Greece are political refugees. The majority, the article says, are economic migrants. They are people moving, in other words, in response to the brute facts of uneven economic development. As Chapter 1 has shown, uneven development and migration are intimately related: 'Many international migrations closely reflect the global economic distribution of power, in particular, the demand for … labour by the centres of capital accumulation …' (Chapter 1, section 1.6). But at the other end of the process, so to speak, are the places where people leave, where there is no need for labour, where globalization does not reach. In **Allen and Hamnett (eds, 1995)**, **Lockwood (1995)** and **Hall (1995)**, it became clear that among those vast areas of the world which are 'omitted' by the globalization of the more prosperous is Africa. For many people in Africa the only immediate possibility of joining in the supposedly globalized world is to migrate to it. In northern Africa, with the Mediterranean just to the north, the nearest place to turn is Europe. And for many north African countries which were once French imperial possessions, the most obvious place of all is France. Indeed north African workers have long fuelled the French economy in much the same way as Caribbean and Asian workers have fuelled the British, and Turkish and others the German. In the case below, the facts of the imperial connections of history and the pressures of the uneven development of today combine.

FRENCH GET TOUGH ON ILLEGAL IMMIGRANTS

By Suzanne Lowry in Paris

France is forming a special police unit to fight illegal immigration and will resume deportations of illegal aliens to discourage the world's poor from flooding the country.

The new force, to be called the Central Directorate of Immigration Control and of the Fight Against the Employment of Illegal Immigrants (Dicilec), will come into being a week tomorrow.

It will be headed by one of the most celebrated of French policemen, M Robert Broussard, who formerly ran the anti-gangster brigade.

M Charles Pasqua, Interior Minister, who announced the move on television on Wednesday night, said the government was "obliged to take coercive and administrative measures" to stem the tide of illegal aliens.

"Once we have sent back several planeloads or boat-loads, the world will get the message," he said, referring to the deportation of aliens aboard government-chartered transportation.

The government was forced to give up this method after the deportation of 101 Malians in 1986 caused a uproar in France. Arguing that France "cannot take on the misery of the entire world", M Pasqua said the immigration problems could only get bigger.

The system in eastern Europe had disintegrated, and "if clashes break out there, we will not avoid a huge wave of immigration", he said.

In Algeria, Tunisia and Morocco, M Pasqua said that "by the end of the decade there will be 130 million North Africans, including nearly 60 million under 20 with no prospects and, further south, one billion other Africans." But coercion and new rules would "not solve the problem alone". France should lead a "crusade for development" in countries where the emigrants came from to encourage people to see their futures there.

The recent immigration law changes are beginning to cause serious difficulties for French citizens who marry foreigners from non-EU countries.

No distinction is being made between couples truly in love and those marrying for the right to stay in France.

All foreign brides or bridegrooms without *cartes de sejour* have to leave the country after their weddings to wait for long-term visas. This can take three months' minimum.

The new force, said M Pasqua, would have a role to play in the future application of the Schengen Accords.

These are the EU agreements on the opening of frontiers that were due to come into force a year ago but were effectively delayed by the French.

France has a 3.6 million legal immigrants, of whom two million are North Africans and up to one million illegal immigrants.

Source: The *Daily Telegraph*, 7 January 1994

Activity 10 What is being said in the article above, if only implicitly, about French and Frenchness? Who has rights to reside in France?

As we discussed above, immigrants only become 'illegal' because of the existence and nature of states' restrictions on the movement of people. These restrictions reflect ideas about inclusion and exclusion, 'us' and 'them'. Identity, in this case French identity, is based on difference. 'We' know who 'we' are by defining who we are not. Note the use of the term 'aliens' at the end of the fourth paragraph. This also demonstrates the way language can be used to reinforce ideas of exclusivity. In fact, language plays a strong role in this particular case: Pasqua is quoted as using phrases which score highly on emotive rhetoric.

Not only is Pasqua concerned about keeping out illegal immigrants, he is interested in getting rid of people who are already in France. This is a further reinforcement of the idea of 'Fortress Europe'. Furthermore, he is constructing a special police unit to deal with those classified as immigrants, 'aliens', 'the world's poor' and 'foreigners'. This is linked, according to the article, to 'the future application of the Schengen Accords'. These measures have been mentioned in one of the other articles ('Europe to force visa laws on UK'). Basically, they amount to an agreed set of rules aimed at strengthening the frontiers of the EU against incomers. With this definition of 'Fortress Europe', what about the idea that movement on 'planet Earth' should be a basic human right? Is it? And if not, why not? Finally in this case study, note that Pasqua is not suggesting that 'coercion and new rules' will 'solve the problem alone'. What do you make of his parallel proposal? Does the suggestion of 'a crusade for development' in the 'sending countries' provide a solution? How is this to be reconciled with what you have already learned about 'uneven development'?

4.6   Concluding points

This chapter has been about struggles over the nature of place, about the process – or part of the process – of *making* places. Whether those places be local communities or groups of nation-states, such contests occur continually.

What is clear from all the case studies is the intimate relationship which may exist between constructions of cultural and even personal identity, the process of differentiation from others, and our geographical imaginations. All the different constructions of place in the case studies were contested images, contested representations of places in which each protagonist was arguing the case for *their* representation to prevail. These representations are like snapshots of a place at a particular period in time, images of how people 'see' or interpret the place. In general, by laying claim to a particular interpretation of the present identity of the place, which usually in turn drew also upon a particular interpretation of its past, each of the protagonists makes an argument, usually asserting the desirability of continuity, for what should be the future of the place. The 'snapshot of space–time' forms the basis of this argument. If we think back to the notion of social space as expressed in **Allen and Hamnett** (eds, 1995) – space as the complexity of stretched-out social relations – and if we remember also the notion of place developed in Chapter 2 of this book – place as a subset of this complexity, as a particular locus of intersections and interactions – then one way of interpreting these contests over place is as battles over *the claiming and naming of particular envelopes of space–time.* Is 'the Wye Valley' over the past few centuries, through the present and into the future, to be interpreted as a secluded place, an area of peace for the contemplation of nature; or is it to be seen as a place of production and of people earning their livings, whether through iron-making, farming or the tourist industry? These competing imaginary geographies, these differing claims over the labelling of envelopes of space–time, are at the centre of all the cases we have studied in this chapter. Contestation is a process, not just an occasional battle; it occurs constantly and at all geographical scales. It may take the form of a local tussle over whether or not to allow a McDonald's in Hampstead; it may concern major world-historical conflicts, such as struggles for national liberation from a colonial power, or for the rights to live in certain pieces of territory (think of the long conflicts in the Middle East); or it may be a debate over what should be the future character of 'Europe'. But in all of these are in play issues of identity, the construction of difference, and the question of how we are going to develop our geographical imaginations.

Activity 11 Pause here for a few minutes, and consider how *you* think 'European identity' might best be defined?

Think back to Chapter 3, section 3.2.2, and Reading A by Morley and Robins. But think also of the 'global' construction of Europe, the contribution of the rest of the world to what we today recognize as European.

One thread of analysis which emerged from the case study of Europe in this chapter is the sometimes close relationship between claims over the identity of place on the one hand and the brute facts of uneven development on the other. Charles Pasqua recognizes this when he argues that France should lead a 'crusade for development' in countries where the emigrants come from, in order to encourage people to see their futures there. This harks back to Chapter 1 of this book. While there is such yawning uneven development in the world, at least one of the major pressures for migration will continue. And if there *is* 'a world economy', if we are all involved in globalization, and *if* we accept the argument that there should be free movement of capital and of trade (though by no means everyone does), then what are the arguments against the free movement of people?

Another thread which emerges from these case studies is, once again, the complexity of the relations between the local and global. It is often tempting to interpret the two concepts in terms of 'plucky little local area resists global forces'. That is, maybe, how you may have interpreted the conflict in Honduras. But then what of Wye? Did you feel the same in that case? Or Elveden? Moreover in each case, the local and global were *already thoroughly interrelated*. Even in Honduras the localness of the locals was not absolute and they were busily and quite successfully striving to build wider alliances, to turn this into a more global issue and to draw on wider arguments. In Wye the locals, in the sense of those embattled over the new development, were divided, with the opposers in fact being precisely *not* local in terms of length of residence. In Elveden the local residents were putting forward any argument they could think of to avoid fully recognizing that their local village *already had* connections with Sikhism, that the global was already part of the constitution of the local. The uniqueness of the local place is in part constructed out of wider relations.

But, finally, perhaps the most general conclusion to be drawn is that each case raises different issues and should be evaluated in its own terms. This is not the trite point it might seem at first reading. For what it implies is that it would be extremely difficult to argue for any *general* right for 'local' people to have unquestionable control over particular parts of the Earth. In each case, unique relations of space and place are at issue. We may *in certain cases* feel that such rights should in fact be granted – the right to particular areas of land for certain aboriginal and indigenous groups, maybe. But the case for this will be made on the basis of arguments specific to this instance: the relative powerlessness of indigenous peoples and the great losses which they have already suffered might be a consideration in this case, for instance. But the point is that the claim cannot be made by reference to any general principle of the rights of exclusivity and control being in the hands of 'those who got there first'. As we wrote in the discussion of Honduras, 'It is difficult *always* to defend the locals, or *always* to defend "mixing" [and that means one cannot defend people simply on the basis that they *are* locals]. And that is because *in each case what is at issue is a different set of relations to place and to the power relations which construct social space.*'

And anyway, as we have seen, the very definition of 'local' people is in itself usually one of the issues at stake. In fact, the cultures of the world are all already the product of contact and of mixing, to some degree or other. And it is to that – the issue of mixing and hybridity – that the next chapter now turns.

References

ALLEN, J. and HAMNETT, C. (eds) (1995) *A Shrinking World? Global Unevenness and Inequality*, Oxford, Oxford University Press/The Open University (Volume 2 in the series).

HALL, R. (1995) 'Stabilizing population growth: the European experience' in Sarre, P. and Blunden, J. (eds).

LOCKWOOD, M. (1995) 'Population and environmental change: the case of Africa' in Sarre, P. and Blunden, J. (eds).

MASSEY, D. (1995) 'Imagining the world' in Allen, J. and Massey, D. (eds) *Geographical Worlds*, Oxford, Oxford University Press/The Open University (Volume 1 in the series).

SARRE, P. (1995) 'Paradise lost, or the conquest of the wilderness' in Sarre, P. and Blunden, J. (eds).

SARRE, P. and BLUNDEN, J. (eds) (1995) *An Overcrowded World? Population, Resources and the Environment,* Oxford, Oxford University Press/The Open University (Volume 3 in the series).

New cultures for old

by Stuart Hall

Chapter 5

5.1   Introduction

We have seen, in the four previous chapters, how migration redistributes peoples and their cultures in new ways, in relation both to one another and to places of settlement; and how globalization reconstructs the relationship between 'the local' and 'the global', transforming both what it is actually like to live in a place and the sense we have of, the meanings we give to, 'place'. This chapter takes the story one step further by looking at the impact of globalization and migration on *culture*. In particular, it focuses on the new cultural formations and identities to which these global processes are giving rise.

culture   Here, many of the questions which were examined in earlier chapters are revisited – but now from the perspective of 'culture'. By *culture* we mean the systems of shared meanings which people who belong to the same community, group, or nation use to help them interpret and make sense of the world. These meanings are not free-floating ideas. They are embodied in the material and social world. The term 'culture' includes the social practices which produce meaning as well as the practices which are regulated and organized by those shared meanings. Sharing the same 'maps of meaning' gives us a sense of belonging to a culture, creates a common bond, a sense of community or identity with others. Having a position within a set of shared meanings gives us a sense of 'who we are', 'where we belong' – a sense of our own identity. Culture is thus one of the principal means by which identities are constructed, sustained and transformed.

Cultures are usually thought of as relatively stable or fixed sets of meanings and practices which have achieved a settled continuity over time and place. To think of oneself as 'English' or 'British' is inevitably to place oneself within a set of meanings that have a long history and continuity. Cultures pre-date the individual. They seem to provide a frame of reference or a tradition which connects one's present mode of existence to the way of life of one's ancestors, thereby giving a culture a distinctive coherence and shape over time and making it internally homogeneous. Those who identify with a culture, who share a cultural identity, are assumed to be the same (identical) by virtue of this membership. Cultures are usually seen as well-bounded formations, clearly marked off from 'other' cultures. This marking of cultural difference both increases the sense of community or group solidarity ('us') amongst those who belong and (as Gillian Rose argued in Chapter 3) sharpens the sense of difference from 'other cultures' ('them').

Given that cultures are defined and perceived in this way, it is hardly surprising that the impact of globalization is seen by many commentators as profoundly unsettling for cultures and cultural identity. With its accelerated flows of goods, peoples, ideas, and images, the 'stretching' of social relations, its time and space convergences, its migrating movements of people and cultures, globalization is calculated to disturb culture's settled contours (Harvey, 1989). Established traditions and customary ways of life are dislocated by the invasion of foreign influences and images from the new global cultural industries which traditional communities find enormously seductive, impossible to reject, yet difficult to contain. Global consumerism, though limited by its uneven 'geography of power' (Massey, 1991), spreads the same thin cultural film over everything – Big Macs, Coca Cola and Nike trainers everywhere – inviting everyone to take on western consumer identities and obscuring profound differences of history and tradition between cultures. Migration, which is part of the same process, moves peoples of very different backgrounds and traditions into the same space and time-frame. Sometimes, cultures are caught between, on the one hand, the desire for the mobility and material rewards of modernity and, on the other, the nostalgia for a lost purity, stability and traditional coherence which the present no longer provides, and consequently they splinter and fragment. The consequences of globalization for culture and cultural identity are profound. They are also contradictory, moving in different directions, and difficult to understand or predict. The main purpose of this chapter is to trace some of these new cultural patterns and explore some of the tensions which globalization has triggered.

Reading B in Chapter 2 contains the following passage in which Kevin Robins attempts to capture the radical impact of globalization on culture:

Globalization is profoundly transforming our apprehension of the world: it is provoking a new experience of orientation and disorientation, new senses of placed and placeless identity. The global–local nexus is associated with new relations between space and place, fixity and mobility, centre and periphery, 'real' and 'virtual' space, 'inside' and 'outside', frontier and territory.

(Robins, 1991, p. 41)

'Globalization', Robins claims, 'as it dissolves the barriers of distance, makes the encounter of colonial centre and colonized periphery immediate and intense' (*ibid.*, p. 25). As was pointed out in Chapter 2, Robins may tend to exaggerate both the scale and the novelty of the phenomenon. Nevertheless, there are new forms associated with the contemporary phase of globalization, and the process may be being experienced now in new ways or with a new intensity.

How, then, are we to understand the changing shape of the cultural map in the most recent phase of the age of globalization? How are the new linkages of 'global' and 'local' affecting cultures? Are cultural differences being strengthened or eroded? Are new local cultures emerging as the older local cultures decline? How should we think about or re-conceptualize cultural identity in these more global times?

The next section will pursue these questions further. It examines the concept of *culture* itself. How does it work? What does it mean? I look at the role of language in culture. Language, the system we use to construct and communicate meaning to one another, is one of the fundamental practices of culture. But also, more broadly, language provides us with a useful model of culture. Cultures work 'like a language'. Then I turn to another aspect of culture: place. I discuss the relationship (also explored earlier in Chapters 2 and 3) between culture, identity and place. Since cultures do not necessarily depend on place, why do we continue to think or imagine cultures as 'placed'? Later in the chapter, I turn to one of the most fundamental 'placings' of culture in modern times: the nation-state. Are national cultures really the 'placed', well-bounded and internally unified entities we imagine them to be?

Activity 1 Before you start section 5.1.1, try this exercise. Jot down on a piece of paper a list of some of the things that come to mind when you think of what you *share* with those people whom you regard as members of your own culture.

When you have done so, see whether you can identify the *places* which you mainly associate with these cultural traits. So, if you put 'speaking English', what place would you associate it with? Home and family, where you first learned to speak? Or school which taught you the language? What about your favourite television programme? You share this with many people, but they all live in many different places …

There is no right answer to this exercise. But it may help to get you thinking about how the general themes of the chapter relate to your own personal experience.

5.1.1   Culture, place and identity

You may have noticed that rather similar questions about the relationship between culture, place and identity were posed earlier by Doreen Massey, when she asked what constitutes 'place' and how should we conceptualize it (in Chapter 2); and by Gillian Rose, about the 'sense of place' and the cultural meanings which people give to place (in Chapter 3). This chapter extends this enquiry to questions of culture in general and specifically to the cultural aspects of identity.

My argument, briefly, is that globalization forces us to question many of our commonsense ideas about cultural identity and obliges us to conceptualize culture in new ways. We can start the process of dismantling some older notions of cultural identity, and putting some alternative notions in play, by revisiting the idea which has played such an organizing role in the previous chapters: the concept of place. What is involved in thinking further about the changing relationships between culture, identity and place?

In Chapter 3, Gillian Rose argued that territory and settlement are seen by some writers as fundamental to human existence. Having or wanting a place where you feel you belong, they say, is often experienced as a natural human attribute, a basic human instinct. However, she went on to argue that a sense of place is almost certainly *not* 'natural' (not part of our 'given' human nature, not biologically or genetically programmed) but cultural. That is to say, it is part of, and is produced by, the systems of meaning through which we make sense of the world and thus is open to being reworked and transformed.

meaning systems What do we mean when we say cultures are *systems of meaning*? How do they work? One way of understanding how such systems of meaning work, is to think of culture in terms of a model of language. Things – objects, events, people – don't have a fixed meaning, a single truth, which exists for all to see and which we simply reflect in the language we use about them. Rather, it is through language that we *give meaning* to the world. Snow does not know that it is 'snow'. It is we who agree, within the conventions of our language code, to call that soft, cold, frozen white water from the sky 'snow'; and by doing so we give it a meaning by distinguishing it from two other closely related phenomena, 'rain' and 'hail'. The Inuit people, who have rather a lot of the stuff, are said to have many more words in their language for distinguishing between different kinds of 'snow'.

So cultures consist of different systems which produce meaning, which classify the world *meaningfully*. Thus, there is a very close relationship between the sorts of meanings and resonances embodied in the English language and English culture. Systems of meanings or cultures work like languages. They provide us with interpretive frameworks through which we make sense of the world. Using the same language code or system of meanings to make sense of the world places us English-speakers within what is sometimes called the same 'interpretive community'. Individuals can't change language – the meanings of words – by an act of will; nevertheless, language is constantly changing, historically. This suggests that language is a shared, a collective social construction, though each of us can use it individually to say what we mean.

In the same way, systems of meaning or cultures cannot be fixed since there is no way of insisting that events, practices, rituals or relationships mean only one thing or of preventing them, over time, or in different contexts, from taking on new meanings. In culture, as in language, each usage changes or inflects the meaning in new ways; and over time (in different periods or different contexts, in relation to new topics or situations) new meanings or inflections will establish themselves in common usage. Think of the very different meanings carried by 'having a cup of tea' in Tunbridge Wells, Hunslett or Edinburgh. Or among the British expatriates in the Himalayas or Torremolinos. Or in Buckingham Palace, Wimbledon or 'Coronation Street'. Some novel meanings will emerge by combining older meanings, while others will simply fall away or become archaic, useless for communicative exchange, through lack of use or relevance to a changing situation. We may try to use these systems of meaning like we use language, as accurately as we can, in order to say what we mean, to express ourselves perfectly. But we know that every statement will slip a little when it is appropriated or interpreted or translated into their own frame of reference by the persons with whom we are communicating. Meanings shift and are always open to interpretation – and other people never understand perfectly everything we say or catch every nuance of meaning we try to express. On the other hand, just as to communicate to a Swahili speaker requires us to use a common Swahili language code, so to express a cultural meaning requires us to position ourselves within a shared cultural meaning system, and then to use it to say or mean something – even if the idea may not have been expressed quite like that before, and often goes beyond the established tradition or conventions of the culture. A reference to 'the cross' will carry a very different meaning in a Christian, as opposed to a Muslim, country. The Union Jack evokes very different sentiments in Dublin and London.

We have been using language as a model of how cultural systems work. But language, we must remind ourselves, is also itself one of the fundamental cultural systems. People who share a language can communicate with or 'make sense' about the world to one another. A shared language is something which helps to give a person a cultural identity – being a Gaelic or Basque or Standard English or Urdu or patois speaker is to *be* a certain kind of person. It places one in a particular part of the language map: the community of English or Gaelic or Basque or Urdu or patois speakers to which one 'belongs'. Speaking a language means that you are familiar with, even if you do not share, the values of other language-users. That is why the right to use a particular language has been, historically, so significant a part of the struggles for national independence; and why being obliged to speak someone else's language – the language of the conqueror or colonizer, for example – is such a powerful symbol of cultural subjugation.

However, language is only one of the systems of meaning which produce culture. A culture is composed of many such systems. For example, religion is a powerful bearer of shared meanings about the sacred which carries a great deal of symbolic meaning and authority in many cultures. Again, religion has traditionally been a powerful source of 'belongingness', and, perhaps for that very reason, also a source of division and the marking of difference and 'otherness' (for example, between Hindus and Muslims during the partition of India; or between Protestants and Catholics in Northern Ireland today). Another powerful source of cultural meanings and cultural identities is custom and tradition: the distinctive, traditional ways things are done in 'this' part of the country or world as opposed to 'that'; the everyday rituals and practices which establish what the 'folkways' have been down the ages, or which mark special occasions (births, puberty, marriages, deaths, anniversaries), and connect present forms of life with the distinctive ways of life of one's ancestors. There are also shared traditions of representation: *genres* of painting or decoration; narratives about the past of the 'tribe'; sculptures or crafts which have a special significance in the working, familial or sacred life of the group; forms of dress and adornment; or stories (popular or highbrow) which maintain in collective memory the historical record of the group.

'Place' is another of those cultural systems, as Gillian Rose argued in Chapter 3. We use a discourse of 'place' to give meaning to life and to position ourselves in certain definite ways within society and its belief system. I would argue that cultures are often understood as 'placed' in at least two senses:

1 First, we associate 'place' with an actual location where many different relationships have overlapped over time, producing a dense, richly textured sense of life. Until recently, it had been assumed that the idea of place was a significant, though not a necessary, element in the way we understand cultures. In fact, it is the case that shared meaning systems can develop between people who live in very different places – across time and space. Indeed, this tendency may be increasing under the most recent forms of globalization where, for example, transnational migrants maintain important linkages between place of origin and place of settlement. Modern communications systems give rise to shared 'communities of interest' (e.g. chess players), or shared 'communities of taste' (e.g. opera lovers, jazz enthusiasts, *Neighbours* or *Eastenders* addicts), or shared consumer tastes (e.g. youth fashions) amongst people who are widely separated, who do not actually share a place, and who may indeed have never met one another. Shared systems of meaning can also survive lengthy spatial separation. Think of the successful struggle to keep traditions and folkways alive among many exiled or migrant communities (e.g. black slaves in the New World, orthodox diaspora Jews in Europe, Puerto Ricans or Sicilians in New York, Latvians and Rumanians in Milwaukee). Nevertheless, it is still common to *think* of cultures as if they depended on the stable interaction of the same people, doing the same sorts of things, over and over again, in the same geographical location – a set of meanings which we traditionally associate with 'place'.

2 In other words, while not literally necessary to culture, 'place' seems to act as a sort of symbolic guarantee of cultural belongingness. It establishes

symbolic boundaries around a culture, marking off those who belong from those who do not, as Gillian Rose argued in Chapter 3. It ensures the continuity of patterns of life and of tradition amongst a gathered and interrelated population who have been together, living in the same spatial environment, since 'time immemorial'. Again, let us emphasize that it is possible to think of many cultures which are maintained by groups that are *not* settled in one place, and by cultural influences between groups that have never shared the same place. However, physical settlement, continuity of occupation, the long-lasting effects on ways of life arising from the shaping influence of location and physical environment, coupled with the idea that these cultural influences have been exercised amongst a population which is settled and deeply interrelated through marriage and kinship relations, are meanings which we closely associate with the idea of culture and which provide powerful ways of conceptualizing what 'culture' is, how it works, and how it is transmitted and preserved.

When shared meaning systems are underpinned by long, historical settlement of a population and 'shaping' in one physical environment, with strong kinship links as a result of continuous intermarriage over generations, we get a *very* strong and *strongly bounded* idea of culture and cultural identity. This definition of culture, though not actually genetic or biological, is often experienced as if it were a part of our biological nature because it is tied up with the sharing of the culture between members with a long and unbroken common genealogy, kinship, residence and descent.

We call this very strong, well-bounded version of cultural identity *ethnicity*. Ethnicity arises wherever shared activities and meaning systems in one place are underpinned by shared kinship and blood-ties, evidence of which can sometimes be 'read' into certain shared physical features and characteristics of a population. Where people share not only a culture but an *ethnos*, their belongingness or binding into group and place, and their sense of cultural identity, are very strongly defined. Indeed, ethnicity is a form of cultural identity which, though historically constructed like all cultural identities, is so unified on so many levels over such a long period that it is experienced as if it were imprinted and transmitted by Nature, outside what we would call Culture or History. This is where culture appears, and is defended as, part of one's kith and kin, and cultural identity is based on ideas of 'Blood and Soil'.

ethnicity

Place, in short, is one of the key discourses in the systems of meaning we call culture, and it functions to help stabilize cultural patterns and fix cultural identities, as they say, 'beyond the play of history'.

5.1.2 Landscaping culture

There is little doubt that this association with place is one, very powerful, version of our commonsense understanding about culture. It seems to persist even when it has no strong historical basis in fact. We are therefore driven to the conclusion that we think of cultures as strongly placed, not because all cultures *are* but *because that is how we imagine them*. To put the point simply, when we think of or imagine cultural identity, we tend to 'see' it in a place, in a setting, as part of an imaginary landscape or 'scene'. We *give* it a background, we put it in a frame, in order to make sense of it. Can we think of 'Englishness' without seeing, somewhere, in our mind's eye, England's 'green and pleasant land', rose-trellised thatched cottages, village green and church steeple, a 'sceptred isle', 'this precious stone set in a silver sea' (Taylor, 1994)? Can we think of what it is like to be typically 'Greek' or 'Italian' without a Mediterranean scenario – white beaches, azure-blue sea – flashing before us? These are stereotyped representations of *national* identities; but I am suggesting that all cultural identities tend to have what Edward Said calls their 'landscapes of the mind', their 'imaginary geographies' (Said, 1990). There is a strong tendency to 'landscape' cultural identities, to give them an imagined place or 'home', whose characteristics echo or mirror the characteristics of the identity in question. Identity, Jacqueline Rose suggests, takes shape 'in the field of vision', and vision always has its spatial coordinates, a field or screen (real or imaginary) in which the subject is 'placed' (Rose, 1986). (Remember Gillian Rose's discussion of 'Englishness', the rural idyll and the Gainsborough portrait of Mr and Mrs Andrews in Chapter 3.) As Daniels put it:

National identities are coordinated, often largely defined, by 'legends and landscapes'; by stories of golden ages, enduring traditions, heroic deeds and dramatic destinies located in ancient or promised home-lands with hallowed sites and scenery … Landscapes … provide visible shape; they picture the nation …

(Daniels, 1993, p. 5)

The association of national cultures and identities with particular landscapes therefore helps to construct and to fix in place a powerful association between culture and 'home'. We think of our culture as a *home* – a place where we naturally belong, where we originally came from, which first stamped us with our identity, to which we are powerfully bonded, as we are to our families, by ties that are inherited, obligatory and unquestioning. To be among those who share the same cultural identity makes us feel, culturally, *at home*. Cultures give us a powerful sense of belongingness, of security and familiarity.

You *may* say that cultures are not actually, certainly not always, like that. But this is how we often imagine and talk about them. Benedict Anderson calls national cultures *imagined communities*. Since we can't possibly actually know or meet all the other people who belong to the same national community, what we share, Anderson argues, is really an *idea or a narrative of the nation* – sustained by the different cultural systems which *represent* the nation and give it meaning, which represent what sorts of people 'belong' (and don't belong) to it. Nations, he argues, differ from one another largely because of the different ways in which they are imagined (Anderson, 1983).

imagined communities

This is not to say that communities do not exist, or that we cannot analyse the institutions, social relations and material artifacts that hold communities together. But it does mean that a community also includes the idea we have of it, the images we use to conceptualize it, the meanings we associate with it, the sense of community with others we carry inside us. These are the ways communities are imagined – and thus how we give the idea of community meaning. As that renowned British patriot, Enoch Powell, once observed, 'the life of nations no less than that of men [*sic*] is lived largely in the imagination' (Powell, 1969, p. 245). Hence the importance of those mythical landscapes, invented traditions, stories and ceremonies which define the nation (or the National Heritage, as it is called these days), which span time and space and 'make up the threads that bind us invisibly to the past' (Schwarz, 1986, p. 155). These threads, as Homi Bhabha remarked, 'typically lose their origins in the myths of time and only fully realize their horizons in the mind's eye' (Bhabha, 1990, p. 1). They give us an imagined origin – a place where we began, and an imagined place (the same place) to go back home to.

Summary of section 5.1

o   Cultures are meaning systems or interpretive frameworks which, like languages, enable us to make sense of the world.

o   Meaning is not fixed *in* things – objects, events, relationships. We give them meaning by bringing to bear our shared cultural frameworks.

o   Cultures work like languages. They cannot be fixed, but shift and change historically.

o   Language itself is one of the principal means for constructing meaning. There are others – religion, custom, tradition, ritual …

o   Place is another key feature of all meaning systems. In fact, culture does not require place – cultures can be sustained by peoples who do not live in the same place and who have never met.

o   Nevertheless, we continue to *imagine* cultures as 'placed', to landscape cultures in our mind's eye. They are 'imagined communities'.

o   Place helps to stabilize cultures, to give them a 'home', to fix our identities in place, to make cultures seem well-bounded, self-sufficient, unified entities.

o   We call very strongly bounded, homogeneous cultural identities, firmly associated with a particular 'homeland' and rooted in strong kinship ties, an *ethnicity.*

5.2   Representing the nation

I have been arguing that we tend to think of or imagine cultures as 'placed'. However, even if we restrict ourselves to the example of the nation-states of Western Europe, with their powerful national cultures, their strongly marked national cultural identities (British, French, German, Italian, Spanish, etc.), and their hegemonic role in shaping the modern world, a little thought will suggest that nations are not really as solidly 'placed', well-bounded or internally unified as we imagine them to be.

Activity 2   Before you proceed, try answering the following questions:

1   When would you say, at a rough guess, that the people living in England became 'English'?

2   What is the difference between being 'English' and being 'British'? Construct a simple sentence using both words, bringing out the difference in meaning between them.

3 How does your definition of 'Englishness' accommodate the following peoples, all of whom at one time or another have occupied parts of England: Saxons; Romans; Norsemen; Normans; Bangladeshis; Jamaicans?

The questions in Activity 2 were designed to make you reflect on the meanings we attach to national cultural identities, the way these meanings change over time, and influence how we think of or 'imagine' Englishness. Who belongs, who doesn't? When did the many different peoples and nations coalesce into *one* identity? Does the use of different terms, like 'English' and 'British', signal differences within the 'United Kingdom' which still persist? The Scots, the Welsh and the Northern Irish are 'British' too, but 'Englishness' seems to have a quintessential relation to 'Britishness' which the others don't quite carry. Is national identity, then, also a power relationship? And if the Romans and Normans have 'become' English, how about more recent settler populations? How long does it take to *become* 'English'? Can you be 'black *and* English'? Great Britain has been a relatively unified political entity for centuries (at least since the Act of Union), but it would be hard to prove that the 'political roof' of the British nation-state covers what were originally a single people belonging to a single culture (*ethnos*). The UK is in fact the product of a series of invasions, settlements and conquests, by different ethnic groups, belonging to different cultures, speaking different languages and worshipping different gods – it evolved only gradually into one composite nation. The job of the national culture was therefore not to reflect in its political arrangements an already unified people and culture but to *produce* a culture in which, with luck, the different elements could gradually be unified into a sense of common belongingness – a process of cultural unification which has been, at best, *only partly successful.* One has only to think of the regional, cultural, class, gender, 'racial', economic and linguistic differences which still persist within its boundaries; of the tensions which now accompany this idea of a 'united' kingdom; and of the role of 'Englishness' as the hegemonic culture in relation to the other 'nations' within the kingdom – a fact which irritates many Scots, Welsh and Northern Irish people, and which fuels nationalist sentiment and aspirations in different parts of the UK. Even after centuries, the 'unity' of the United Kingdom remains somewhat precarious. Indeed, it has become in recent years, as a result of the move toward the EU and the growth of nationalist sentiment within the UK, a source of growing public anxiety and debate.

The role of the national culture – perhaps of cultures in general – is therefore not to express the unitary feelings of belongingness which are 'always there in the culture', but to represent what are, in fact, real differences *as a unity*; to produce, through its ongoing 'narrative of the nation' (in education, literature, painting, the media, popular culture, the historical heritage, the leisure industry, advertising, marketing, etc.) an identification, a sense of belongingness which, without constant nurturing, would not be sufficient to bind the nation together across the divisions of class, region, gender, 'race' and the unevenness of economic development.

If this is true of the culture of the United Kingdom, a relatively stable nation-state which has not suffered invasion or conquest for several centuries, how much more so is it true of other Western European national cultures, many of which (like Germany and Italy) were not unified until the nineteenth century, and which within their sovereign borders include very sharp ethnic and cultural differences between regions, especially between 'North' and

'South'. Europe is the product of successive conquests, and of the subjugation of peoples, often within the framework of empires which long preceded the formation of the nation-state (e.g. the Holy Roman Empire). This is certainly not to deny that there are shared cultural features between the peoples and cultures clustered under the roof of these 'core' Western European nation-states. But it is to insist on the profound *differences* which persist and which these shared national cultures have constantly had to negotiate. This points us towards a rather different conception of culture – one where 'a culture' is never a simple, unified entity, but always has to be thought of as composed of similarities and differences, continuities and new elements, marked by ruptures and always crosscut by *difference*. Its meanings are the result of a constant, ongoing *process* of cultural negotiation which is constantly shifting and changing its contours to accommodate continuing tensions. Cultures conceptualized in this way do *not* stretch backwards, unchanged, into 'time immemorial'. They offer no fixed, single point of origin which can stabilize cultural identities forever, thereby guaranteeing that all those who ever belong to them were, have become, or are destined to remain *the same* (i.e. identical).

This suggests that what we call nationalism – the ideology of belongingness as one people to what is sometimes referred to as the 'family' of the nation and national culture – arises not (as the national story tells us) because that is what it always was in the past. Rather, it is a key element in the ongoing *process* of unifying or binding people together, creating through these discourses an idea of the nation with which they can identify, and in that way binding up differences and cementing the nation in the present, for the sake of the future. Nationalism often invokes a return to past glories or virtues (think of Mrs Thatcher's remark at the time of the Falklands War, that 'Britain can be "Great" again'). But its aim is really to produce something – a unified culture – in the future. Nationalism is always rehearsing the 'narrative of the nation' as a return to lost or forgotten origins. But its project is actually to create something which does not yet fully exist – a unified culture.

The Western European nation-states which we think of now as the 'motors' of modernity and world development are, in fact, all culturally and ethnically mixed formations – 'hybridized', to use a term we shall examine at greater length below. The situation in Central and Eastern Europe, and in what was formerly the Soviet Union, is even more complicated. Here, nation-states were often the relatively recent product of the disintegration of former empires (the Austro-Hungarian and Ottoman empires, for example); or of the expansion and forcible absorption of one people by another (the Baltic States); or of the arbitrary solutions which the 'Great Powers' reached at conference tables (the former Czechoslovakia). The framework of a national culture has proved even less durable here than it has in the West. It has proved itself incapable of unifying peoples of different cultures, languages, ethnic origins or religious persuasions, many of whom have lived for decades in 'multicultural' communities – as recent events in the former Yugoslavia tragically demonstrate.

Europe, East and West, is so culturally mixed that the effort to oblige each 'homeland' to contain only one ethnic group, to constitute nations out of one culture, or, as Ernest Gellner remarked, to unify one people, one ethnos, under one 'political roof', only encounters the many minorities living in the same 'place', who are *not* of the same culture but persist in considering that place to be their 'home' too. As John Fine recently remarked, reviewing Noel Malcolm's *Bosnia: A Short History* (Malcolm, 1994): 'He [Malcolm] describes well the religious communities in the medieval and Ottoman periods and the tolerant relations between them. He also acknowledges that the "Serb" and "Croat" identities of those Bosnians who assumed them are of recent origin' (Fine, 1994, p. 10). A unified, well-bounded, internally coherent 'Serb' culture can only at this late stage of history be carved out of this hotchpotch by violence – the sort of 'ethnic cleansing' we have seen in Bosnia-Hercegovina is its direct result.

In short, though cultures are sometimes 'placed' and we tend to imagine them as strongly unified and homogeneous, integrated by tradition in a landscape and tied to a 'homeland', the effort – against the complex and tortured background of modern history – to actually *make* 'culture' and 'place' correspond with one another turns out to be a hopeless, expensive and sometimes violent and dangerous illusion.

5.2.1   Making culture a 'contested concept'

I started section 5.2 by taking the example of the nation and the national identities of European nation-states. I asked whether the conception of these 'cultures' as strong, fixed, bounded, permanent and homogeneous formations of cultural practices and meanings actually corresponds to what we know of the history of Europe; and thus whether it might be possible to retreat from our present complexities by returning to or attempting to reconstitute such unified cultures of the past (or rather, of the past as we imagine it to have been) out of the hotchpotch of the present. But it seems that this is increasingly difficult if not impossible to do because these cultures are hybridized beyond repair. However, as was suggested, there are powerful reasons why people persist in trying to retreat defensively from the fact of cultural hybridity and difference into closed definitions of 'culture'.

In the next section, we shall look at these two, apparently contradictory, tendencies – the attempt to secure the purity of a culture and the hybridity of most culture – in the context of globalization. However, we can already draw one important conclusion. Our considerations lead us to question the very way in which culture is usually conceptualized. As a result of our preliminary investigation, we are obliged to treat culture as a 'contested concept'.

To put this another way: what Doreen Massey has argued about *place*, both in her Chapter 2 in this book and elsewhere, and what is echoed in Gillian Rose's chapter, can now be said about *culture*, and the imagined relation between *culture* and *place*. Our sense of place is really part of our cultural systems of meaning. We usually think about or imagine cultures as 'placed' – landscaped, even if only in the mind. This helps to give shape and to give a foundation to our identities. However, the ways in which culture, place and identity are imagined and conceptualized are increasingly untenable in the light of the historical and contemporary evidence. Doreen Massey therefore proposed (in Chapter 2, section 2.2.1) that we abandon 'the notion of place simply as settled, enclosed and internally coherent ... and its replacement or supplementation by a concept of place as a meeting place, the location of the intersections of particular bundles of activity spaces, of connections and interrelations, of influences and movements'. Place, she argued elsewhere (Massey, 1994, p. 12), 'is the vast complexity of the interlocking and articulating nets of social relations which is ... formed by the juxtaposition and co-presence there of particular sets of social interrelations and by the effects which that juxtaposition and co-presence produce'. The same can now be said of *culture*.

Summary of section 5.2

In this section I have argued that:

o   Nation-states are not in fact unified, culturally. Most of them are the result of conquests, invasions, settlements and empires and contain within their borders peoples of different cultural and ethnic origin.

o   National cultures, however, represent nations as if they have always been unified and homogeneous. They tell the story of the nation as a unified entity – and thereby help to produce the unified culture which they proclaim already exists.

o   Western European nation-states in particular evolved out of a succession of empires, conquests and settlements. However, new peoples with aspirations to join 'Europe' and thus enter modernity aspire to carve out of this hybrid past a form of nation-state in which there would be one 'political roof' to each people or *ethnos*.

o   Nations generally continue to narrate themselves in terms of cultural homogeneity because that helps to focus the identification and loyalty of their citizens and create among their populations a sense of identity and belongingness.

In much the same spirit of revision as we found in Doreen Massey's Chapter 2 with respect to 'place', I would propose to re-conceptualize 'culture' along the following lines:

o   Culture is not settled, enclosed or internally coherent. In the modern world, culture, like place, is a meeting point where different influences, traditions and forces intersect.

o   A culture is formed by the juxtaposition and co-presence of different cultural forces and discourses and their effects. It does not consist of fixed elements but of the process of changing cultural practices and meanings.

o   The identities which culture helps to construct are not guaranteed in their 'sameness' by some simple origin or fixed in their eternal belongingness to shared values and meanings.

However, the fact that cultures are not as unified, fixed or homogeneous as we imagine does not mean that we will stop thinking of them in this way. Why is this so?

o   The nationalist passion for 'belongingness' and the security which such closed conceptions of culture provide are not easily shifted by rational reflection.

o Closed conceptions of culture persist because they have a real purpose and function. Their purpose is to represent 'differences' *as* a 'unity', and this has real effects in the world (i.e. they keep nations together) even if the unity is more imagined than real.

o Above all, closed conceptions of culture help to bind up and unify nations which might otherwise fall apart because of their many internal tensions and historic differences.

o In short, cultures *produce* (rather than simply reflect) national identity.

The question then is: what would a revised conception of culture and cultural identity, which took these qualifications into account, look like? How do such cultures actually emerge and change? In what ways are these changes connected to, or even profoundly influenced by, the process I have been calling globalization?

5.3   Globalization and cultural diversity

In some accounts, a more open and diverse conception of culture is closely linked with the process of globalization. It is often argued that the *pace* of globalization in the last few decades is particularly intense. Time and space have been globally condensed in ways which were unimaginable a few decades ago, and many of the forms which organize the latest phase of globalization are novel. However, as discussed in **Allen and Hamnett (eds, 1995)**, globalization is not a new or recent process. It is more or less coterminous with the whole of the historical period we now call 'modernity'.

The Europe of the nation-states which we were discussing in the previous section was a relative late-comer, historically. Before that there was no such thing as 'Europe' or a European culture or a European identity, at least as a single or unified object. Greece, the so-called cradle of European civilization, was a series of city-states, with closer connections to North Africa than to the countries bordering the North Sea (Bernal, 1991). In pre-classical times, the territory we call Europe was occupied by dispersed tribes and peoples and formed no single unity of any kind. Europe took shape through a succession of larger groupings, mostly of an imperial kind, which were very extensive in spatial terms: the conquests of Alexander the Great spread all over the eastern and much of the western Mediterranean and a large part of the Near East; the Roman Empire stretched from Scotland to the African Sahara and from Gibraltar to the Euphrates, and its trade routes reached India, Indo-China and the Far East. By definition, these empires ruled over many different cultures and peoples.

Charlemagne (747–814), the first post-classical western emperor, who is now honoured in the European Union as 'the father of Europe', inherited his original title from a Germanic people called the Franks. Having conquered most of western Christendom he was crowned a Christian Emperor of the West in Rome by Pope Leo III on Christmas Day 800. Through conquest he created the Holy Roman Empire, which included the Frankish parts of Germany and France, Colonial Spain, Burgundy, Northern Italy and Lombardy, and among his subjects were 'Bavarians, Carinthians, Bohemians,

Wends, Avars, Saxons and Danes'. Roberts (1985, p. 89) adds that the shape of his *imperium* was as large as the Roman Empire, and 'somewhat like the original EEC in shape and extent'. He himself was a Serb.

The 'Europe' of Charlemagne was not a product of 'globalization' as we conceive it today. But nor was it a continent of powerful, unified, internally coherent and homogeneous nation-state cultures which we somehow imagine *always* underpinned European national identities.

Europe itself *as a cultural idea* (i.e. 'Europe' as an imagined community) gradually took shape as a consequence of four main processes. First, there was the succession of imperial formations or empires, linking under a single rule many different peoples, landscapes and cultures, to which I have just referred. Secondly, there was the evolution of a broadly common basis of belief and spiritual governance – the spread of Christianity. This was a cultural system as well as a theological one, and a cultural system which included many variations. It only succeeded by absorbing and coming to terms with (and being transformed by) many pagan influences, and was soon to be divided by an unbridgeable schism into its Roman and Orthodox halves, the two very different Christian churches which underpinned the very different cultural development of Western and Eastern Europe. Thirdly, there was the hegemony of Latin – the common language of the clergy and the scholars, of learning and ideas, and the basis of a learned culture which criss-crossed national boundaries. Charlemagne, however, we are told, learned Latin with considerable difficulty. Though it served as a powerful force for cultural unification, Latin was surrounded by many other languages and dialects, to which it finally succumbed. Indeed, Benedict Anderson attributes the rise of nationalism in Europe partly to the triumph of the vernacular languages over Latin (Anderson, 1983). Fourthly, there was the way Christian Europe as an identity emerged through the process of measuring itself against a succession of internal and external 'enemies' – those 'Others' which served as the anvil against which a conception of a distinctive European identity closely associated with a Christian culture was hammered into shape.

Christian Europe's principal adversary was, of course, Islam which had expanded into North Africa, parts of Eastern and Mediterranean Europe and the Spanish peninsula, and which thus became part of the internal history of Europe from the eighth to the fifteenth centuries. It was out of the struggle to expel Islam from Europe that a militant Christian 'Spain' emerged, at the end of the fifteenth century. The Portuguese voyages of exploration, down the coast of Africa, round the Cape and into the Indian Ocean, took place as the Moors were being slowly pushed back. Symbolically, the voyage of Columbus to the New World, which inaugurated the great process of European expansion, occurred in the same year as the expulsion of Islam from Spanish shores and the forced conversion of Spanish Jews in 1492. This was the inaugurating moment of what Mary Louise Pratt (1992) calls the 'Euro-imperial adventure' – and as convenient a date as any with which to mark the beginning of modernity, the birth of merchant capitalism as a global force, and the decisive event in the early stages of globalization.

You will recall, here, the discussion of globalization and time–space compression in Chapter 2 of this book (the process of globalization is also dealt with in **Allen, 1995**). What do we mean by using the word 'globalization' in the context of *this* discussion of culture?

globalization　　*Globalization* is the process by which the relatively separate areas of the globe come to intersect in a single imaginary 'space'; when their respective histories are convened in a time-zone or time-frame dominated by the time of the West; when the sharp boundaries reinforced by space and distance are bridged by connections (travel, trade, conquest, colonization, markets, capital and the flows of labour, goods and profits) which gradually eroded the clear-cut distinction between 'inside' and 'outside'. The history of the New World, of India, Asia and Africa gradually became a subordinated part of the 'internal' history of the West. It was the beginning of that very uneven time-frame we call 'global' time.

By globalization we refer, in a long historical perspective, to a number of different processes:

o　The exploration by the West of hitherto 'unknown' parts of the globe (unknown to Europe, that is).

o　The expansion of world trade and the early stages of the construction of a 'world market'.

o　The movements of capital investment and the transfer of profits and resources between metropolis and periphery.

o　The large-scale production of raw materials, food, minerals and commodities for industries and markets elsewhere.

o　The process of conquest and colonization which imposed systems of rule and other cultural norms and practices on subordinated cultures.

o　The migrations which were set in motion and the settlements and colonized outposts which were established.

o　The establishment, even where direct colonization was avoided, of powerful imperial spheres of cultural influence: Britain, France, the Netherlands and Portugal in the Middle East and the Far East; the British, Spanish, Portuguese and Dutch in Latin America; the colonizations by the Dutch, British and French of the Pacific; the scramble by the great powers for colonies in Africa.

In its wake, the idea of culture as a set of autonomous, self-enclosed meaning systems and practices begins to seem anachronistic. The cultures of many parts of the world had for the first time to negotiate with the colonizing cultures imposed on them through conquest, settlement, trade or direct administration and government. The colonizers exported European culture to the places they conquered. Other cultural influences – religion, language, education, legal systems, conceptions of property – followed the flag. The indigenous ways of life were often broken up and destroyed; new habits and values were implanted in their place. Movements of populations, planned and unplanned, followed the shifts in power. Cultures began to be defined, not in terms of their own indigenous values, but by their relationship (usually of power) with *other* cultures. Culture began to form one of the critical circuits through which power of different kinds – economic, political, religious, gendered, racial – circulated. The world, we might say, became, through this process, 'global' for the first time.

In the New World, for example, this meant: the long and complex attempt to found a 'new' Spanish civilization (New Spain) in the New World, on the ruins of the indigenous empires which were destroyed and whose peoples were scattered, driven into the hinterlands and forests, subjugated or destroyed by the conquest; the lengthy process of European rivalry between the great powers that carved up Latin America and the Caribbean between the British, Spanish, French, Dutch and the Portuguese; the long struggle between the British and the French for hegemony in North America; the cultural transformation which followed the largest forced migration of modern history – the Atlantic slave trade; the flow of Indian indentured labour which followed the abolition of slavery; and, threaded across all these stories, the confinement and decimation of Native American peoples. The cultural upheavals, the forced and casual mixing of peoples, languages and cultures which accompanied this colonizing history, are difficult to imagine.

Far from some gentle movement of ideas, culture and power were intimately connected in the process of globalization from its early inception. The establishment of spheres of cultural influence, the hierarchical relations of dominance and subordination between colonizing and colonized cultures, between different racial groups, between the 'civilized' and 'the barbarians', the shifting relations of cultural power which followed in the wake of the successive phases of globalization, are difficult to exaggerate. Much the same process was set in train elsewhere around the globe – for example, in the Indian subcontinent, in South East Asia and in Africa – in the wake of the 'Euro-imperial adventure'.

In what follows, we shall be pursuing some examples of the impact of globalization on culture drawn from this colonizing, Euro-imperial process. We shall be looking at the process from both ends: both how the relationship between colonizing and colonized cultures evolved in the 'contact zones' of the periphery, and then what happens when the colonized cultures come 'home' to the metropolitan country. However, it is worth remarking here that this is only *one type* of cultural interrelationship selected from a much wider range. Cultures can be 'connected' with one another, and influences can flow in both directions, even when there is no direct face-to-face contact, no colonization or forced occupation, no direct administration of one society by another, such as we find in the colonizing and migration moments. Slavery in the Caribbean influenced the lives, feelings and attitudes of young ladies like the heroine of Jane Austen's *Mansfield Park* because her father, like so many other English gentlemen, had 'West India interests', though she never went to the Caribbean, hardly thought about it, knew nothing of its peoples and customs, and probably never laid eyes on a black person (Said, 1993).

5.3.1 Re-conceptualizing culture

How then can we best understand the cultural processes which this early phase of globalization engendered? Mary Louise Pratt has contributed two important concepts which help us to grasp analytically what was happening to culture in this period. The first is the idea of the *contact zone*, which refers to: contact zone

the space of colonial encounters – in which peoples geographically and historically separated came into contact with each other and established ongoing relations usually involving conditions of coercion, radical inequality and intractable conflict ... 'Contact zone' ... is often synonymous with 'colonial frontier'. But while the latter term is grounded within a European expansionist perspective ... 'Contact zone' is an attempt to invoke the spatial and temporal co-presence of subjects previously separated by geographic and historical disjunctures, and whose trajectories now intersect.

(Pratt, 1992, pp. 6–7)

Though I shall illustrate the term in this chapter mainly with reference to 'colonial encounters', its use is broader, covering all those cultural spaces characterized by 'the co-presence of subjects previously separated by geographic and historical disjunctures … whose trajectories now intersect'.

The second concept is a term borrowed from the work of ethnographers, when trying to describe 'how subordinated and marginal groups select and invent from materials transmitted to them by a dominant and metropolitan culture' (Pratt, 1992, p. 7):

While subjugated peoples cannot readily control what emanates from the dominant culture, they do determine to varying extents what they absorb into their own and what they use it for. Transculturation is a phenomenon of the contact zone.

(ibid., p. 6)

Life in the 'contact zone': slave-owners watching slaves celebrating a 'festival'

Transculturation describes one of the key cultural processes which operate between hitherto sharply differentiated cultures and peoples who are forced to interact – often in profoundly asymmetrical ways in terms of their relative power.

transculturation

A third, related, term which I shall use in subsequent sections is the concept of *diaspora*. Diaspora refers to the long-term settlement of peoples in 'foreign' places which follows their scattering or dispersal from their 'original' homeland (I put this in quotation marks as a reminder that they may well, long before the dispersal, have 'originated' from somewhere else).

diaspora

Not all diasporas are the consequences of the 'Euro-imperial adventure'. The most famous in modern history is probably the scattering of the Jewish people as a consequence of their long history of exile, oppression and the ravages of anti-semitism. But diasporas are generally the effect of migrations, whether forced or 'free', and the Euro-imperial adventure and its associated processes of globalization set many migrating movements in train, as Russell King charted in Chapter 1 of this book. Trade and conquest have contributed significantly to the creation of diaspora settlements and the presence of large minority cultures in unexpected places. Following Mary Louise Pratt's definition, diasporas are classic 'contact zones' in which, characteristically, the transculturation process takes place.

What is distinctive about the cultures of contact zones or diasporas is that they never remain 'pure' to their origin. The new circumstances in which these cultures must survive begin to have consequences for how the 'original' culture is changed and adapted over time. The original cultures of the displaced groups come into contact and are obliged to negotiate with the cultures of the other groups with whom – on whatever terms – they establish a 'co-presence'. The culture which evolves in diasporas is therefore usually the result of some never-completed, complex process of combining elements from different cultural repertoires to form 'new' cultures which are related to but which are not exactly like any of the originals. As with the crossbreeding of a plant from different strains, this process of transculturation is sometimes referred to as *hybridization*.

hybridization

5.3.2 'Cricket, lovely cricket'

Let us take an example which will help to illustrate these concepts of contact zones, transculturation, diaspora and hybridity.

In the British Caribbean, British colonial rule displaced earlier colonization by the Spanish (Jamaica) and the French (St Lucia). The population was composed of the offspring of these European colonizers, plus the descendants of African slaves, Indian and Chinese indentured workers, and people of mixed descent (from different combinations of these cultures). It is a classic colonized 'contact zone'.

Wherever the British colonized (not only here but also in Asia, Africa and the Pacific), there was *cricket*. Cricket is, culturally, a quintessentially 'English' game, with its leisurely unfolding, its gentlemanly formality (cricketing whites), its intricately rule-governed and orderly conduct, its tradition of amateurism, its deference to authority (umpires), respect and hierarchy (landowners and grooms played in the same team, but would not fraternize

Cartoon from The Guardian, *2 April 1994*

socially), its attachment to public school codes of sportsmanship ('play up, play up and play the game'), its stiff-lipped refusal to give in when all the odds are against you, and of course its imaginative 'landscaping'. It is also strongly marked by gender – being essentially a game for 'gentlemen' which 'the ladies' watch. (This image has not been significantly affected by the growth of women's cricket.) Cricket is classically associated with a particular idea of the English landscape – village greens, trimmed hedgerows, the slanting light and lengthening shadows of lazy, English summer afternoons.

The British introduced it to their colonial outposts (including the Southern States of the US, where it was played until the nineteenth century) and considered the initiation of 'the locals' into the arcane mysteries of this most masculine of sports as an informal way of 'assimilating them' – that is, teaching them to adopt the ways and acknowledge the superior cultural models of the colonizers. Cricket flourished in the 'contact zones' of the Empire (and is still played only where British imperial culture flourished – the Caribbean, Australia, New Zealand, India, Pakistan, South Africa, Sri Lanka). It was one of the spheres of life in which it was hoped that the clear civilizing superiority of the colonizing culture would be demonstrated to 'the natives' – not simply the superiority of technical athletic skill but of the whole 'way of life' which the game symbolized. Though not consciously planned as such, it nevertheless functioned as a source of cultural authority and cultural power.

Frank Keating records that when Lord Hawke led the first English touring side to the Caribbean in 1897 they were obliged in Trinidad to play a multiracial side, which beat them. Pelham Warner, son of a plantation-owning family in the Caribbean, noted in *Wisden*, the cricket annual:

'The fielding of the Trinidad team was splendid. Black men are especially fine fielders: they throw well and seldom miss a catch.' I suppose he felt it superfluous to explain that the black men, at least in the Trinidad team on those two days, had all been mighty well practised in the fielding arts by regular and compulsory fielding at games played by the garrison officers of the British army stationed in Trinidad, or by the sons of the well-to-do plantation owners – games in which, it goes without saying, native sons of the soil were not allowed an innings or a turn of the ball themselves.

Warner's brother led the first 'unofficial' return tour to England three years later. During the match against Gloucestershire, Woods, the black bowler,

who had so impressed Warner Jr three years ago in Trinidad marked up his run in boots for the first time. Two whacking great cornish-pasty-like things at the end of his legs. It must have been, to him, like running in concrete. Gloucester's crouching demon of a hitter, Gilbert Jessop, sprang at poor Woods mercilessly, flailing an astonishing 157 in just over an hour.

Early on in the assault, Woods approached his white-man captain at mid-off – 'Please, Mr Warner, sir, I have only ever bowled if I can feel the pitch with my toes. May I take my boots off – even for just one over, sir, then I am sure I can get this man out?' 'Certainly not, my good man. This is England. You are playing cricket against a first-class county, sir!'

(Keating, 1991, p. 30)

The cricket pitches which mark these very different parts of the globe are symbolic of, and could not have existed outside, the transculturation process of the colonial encounter. C.L.R. James, the West Indian historian and political philosopher, in what is perhaps the best history of cricket ever written, *Beyond a Boundary* (1963), shows how the game evolved differently in its colonial transplantation from its evolution in its native English soil. Gradually, the 'locals' learned to play it – assimilating some of the lessons of the colonizing culture, and slowly beginning to participate in it – though still, as Keating makes clear, within the strict power-hierarchy of colonizer/colonized. However, little by little, they not only 'took on' the rules and spirit of the colonizer's game, but began to infuse and inform it with attitudes, skills, values, temperaments formed *outside* of English 'cricketing culture' – that is, with cultural skills they brought *to* cricket from the very different cultures of Africa, of the plantation and the colonial ethos. James argues that the very effort to 'submit' to the game and its rules helped the colonized players to develop precisely those disciplined skills of self-mastery and control, craft and judgement, which tempered them into world-class players. Finally, of course, James records with pride how cricket became a site of resistance. He records with pleasure the symbolic victories scored in post-war cricket by the West Indies, as the 'underdogs' turned the tables and defeated their colonial masters at Lords, the 'home' of English cricket (for the first time and in the same moment – the 1950s – as the tide of Caribbean decolonization and the independence movement was gathering pace). The famous post-war victory of the West Indian side, including the three 'W's' (Worrell, Walcott and Weekes) and the bowlers, Ramadhin and Valentine, had a 'carnival' atmosphere – and was immortalized in that classic carnival form, the Calypso, in one by Lord Beginner entitled 'Cricket, lovely cricket'.

The result of this transculturation process, then, was to produce in the Caribbean *neither* exact replicas or mimics of the 'master culture' *nor* an entirely different game which could replace the old game of 'the masters', but some hybrid combination of the two: something new, something significantly but not absolutely different – that self-confident, relaxed, almost casual physical style and apparently effortless 'mastery' characteristic (and characteristically un-English) of the outstanding post-war West Indian players, like the remarkable Gary Sobers, the first black professional West Indian captain, about whom C.L.R. James wrote with such pride, or, later, the much admired and 'characteristically West Indian players', such as Viv Richards or Brian Lara.

This friendly-but-serious rivalry has marked every post-war cricketing encounter between England and the West Indies. It is interesting to note that there is only one cricket issue on which these two opposing sides have *always* agreed – that is, that cricket is a 'man's game' and that the idea of 'women's cricket' is absurd! This is a good example of how one area of social contestation (gender) intersects and crosscuts another (the legacy of colonization) producing contradictory alignments.

The process described above exactly exemplifies what Mary Louise Pratt defined as transculturation: '… how subordinated and marginal groups select and invent from materials transmitted to them by a dominant or metropolitan culture. While the subjugated peoples cannot readily control what emanates from the dominant culture, they do determine to varying extents what they absorb into their own and what they use it for' (Pratt, 1992, p. 23). We may call transculturation *a cultural strategy*. Kobena Mercer, the cultural critic, suggests that this strategy has long been associated with diasporas and other 'colonial' and post-colonial contact zones. Mercer describes this cultural strategy in the following terms:

There is, however, a response … inscribed in aesthetic practices of everyday life among black peoples of the African diaspora in the 'new world' of the capitalist West, which explores and exploits the creative contradictions of the clash of cultures. Across a whole range of cultural forms there is a 'syncretic' dynamic which critically appropriates elements from the master-codes of the dominant culture and 'creolises' them, disarticulating given signs and re-articulating their symbolic meaning otherwise. The subversive force of this hybridising tendency is most apparent at the level of language itself where creole, patois and Black English decentre, destabilise and carnivalise the linguistic domination of 'English' – the nation-language of master-discourse – through strategic inflections, reaccentuations and other performative moves in semantic, syntactic and lexical codes. Creolising practices of counter-appropriation exemplify the critical process of dialogism as they are self-consciously aware that, in Bakhtin's terms,

> *The word in language is half someone else's. It becomes 'one's own' only when … the speaker appropriates the word adapting it to his own semantic and expressive intention. Prior to this moment of appropriation the word does not exist in a neutral or impersonal language … but rather it exists in other people's mouths, serving other people's intentions: it is from there that one must take the word and make it one's own.*

(Mercer, 1988, p. 57)

Activity 3 This is a difficult paragraph – some of the terminology may be unfamiliar to you. But it is worth spending some time on it. This activity is designed to help you get the most out of it and to help you understand the concepts. Kobena Mercer is describing the process of *transculturation* characteristic of this type of 'contact zone'. Note the following points which will help to clarify the meaning of the passage:

1   Kobena Mercer speaks of a 'syncretic' dynamic. Syncretism is another name for the process by which elements from different cultures are fused together to produce a new meaning. An example of syncretism is the combination of Christian Catholic and African 'folk' religions which is found throughout Latin America and the Caribbean.

2   The particular version of syncretism described here is where the colonized culture 'borrows' a dominant cultural form (e.g. cricket), appropriates it to its own uses, disconnects it from its dominant cultural associations (with the English way of life), and re-articulates it to a new set of meanings (i.e. as an expression of West Indian culture).

3   Mercer defines this as a process of cultural struggle and resistance ('a subversive force'). Language is a good example, where slaves 'borrow' the English of the slave-master and 're-code' it to express their own meanings; or, as the American critic, Henry Louis Gates puts it, slaves use the master-language but make fun of or parody it, to 'signify or sign-ify differently' (Gates, 1988). This giving of a 'native' inflexion to something borrowed from the master-code and transformed produces the Creole languages (mixtures of African and European languages) – the basis of contemporary Caribbean dialects as well as the many forms of parody to be found in slave and black vernacular cultures.

4   The word thus becomes something different when it is so expropriated. Mercer borrows this idea from the Russian linguistic philosopher, Mikhail Bakhtin (1984), who argued that *all* meaning is constructed in the process of *dialogue* between two speakers. Meaning, he said, was 'dialogic' – hence Mercer's phrase 'the critical process of dialogism'.

5   Meaning, you will notice, is not simply 'there' to be expressed. It is created and transformed – in the give-and-take, the contestation, over meaning.

6   This process, Mercer adds, 'carnivalizes' the linguistic master-code of English. To understand what this means, you must know something about the rest of Bakhtin's argument. Bakhtin argued that popular carnivals were festivals where, symbolically, the tables were turned: master and servant or slave changed places for a day and the underdog had a licence to say and do what he/she pleased. There were such occasions even during slavery, especially at Easter and Christmas, and the phenomenon survives in the Caribbean and Latin America in the famous Trinidad, Haitian, Martiniquan and Brazilian carnivals culminating at Easter, when everyone, including the poor, dresses up, parades in masks and costumes, and Calypso singers have the licence to sing about and 'scandalize' public figures. Caribbean carnival, however, is itself a hybrid cultural form, since it combines this tradition of slave celebration with the European tradition of Mardi Gras and the Catholic Easter festival leading up to the fasting of Ash Wednesday and Lent. The Notting Hill Carnival which is held in London in August – the anniversary date of the abolition of slavery – celebrates the black presence *in Britain*. It, too, turns the tables or 'carnivalizes' everyday relationships, appropriates the streets of North Kensington for its own purposes of making music, dancing in the streets and feasting – and gives the whole transculturation process a further twist.

Now, read the passage from Kobena Mercer carefully, again.

Modern Caribbean carnival in Trinidad: a hybrid cultural form

5.4   The 'return to roots'

In a rather simplistic way, for the sake of the argument, I have set up two,
contrasting, models of culture and their relation to 'place', both real and
imagined. First, there is the model of culture which we discussed in section
5.1: culture as a relatively fixed set of meanings, which stabilizes cultural
identities and guarantees that the way of life of those who share it remains
homogeneous. This model is firmly attached to the idea of a 'place' or home
of origin to which we are connected by *tradition*. Secondly, there is the model   tradition
of which cricket was the main example: where meanings are not fixed, but
are constantly being negotiated, contested and transformed; where cultural
forms and practices are not 'pure' but combine with elements of other
cultures; and where identities are not stable and invariable because of where
they came from, but are constantly producing themselves in new forms, in
new places, out of combinations of elements and meanings.

The argument is that globalization, seen in a longer historical perspective
than is usually adopted, has been gradually, if very unevenly across the
globe, pushing us away from the first towards the second, more syncretic,
model. This trend, it is said, has accelerated in recent decades, as the pace
of globalization has qualitatively increased. As time and space compression
has deepened, so the cultures of more and more places become
'translated'. As modern migration has stimulated the flows of peoples,
cultures have characteristically become composed not of single but of
diverse cultural traditions and patterns. There is a further argument that,
whereas globalization in the earlier phases of colonial expansion tended to
impose metropolitan cultural values and norms on the cultures of the
periphery, the process – greatly supplemented by the global character of
modern communications and consumer industries – is now complicated by
the reverse flow: from the impoverished cultures of the 'margins' to the
metropolitan centres. In that sense, the transculturation typical of the old
colonial cities like Kingston, Mombasa, Bombay, Saigon or Hong Kong is
now supplemented and expanded by the multicultural processes which are
reshaping and hybridizing London, Paris, Los Angeles and New York (what
have been called the new 'global cities' – see **Hamnett, 1995**), and 'third
world' cities of the first world like Toronto, Marseilles or Miami.

5.4.1   Cultural fundamentalism: 'back to basics'?

However, this is too evolutionary a way of describing what are in fact bitterly
contested *alternative strategies* in the process of cultural change. It makes it
sound as if societies will smoothly and unproblematically 'evolve' from one of
our models to the other. What such an account leaves out is the question of
cultural power and *cultural resistance*; the issues of cultural politics which
underpin such transitions; the different, often contradictory, currents which
are at play in the modern version of 'the culture wars'; the way in which the
question of cultural identity has become *the* key issue – what is ultimately at
stake, being struggled over, in these cultural shifts.

For many groups, cultural survival has always been seen to depend on
keeping the culture 'closed' – intact, homogeneous, unified within, and with
strongly marked boundaries separating it from 'others'. Creolization,
transculturation, hybridization – whichever of these terms we wish to use to

describe culture under the impact of globalization – is seen as threatening the integrity of the culture and weakening the sense of cultural identity that holds the group together. From this perspective, migration weakens the bonds of belongingness, and creolization is seen as a form of dilution – even, perhaps, of cultural pollution. The only viable strategy is to hold fast to cultural traditions, to reaffirm those elements of the culture which maintain the links to one's past, to keep the connection 'pure', to resist all forms of syncretism as, in effect, a 'loss of identity', to counter this potential loss by a 'return' to one's cultural roots, to hold fast to one's founding identity; and thus in these ways to *close up the community around its foundational cultural beliefs and values.*

We may call this strategy the *revival of ethnicity* – the attempt to restore strong, closed definitions of what constitutes a culture. The surprising thing is that this response to globalization is to be found in the late twentieth century in *both* 'colonizing' and 'colonized' peoples, at *both* the 'centre' and the 'periphery', in what are usually thought of as *both* traditional and modern societies. Indeed, it has made a strong, and somewhat unexpected, return in recent years to the world stage. It cuts across the usual political alignments of 'left' and 'right' and it sometimes divides members of the same cultural community from one another.

Thus, we can see evidence of this tendency in the revival of nationalism which is to be found in resurgent forms in Central and Eastern Europe and in the former Soviet Union. But you can also see it in the 'Little England' reaction in Britain to the fear of losing sovereignty to 'Europe'; and it is very much in evidence in the growth of racism and the rebirth of racist and neo-fascist movements across the New Europe, focused on the threat of migrants coming into Europe from Africa, the Middle East, the Caribbean, Asia, or the fear of Europe being overrun by 'economic migrants' in search of a better life, or by the refugee problem. Forms of cultural racism have appeared in recent years, not only in the so-called 'backward' parts of Europe in the East, but right in the centre of *modern* Europe – in Britain, Germany, France, Spain and Italy. You can certainly find an equally exclusive definition of 'culture' – this time with religion rather than 'race' or ethnicity providing the focus – in the versions of Islamic fundamentalism which have gained ground in recent years in Iran, Egypt and Algeria, as well as in the success of the Hindu fundamentalist movement in India. But 'fundamentalism' is not confined to the so-called 'third world'. We can see a respectable version (though not perhaps so closely related to religion) beginning to attract support amongst those groups in both the US and the UK who want to roll back 'multiculturalism' in education and go back to much more traditional and exclusivist definitions of 'Englishness'; or among those who have reacted strongly against including the literatures of other peoples, or indeed works by women writers from other cultures, in the literary canon being taught in colleges and schools – despite the fact that British and American urban schools and campuses have been transformed in recent years by migrations from Latin America, the Caribbean and Asia.

These are all, of course, very different examples with different specific histories, and I am not trying to represent them as all the same. What I am suggesting, however, is that they do all share *one* important feature in common: their response to globalization is to turn back to more 'closed' definitions of culture, in the face of what they see as the threats to cultural identity which globalization in its late-twentieth-century forms represents. They mark the revival of an attachment to more 'local', or fixed, or placed aspects of culture. This may not be such a surprising turn in a world where globalization is increasingly transgressing boundaries, mixing up traditions, confusing 'us' and 'them', 'inside' and 'outside', and constructing identities based on less 'grounded' forms of identification.

The fact that this return to more 'closed' conceptions of culture can also *divide* communities is well illustrated by the so-called Salman Rushdie affair. Rushdie's novel, *The Satanic Verses*, was written by someone who is a secularized Muslim intellectual living for many years in England as an exile from India. He was held by some Muslims in Britain to have blasphemed against Islam by writing ironically about the Prophet Mohammed, which resulted in the issuing of a *fatwa* (legal ruling), sentencing him to death, by the fundamentalist regime in Iran. Other Muslims, however, have argued that Islamic culture has always included a tradition of satire and, in any event, a writer should not be condemned to death for holding unorthodox opinions.

Before pursuing this argument further, it would be useful to ask you to examine two, contrasting, contemporary examples of these tendencies.

Activity 4 Now read Reading A, 'English teaching in the National Curriculum', which you will find at the end of the chapter. This extract from *The Observer* (8 May 1994) reports on the new proposals for the English curriculum in the National Curriculum in schools which the then Education Secretary, following a major review, proposed in 1994. It also notes some critical observations on these proposals by teachers. Bear in mind the following questions as you read:

1   What are your thoughts about this controversy?

2   Which side, in your view, has the stronger argument?

3   How much should the established canon of literary works, which symbolizes
    · certain key 'English' values, be sacrificed to the multicultural context in which
    most schools in Britain (and other western societies) now operate?

There is, of course, no *right* answer to these questions. The point of the exercise is to help you to see how these general issues of 'cultural politics' arise and are being contested in everyday contemporary situations.

Activity 5 Now read Reading B, 'Accept African identity, Grant tells blacks'. This is a report, from *The Independent on Sunday* (12 December 1993), of a speech delivered by Bernie Grant, Labour MP for Tottenham. It repeats his argument that, since racism is once more on the increase in Britain, the government should offer financial help to blacks in Britain (including black children born here) to emigrate back to the Caribbean. British blacks, he argues in the article, should build a new political agenda with an 'African identity at its heart'. The article reports more widely on the growth of 'Afrocentric' movements in the UK as a reaction against racism, as well as the responses of some people who have actually emigrated. You should bear in mind the following questions as you read:

1   Do you find Bernie Grant's argument a persuasive one?

2   What does it mean to invite Afro-Caribbeans who are born or long resident in
    the UK to accept their African identity?

3   In what sense are third generation black British youth 'Africans of England'?

4   How much do you think the growth of this position is a response to the growth
of racism in Europe?

Again, there is no right answer. The point is to see how and where this return to
'closed' conceptions of culture is arising, and what assumptions underpin the
position.

The idea that black British youth should think of themselves as 'Africans'
may seem like a very defensive cultural response; but such strategies for
recovering one's past cultural identity are not always or *necessarily* reactionary.
The idea that some colonized peoples belong to an ancient culture which
predates the onset of globalization and the Euro-imperial adventure has
often been a source of pride, solidarity, and resistance to domination. All the
decolonizing movements of the post-war period, which led to the
independence of the colonies of the former British, French, Dutch and
Spanish empires, were motivated either by such an idea of an 'imagined
community' of the past or by the desire to set up an independent nation and
autonomous culture in the future where the old cultural traditions could
once again flourish.

Indeed, 'separatism' has been a critical way in which an alternative, more
self-sufficient cultural identity has been *imagined*. From Marcus Garvey's 'Back
to Africa' movement in the US and Jamaica in the 1920s onwards, significant
political movements in the African-American and other African diasporas of
the New World have dreamt 'freedom' in terms of going back to Africa; or in
terms of setting up a 'free state' for displaced slaves in Africa; or in terms of
building an independent black 'nation' within the American nation, like the
Black Nationalists; or in terms of rediscovering their spiritual centre in North
Africa as Black Muslims have long believed. Even where political and social
protest at black poverty and marginalization in American life does not take a
specifically nationalist form, the cultural imagery of blacks belonging to a
wholly separate, black, African-derived culture (Afrocentrism) has been a very
powerful cultural force.

In Jamaica, for example, formal political independence in 1963 did relatively
little at first to make profound cultural changes in the 'colonial' way of life
in the island. A cultural revolution in attitudes and self-images only occurred
when, in the wake of the American civil rights movement, 'black pride' and
'black consciousness' began to take root. Black Jamaicans began (at last) to
recognize and acknowledge their African heritage and descent. Slavery and
colonization could be openly spoken about for the first time by ordinary
people; and the population, the overwhelming majority of whom were black,
of African or mixed-race descent, for the first time experienced themselves as
a 'black' people. This African consciousness often took the form of adopting
African names, dress, customs and hairstyles.

One of the principal means of restoring these lost connections with 'Africa'
was represented by the growth of the Rastafarian religion, which until the
1960s had been a small and much despised religious sect. Rastafarianism
derived its message from a certain reading or interpretation of the Bible.
Rastafarians saw their salvation in Haile Selassie, the first black king of
Ethiopia (the first independent black African kingdom), whom they revered
as 'Ja', the Living God. Large numbers of Jamaicans who never became
converts to Rastafarian beliefs were nevertheless profoundly influenced by its
cultural values, language and cultural symbolism. Rastafarian symbols, beliefs

and forms of language were transmitted especially through the new Jamaican 'world music', reggae, which carried the message that the Jamaicans were a 'chosen people', who still languished in 'slavery', and who looked forward to being led out of bondage in Babylon into the Promised Land. 'Africa', as much a metaphor for 'freedom' as a literal place, was the metaphor through which those hopes and aspirations were expressed, the means by which a colonized Jamaican people imagined themselves, in the 1960s, into cultural independence from white, colonial Jamaica.

Return to one's cultural roots, imagining oneself as a member of a closed and sustaining culture which colonization and globalization threatened, but were unable to destroy, has therefore been a powerful strategy of resistance and renewal, as well as a defensive strategy of retreating into the fortress of one's own cultural ghetto. Such metaphors of 'home' and 'homeland' have done profound damage when linked to aggressive nationalist movements (e.g. Bosnia). But they have also functioned as a potential source of cultural resistance and liberation.

5.4.2   Back to the future

However, the 'Jamaican' story does not present quite as simple or as stark a choice between a strategy of defence and a strategy of renewal as we may at first imagine. In the description above, I called the 'rediscovery' of African roots, and the 'return' to an African identity, a *metaphor*. 'African' was counterposed symbolically to 'British', as a way of retelling and giving new meaning to a history which had hitherto been told primarily from the viewpoint of the colonizer. 'Africa' represented all that forced migration and slavery had destroyed. It stood for all the cultural traditions, customs and practices which had survived plantation slavery, and which had kept alive the collective memory of an African heritage amongst the degrading conditions of slave life. It therefore came to embody the dream of one day being released from captivity and bondage. 'Africa' was a discourse through which black people of the diaspora resisted being wholly swallowed up and assimilated as a second-class people (remember the cricket example) in a white colonial culture. Through the metaphor or discourse about Africa, people learned, for the first time, to tell the story of their past – and present – sufferings, to keep alive and honour neglected traditions, and to recapture an aspect of their identities which the culture of colonization had silenced. This 'African' element then entered into the self-image of Jamaican blacks as a powerful source of identity in the twentieth century. Since 'identity' is often a way of telling the story of ourselves, the discourse of Africa made possible new ways of telling a new version of their own history. It produced what is sometimes called a counter-narrative. It has therefore entered, as one major cultural element, into what we would call today the cultural identity of the modern 'black Jamaican'.

But notice some other features. 'Africa' – part of the lost story of people of African descent in the New World – was recovered. But it was recovered *in the Caribbean*. Very few people – even fully committed Rastafarians – ever literally tried to go 'back to Africa'. And the few experiments were not overwhelmingly successful. Too much had happened to them in the New World. They *were* 'people of African descent'. But they were *diaspora* Africans – Afro-Caribbeans. And the hyphen tells the story, for, *culturally*, they were *also* 'people of European descent', in the sense that, for good or ill, the

African element in their culture had been obliged to co-exist, or establish a 'co-presence' with, and over the years had often fused or syncretized with, European elements (transculturation). The whole Rastafarian cult was not, as many thought, an ancient African religion. Though, of course, it revived and retained many elements of African religion, it had first arisen in Jamaica in the 1920s. The key episode in the formation of Rastafarianism was the 'prophesying' which followed the return of Marcus Garvey from the US with his 'Back to Africa' message. And the principal text was a free re-reading of sections of the Bible, which the missionaries had first taught slaves to read. In short, culturally, Jamaica and Jamaicans were irrevocably the product of a process of transculturation, in which 'Africa' played a critical part, but few 'pure' African elements persisted unchanged from the past. Africa in any 'pure' sense could not account for the shape which the culture had assumed.

Language, music and religion provide excellent examples of the same processes at work. The many variants of English, and the English- and African-influenced patois which the Jamaican people speak, or the varieties of musics to be found in Jamaica, in addition to religion, which is an enormously pervasive cultural influence in the lives of the people, clearly demonstrate the transcultural, syncretic or hybrid character of Jamaican culture. Religion in Jamaica today consists of a kaleidoscope of rituals and beliefs covering the entire spectrum, from elements which are retained almost unchanged from African religious ceremonies and practices, to a sort of mimicry of established forms of Church of England or Anglican worship. Much the same syncretism is to be found in all the black religious practices of the Caribbean and Latin America.

To take one specific example, *baptism* plays a key role in many different religious practices in Jamaica today. Baptisms take place in Baptist chapels exactly as they do in such chapels in England; but they also take place in rivers and by the seaside as parts of the ceremonies of Pentecostal, Ethiopian and other 'break-away' sect churches. If you wished to analyse the cultural meaning of this practice in Caribbean religious life today, you would have to piece together elements selected from the following religious cultural strands and the way they have been recombined into new practices and meanings:

1   The growth of a native 'Black Baptism', in both slave and post-slave society (the first Jamaican Baptists were freed slaves from the American plantations).

2   The influence of Baptist missionaries from the UK, who played a key role in Christianizing the slaves and helping them to become literate, and who were active in the movement to abolish slavery and in shaping early post-emancipation Jamaica.

3   The significance of the gods of water and of the river in the cosmology of the African religions which slaves brought with them to the New World and which were retained in many folk forms.

4   The context of plantation slavery, where 'baptism' became a metaphor for the conversion of black slaves into 'free, independent' Christian men and women,

5   The privileged role which all Jamaican Christian religions give to Moses (sometimes more important almost than Jesus), because he 'led the people out of slavery, across the Red Sea, into the Promised Land'.

(For an account of black and white versions of 'Baptism' and their history in the post-emancipation period, see Hall, 1993.)

The 'Africa' which was recalled in Jamaican culture, during the 1960s and 1970s, represented a major turning-point in the 'black consciousness' cultural revolution in post-war Jamaica: but it was a disapora-ized Africa, not a pure one. Moreover, the consciousness it awakened was principally about, not only the suffering which blacks had undergone in the *past*, but the suffering they were undergoing *now*, in the 1960s, in so-called independent Jamaica. The 'local' references – the places which were symbolically invoked in, say, the reggae songs of Bob Marley, which were infused with Rastafarian consciousness and the language of 'Ja' – were *neither* the actual places in West Africa from which slaves were taken, nor the actual country we now know as Ethiopia, but 'Trench Town', which was a tiny, notorious ghetto area in modern West Kingston. The 'good news' about Rastafari was transmitted, not via tom-toms and the bush-telegraph, but via the recording studio, the vinyl disc, the amplified sound system and the transistor radio: the whole technology of the late-twentieth-century global music industry. 'Babylon' was retranslated from the Bible, first to describe the conditions which Jamaicans were suffering in Kingston, and then the conditions which those who had migrated again experienced in the *new* 'contact zones' of the UK – Brixton, Handsworth, Toxteth, St Paul's, or Moss Side. 'Babylon' was also and remains the common name given by British blacks to the British police, when blacks are harassed on the streets and in inner-city areas. To put it simply, the 'return to African roots' did not turn out to be a strategy for actually recreating a closed or self-sufficient African culture in Jamaica. What it produced was a new kind of 'Jamaican', a new kind of black, British 'Afro-Caribbean' culture. It was the means of constructing a new set of 'hybrid' cultural identities, not only in the Caribbean diaspora to which slaves had been transported in the seventeenth and eighteenth centuries, but in the *new diasporas* of Europe that were created through mass migration in the 1980s and 1990s, by late-twentieth-century forms of globalization.

Summary of section 5.4

o Two contrasting 'models' of how the processes of cultural change operate under conditions of globalization can be seen as contested alternative strategies.

o There is a tendency for some nation-states, now challenged by migration, to retreat from 'difference' into 'closed', more racialized and exclusive conceptions of cultural origin and identity (e.g. the 'New Europe').

o The same tendency can be found among some 'colonized' groups, where a closed, homogeneous and unitary idea of cultural origin and identity sometimes functions as a site of resistance (e.g. forms of 'African' consciousness in Jamaica and the US in the 1960s).

o Even this strategy may not be as one-dimensional or unambiguous as it seems. Looked at more closely, it shows clear signs of being the product of 'transculturation'.

The final section will explore the transculturation model as it is increasingly to be found in the contact-zones or diasporas of the late-modern world.

5.5   From 'roots' to routes

We have been considering the 'closed' version of culture and of cultural identities as one, very powerful, way of telling the story of what is happening to culture under the impact of globalization. There are other ways of imagining 'communities of belongingness', which are not centred in the nation-state or the national identity 'story', which cut across and disrupt many of these boundaries and borderlines, and provide alternative resources for constructing identity and fashioning culture.

There are many ways of trying to describe this second, transcultural response to the globalization of culture: the idea of the 'global city' is one way; the notion of 'multiculturalism' and its effects within the hitherto settled cultural frontiers of the western nation-state is another. Yet another way of framing the new relationship between culture, place and identity is to be found in the concept which many cultural critics are beginning to use and which I invoked earlier: the idea of the *diaspora*.

The term *diaspora* can, of course, be used in a 'closed' way, to describe the attempt of peoples who have, for whatever reason, been dispersed from their 'countries of origin', but who maintain links with the past through preserving their traditions intact, and seeking eventually to return to the homeland – the true 'home' of their culture – from which they have been separated. But there is another way of thinking about diasporas. 'Diaspora' also refers to the scattering and dispersal of peoples who will *never* literally be able to return to the places from which they came; who have to make some kind of difficult 'settlement' with the new, often oppressive, cultures with which they were forced into contact; and who have succeeded in remaking themselves and fashioning new kinds of cultural identity by, consciously or unconsciously, drawing on more than one cultural *repertoire*. These are people who, as Salman Rushdie wrote in his essay in *Imaginary Homelands*, 'having been borne across the world ... are translated men (and women)' (Rushdie, 1991, p. 17). They are people who belong to more than one world, speak more than one language (literally and metaphorically), inhabit more than one identity, have more than one home; who have learned to negotiate and translate *between* cultures, and who, because they are irrevocably the product of several interlocking histories and cultures, have learned to live with, and indeed to speak from, *difference*. They speak from the 'in-between' of different cultures, always unsettling the assumptions of one culture from the perspective of another, and thus finding ways of being both *the same as* and at the same time *different from* the others amongst whom they live (Bhabha, 1994). Of course, such people bear the marks of the particular cultures, languages, histories and traditions which 'formed' them; but they do not occupy these as if they were pure, untouched by other influences, or provide a source of fixed identities to which they could ever fully 'return' (Hall, 1990, 1992).

They represent new kinds of identities – new ways of 'being someone' – in the late-modern world. Although they are characteristic of the cultural strategies adopted by marginalized people in the latest phase of globalization, more and more people in general – not only ex-colonized or marginalized people – are beginning to think of themselves, of their identities and their relationship to culture and to place, in these more 'open' ways. It is certainly one of the greatest sources of cultural creativity today – and what much late-modern culture (novels, poems, paintings, images, films, video, etc.) seems to be *about*.

Used in this way, the concept of *diaspora* provides an alternative framework for thinking about 'imagined communities'. It cuts across the traditional boundaries of the nation-state, provides linkages across the borders of national communities, and highlights connections which intersect – and thus disrupt and unsettle – our hitherto settled conceptions of culture, place and identity.

Because it is spatially located, but imagined as belonging not to one but to several different places, the *diaspora* idea actively contests the way in which *place* has been traditionally inserted into the story of *culture* and *identity*. It therefore forges a new relationship between the three key terms – culture, identity and place. From the *diaspora* perspective, identity has many imagined 'homes' (and therefore no one, single, original homeland); it has many different ways of 'being at home' – since it conceives of individuals as capable of drawing on different maps of meaning, and of locating themselves in different imaginary geographies at one and the same time – but is not tied to one, particular place.

It also breaks with a certain conception of *tradition* – the thing which is supposed to link us to our origins in culture, place and time. In the 'closed' version of culture, tradition is thought of as a one-way transmission belt; an umbilical cord, which connects us to our culture of origin. Ultimately, if we keep the links pure, they will lead us back to where we belong. The 'closed' version assumes that the further you get from your origins, the more you are separated from your 'true culture'. It is a *linear* conception of culture. In 'diaspora' conceptions of culture, the connections are not linear but circular. We should think of culture as moving, not in a line but through different circuits. Paul Gilroy argues in his book *The Black Atlantic* (Gilroy, 1994) that, if you wanted to tell the story of black music, you wouldn't construct a story of how 'authentic' black music *started* in Africa and became diluted with each subsequent transformation – the blues, reggae, Afro-Cuban, jazz, soul and rap – all representing 'loss of tradition' the further the music gets dispersed from its *roots*. Instead, you would have to pay attention to the way black music has travelled across and around the diaspora by many, overlapping *routes*.

You would show how *different* were the many 'African' musics and rhythms which slaves originally brought with them from Africa; how much these were transformed, first by life on the slave plantations, then by the impact of different 'European' musics, and especially by the influence of religious music; how in America, in the blues – urban or rural, secular or religious – these already complex musical traditions were further modified, as blacks migrated to the cities; how, in jazz, in soul, in reggae, in rap music, one can see the musical forms being constantly reworked and transformed to produce, not a *diluted* version of 'African' music, but a variety of *new* black diaspora musics (plural). One can also see how all of these were once again transformed in the conditions of post-war migration. Examples would include the influence of American rhythm and blues on Jamaican folk music that produced ska and reggae itself (which was a new, not a traditional music); or the influence of Jamaican music, played on the great 'sound systems' of the 1970s, which was taken to the Bronx by Jamaican DJs, and fused with the tradition of DJ 'talk over' rooted in the powerful black-vernacular traditions of American soul music, and later with rhythms from the Hispanic migrant community to provide the matrix out of which contemporary rap music first emerged. Or one could follow, along a different track, the adaptation of Jamaican 'roots' reggae to British conditions, and the way it was influenced by black soul and other popular music in the UK to create the distinctive sounds of contemporary British black music.

These stories connect the different 'black' diasporas around the Atlantic, linking Africa to the settlements of blacks in the New World created by slavery and to the resettlements in the Old World formed by post-war migration. But they don't connect them in one direction only. There are also contraflows: for example, black British rap artists moving between the UK and the US markets; or black music of the diaspora imported back into Africa, and played there, influencing the growth of *new* kinds of African popular music which are both urban and modern (not 'tribal' and traditional). Each variant of black music takes some 'African' elements – rhythmic and vocal elements especially – from traditions which are continuous and common between all the diasporas. Much of these were already transformed by the culture of plantation slavery. But these musics are, nevertheless, not the *same* because each has also fused these elements with different new elements. Each has taken the shape and imprint of the national contexts in which it developed (compare Afro-Cuban with New Orleans jazz; or American rhythm and blues with British 'Northern Soul'). Thus, what connects one part of the black diaspora to another is *not a tradition which remains the same*, but a complex combination of *continuities and breaks, similarities and differences*: what Gilroy calls a conception of tradition as the 'changing same' (Gilroy, 1994).

5.5.1 New cultures for old?

In this chapter, we started with a definition of culture as a relatively closed, unified and homogeneous structure; and of the centered identities which belongingness to a culture in this sense helped to fix and stabilize. We explored this way of looking at culture in the context of some key concepts which form the central concerns of this book: the relationship between culture, identity and place. However, our discussion of national cultures and notions of identity rooted in the European nation-state helped us to bring this closed conception of culture into question, and to make 'culture' a contested concept. I tried to show that globalization, which is a long historical process, has always challenged and undermined this 'closed' way of looking at culture; and I introduced some new concepts which helped us to begin to re-conceptualize culture – in particular, the concepts of 'contact zone', 'transculturation' and 'diaspora'. Caribbean cricket was the key example of these 'globalized' cultural processes at work.

What, then, has been the impact of globalization on the formation of culture in more recent times? I set up two, rather simple and contrasting models:

'closed' versus transculturation strategies. In section 5.4, we took a closer look at some examples of the first model – the attempt to return to closed conceptions of culture. I suggested that this is *not* restricted to marginalized peoples, or cultures, but is also a strategy to be found in the 'fundamentalism' of so-called advanced western cultures of modernity today when confronted by cultural or ethnic difference. But we also saw how this strategy of 'discovering one's roots' could be deployed by marginalized people as a site of resistance. One such example – the attempt to create a new Jamaican culture by invoking its place of origin, 'Africa' – turned out, in fact, to be another example of *transculturation*.

The account then focused in section 5.5 – through the idea of *diaspora* – upon the second model. I used it to develop a more 'open' conception of culture and of the relationship between culture, identity and place. The main examples here were drawn from the religion and music of the 'black Atlantic' diaspora – a way of rethinking, as a new spatial configuration, the relationships between the different cultures of blacks dispersed from Africa to the New and Old Worlds by slavery, colonization and migration. This diaspora approach does *not* depend on thinking about culture, identity and place in a closed unified or homogeneous way, as a return to roots, but instead redefines culture as a series of overlapping *routes*:

The telling and retelling of these stories plays a special role, organizing the consciousness of the 'racial' groups socially and striking the important balance between inside and outside activity – the different practices, cognitive, habitual and performative, that are required to invent, maintain and renew identity. These have constituted the black Atlantic as a non-traditional tradition, an irreducibly modern, ex-centric, unstable and asymmetrical cultural ensemble that cannot be apprehended through the manichean logic of binary coding. Even when the network used to communicate its volatile contents has been an adjunct to the sale of black popular music, there is a direct relationship between the community of listeners constructed in the course of using that musical culture and the constitution of a tradition that is redefined here as the living memory of 'the changing same'.

(Gilroy, 1994, p. 198)

You may like, in conclusion, to consider for yourself how far the shift which was signalled from 'roots' to 'routes' as a way of thinking about culture applies not only to the ex-colonized, ex-enslaved, marginalized peoples of the diasporas but is slowly and unevenly becoming a more general model of how culture and identity are being reconstructed everywhere in late modernity.

References

ALLEN, J. (1995) 'Global worlds' in Allen, J. and Massey, D. (eds) *Geographical Worlds*, Oxford, Oxford University Press/The Open University (Volume 1 in this series).

ALLEN, J. and HAMNETT, C. (eds) (1995) *A Shrinking World? Global Unevenness and Inequality*, Oxford, Oxford University Press/The Open University (Volume 2 in this series).

ANDERSON, B. (1983) *Imagined Communities: Reflections on the Origins and Spread of Nationalisms*, London, Verso.

BAKHTIN, M. (1984) *The Dialogic Principle*, Manchester, Manchester and Minnesota University Press.

BERNAL, M. (1991) *Black Athena: the Afroasiatic Roots of Classical Civilization*, Vol. 1, London, Free Association Press.

BHABHA, H. (ed.) (1990) *Nations and Narration*, London, Routledge.

BHABHA, H. (1994) *The Location of Culture*, London, Verso.

DANIELS, S. (1993) *Fields of Vision: Landscape Imagery and National Identity in England and the United States*, Cambridge, Polity Press.

FINE, J. (1994) 'What is a Bosnian?', *London Review of Books*, 28 April.

GATES, H. L. (1988) *Signifying Monkey*, New York, Oxford University Press.

GILROY, P. (1994) *The Black Atlantic*, London, Verso.

HALL, C. (1993) *White, Male and Middle-Class*, Cambridge, Polity Press.

HALL, S. (1990) 'Cultural identity and diaspora' in Rutherford, J. (ed.) *Identity: Community, Culture, Difference*, London, Lawrence and Wishart.

HALL, S. (1992) 'Cultural identity in question' in Hall, S., Held, D. and McGrew, T. (eds) *Modernity and its Futures*, Cambridge, Polity Press in association with The Open University.

HAMNETT, C. (1995) 'Controlling space: global cities' in Allen, J. and Hamnett, C. (eds).

HARVEY, D. (1989) *The Condition of Post-Modernity*, Oxford, Oxford University Press.

JAMES, C.L.R. (1963) *Beyond a Boundary*, London, Stanley Paul.

KEATING, F. (1991) 'The Empire strikes back', *Marxism Today*, June, pp. 30–1.

MALCOLM, N. (1994) *Bosnia: A Short History*, London, Macmillan.

MASSEY, D. (1991) 'A global sense of place', *Marxism Today*, June, pp. 24–9.

MASSEY, D. (1994) *Space, Place and Gender*, Cambridge, Polity Press.

MERCER, K. (1988) 'Diaspora and the dialogic imagination' in Cham, M. and Andrake-Watkins, C. (eds) *Blackframes*, Boston, MA, MIT Press.

POWELL, E. (1969) *Freedom and Reality*, Farnham, Elliot Right Way Books.

PRATT, M. L. (1992) *Imperial Eyes: Travel Writing and Transculturation*, London and New York, Routledge.

ROBERTS, J. M. (1985) *The Triumph of the West*, London, BBC Publications.

ROBINS, K. (1991) 'Tradition and translation: national culture in its global context' in Corner, J. and Harvey, S. (eds) *Enterprise and Heritage*, London, Routledge.

ROSE, J. (1986) *Sexuality in the Field of Vision*, London, Verso.

RUSHDIE, S. (1988) *The Satanic Verses*, London, Viking.

RUSHDIE, S. (1991) *Imaginary Homelands*, London, Granta Books.

SAID, E. (1990) 'Narrative and Geography', *New Left Review*, No. 180, March–April, pp. 81–100.

SAID, E. (1993) *Culture and Imperialism*, London, Verso.

SCHWARZ, B. (1986) 'Conservatism, nationalism and imperialism' in Donald, J. and Hall, S. (eds) *Politics and Ideology*, Milton Keynes, Open University Press.

TAYLOR, J. (1994) *A Dream of England*, Manchester, Manchester University Press.

Reading A: 'English teaching in the National Curriculum'

[...] Tomorrow John Patten, the Education Secretary, will unveil details of [...] the new English curriculum. A compulsory 'canon' of great literature, including Shakespeare for all 14-year-olds, will offend many teachers who have argued passionately for the right to choose the texts they teach. There will also be marked emphasis on spelling, grammar and handwriting.

Three English teachers were co-opted on to the working party set up by Mr Patten to plan the details of the new curriculum, but it is understood their recommendations have been ignored.

They asked that the curriculum take account of how English is affected in practice by regional variation, class and ethnic origin – an important issue in schools with many children whose first language is not English.

The teachers also recommended that time be found for media studies, but this will have no place in the compulsory curriculum. [...]

Last night John Hickman, a London comprehensive school teacher who sat on the committee, warned that teachers would be 'extremely angry at prescribed set texts. We all want children to read widely, but fear this approach turns them off.'

English teachers spearheaded last year's boycott of classroom tests, and it is likely that their dislike of the new curriculum will guarantee widespread support for the National Union of Teachers' continuing boycott.

Source: *The Observer*, 8 May 1994

Reading B: 'Accept African identity, Grant tells blacks'

Bernie Grant was again proclaiming the need for British blacks to accept an African identity yesterday. But this time only invited guests were allowed to hear the speech.

The publicity which followed his calls in the autumn for the Government to help black Britons who wanted 'voluntary repatriation', and for some of the Crown Jewels to be sold to compensate African countries for the activities of slavers, had been so bad that the 'white media' were banned from his meeting in Birmingham.

'When Asians and Jews want to talk they are left alone,' he said. 'When blacks get together everyone wants to know what's happening.'

Despite the secrecy, it was clear what was happening. Representatives from about 150 organizations were coming together to discuss a constitution for a British 'African Reparations Movement'.

The Labour MP for Tottenham's theme is that Britain is a dangerous place for blacks. British blacks should not just follow 'the methods of the 1960s and confront racists', but build a new agenda which had African identity at its heart.

The delegates in Birmingham yesterday included representatives from the Nation of Islam, the All African People's Liberation Front and the Ethiopian World Federation. After raising the issue of 'voluntary repatriation' at a fringe meeting at the Labour party conference in October, Mr Grant was subsequently jeered and booed by young and largely black demonstrators at an Anti-Racist Alliance (ARA) protest in Trafalgar Square and came close to making a public apology. Fellow activists made no secret of their horror. 'He's playing with fire,' said Palma Black, spokeswoman for the ARA. 'It's just giving in to the racists.' Embarrassingly, the only major politician to back him was Winston Churchill, a right-wing Conservative MP.

But over the intervening two months, he has grown in confidence. At meetings in Leeds, Manchester and London his message has been the same: blacks at best face a 'lousy' future and should look on themselves as Africans not Britons.

At a rally in Brixton, south London, two weeks ago, he emphasized African identity. 'I'm not talking to you about Indians, Bangladeshis or Pakistanis … I'm talking about black people of African origin. We fought the blackshirts, the brownshirts, the teddy boys, the skinheads of the National Front … and for a while things got better. Now they are back again calling themselves the BNP and black people are saying "take your country, we don't want it".'

He questioned the whole idea that it was possible to be a black Briton. 'We need to find those people who call themselves black Britons. We must give them our message and tell them we need them because they are black African people.'

Mr Grant has been attacked by his own party, and other anti-racist campaigners called his new black nationalist line 'dangerous', 'ill advised' and 'pandering to the worst manifestations of racism'.

But the uncomfortable truth for many on the left is that Mr Grant has found a constituency. Brixton has the fastest-growing black mosque in London. Every Friday, Uthman Ibrahim-Morrison preaches on the need for black separatism to a congregation of converts from Christianity. He rejected his Methodist family and a comfortable middle-class job which took him travelling around Europe in his early thirties.

'I saw what Europe had to offer – its short-sightedness, its consumerism, its shallowness. I wasn't satisfied. They were meant to be the most advanced and most enlightened people … but they were morally and spiritually empty. I said, "Hang on, OK, enough is enough!" I started to study and came to Islam.'

The 'Africans of England', he proclaims, in an unusual interpretation of the Koran, must liberate themselves from the 'cancerous curse of the usurous economy' (paper money). They must also fight a 'false religion' (Christianity), the 'freemason programmers' (who control education, the media and just about everything else), 'Jewish structuralism' (which produces Marxism and most other modern ideas) and 'the wage slavery of the banking centre of the world' (the UK). 'Please don't mistake this for conspiratorialism,' he added, politely.

The mosque, which teaches that most of the African slaves transported to the Americas were Muslims whose descendants have subsequently lost their religion, has seen its membership grow from 20 people in the 1970s to about 300 today.

There are other black Britons who would not dream of converting to Islam or going to one of Mr Grant's meetings, but who have picked up on the idea of emigrating.

The Home Office-supported International Social Service of the United Kingdom receives about 100 enquiries a month from people wanting help to leave Britain. Many are pensioners who have worked here all their lives and plan to go back to friends and relatives. But others are young, British-born and well-qualified.

A spokeswoman for the service said that after racially charged events, such as the election of a BNP councillor or Mr Grant's original speech in October, calls from the young 'flooded in'.

Linda Deane was born in Lincoln and educated at Warwick University. Her father served in the RAF in Britain and the Far East and was relatively well off. Conventional wisdom would assume she would have a successful career in Britain. But last month, aged 30, she and her architect fiancé emigrated to Barbados, her parents' native country.

'Europe isn't so hot any more,' she said. 'I just couldn't take the direct or indirect racism of England. When I waited to cross the street to my home, drivers would shout "black bitch" at me. When I went into shops I would always be followed by the store detectives.

'I thought there are so many troubles in life about jobs and money that at least if I went to Barbados I could get rid of racism and be treated as a first-class citizen. It would be one less hurdle to jump.'

Ms Deane emphasized that she could move to the Caribbean only because she had visited Barbados often and knew what she was letting herself in for.

Ken Douglas, president of the Association of Jamaica's Returning Residents, said that many who emigrated to the Caribbean came back to Britain. 'They did not realize that it's not just all sun,' he said. 'They did not know about the violence and the unemployment in Jamaica.'

But for all the caveats, the underlying fact that a minority of black Britons despair of this country cannot be hidden.

Ms Deane's sister, Sue Beckles, lives in Rugby. She has a master's degree and is married to a doctor.

'At the moment I don't want to bring my children up here,' she said. 'You watch the news about the growth of fascism and it's frightening. Everywhere ordinary people are becoming extreme and mainstream parties are losing out.

'I'll give Britain five years. If it doesn't get better, we'll go.'

Source: *The Independent on Sunday*, 12 December 1993

Places and cultures in an uneven world

Chapter 6

by Doreen Massey and Pat Jess

6.1   Introduction

The familiar claim that 'places are all becoming the same' seems to reflect a notion that everyone everywhere is wearing jeans and trainers and drinking cola out of a metal can. This perception of globalization follows from ideas, prevalent in the 1960s, that the world would become westernized or, perhaps more specifically, that the culture of the USA would spread all over the globe and that, soon, everywhere would have a McDonald's. But although 'fast food' did arrive on the streets of London, Moscow and many other places, it arrived in places which had their own existing character and culture. Sometimes, as in Britain for example, where local characteristics may be reinforced through local planning regulations, some international images have had to be modified to 'fit in' to a local streetscape; sometimes the images and the building-styles that go with the newcomers form a clear reminder of 'the shrinking world' and the multinational corporations. But it is not only American-style burger shops which occupy the High Street; so do Chinese, Italian and Indian restaurants, all of which, in time, become as familiar as the 'local' butcher or greengrocer. In other words, what we have witnessed is a process of global mixing (although an unequal and uneven one) rather than a straightforward, unidirectional notion of westernization.

These representations of the moving and mixing of peoples and cultures run quite contrary to the old idea of places having fixed boundaries and exclusive communities. They suggest instead a permeability of boundaries and an openness to influences from elsewhere, an openness which is multidirectional. The unfamiliar becomes familiar and the familiar is found in unfamiliar places; we now expect to find certain foodstuffs and a host of commodities available in places far from where they were originally produced, and we no longer feel we need to take 'everything' with us when we go on holiday 'abroad'. And not only commodities and places; the process of moving and mixing affects cultures as well. Cultures intersect and influence one another in ways which leave behind any notion of a simple and direct association between culture and place. If ever there was a simple correlation between place and culture, it is no longer so simple. No culture, no place, is 'pure' and there is no authentic version of either to 'go back' to. Globalization is part of major processes of social change, and the multidirectional nature of the moving and mixing involved has produced and reproduced not sameness but hybridity and local uniqueness.

This book has stressed that globalization is not a new phenomenon. From the story of early migrations in Chapter 1 and the issues raised in Chapter 2 about the historical and cultural specificity of our current questioning, through the cases of Honduras and Elveden to the examination of the Euro-Imperialist adventure in Chapter 5, it is clear that the disruptions of place and culture, the contact between peoples and ways of life, are by no means new even at an 'international' level (although, of course, such a concept would literally have been unthinkable before the division of the globe into nation-states).

This does not imply that the current phase of globalization is not distinctive, nor that the process has been even through time. The fact of historical 'bursts' of time–space compression has been emphasized by David Harvey (1989) and in Volume 2 of this series (**Allen and Hamnett, eds, 1995**). Furthermore, each 'burst' has been different. This time the distinctiveness derives in part from the contrasting directions of some of the flows – exemplified, in the context of migration and some cultural influences, by phrases such as 'the arrival of the margins at the centre' and 'the Empire strikes back'. Also distinctive about this current phase is the particular nature of some of the questions being asked, not least about the coherence of places and cultures, questions which have often been provoked by marginalized social groups who were previously excluded from dominant discourses and who now seek to make their claims upon space and place and to assert their own particular identities.

We have, in this book, wanted to insist both upon the particular nature of the current phase of globalization and upon the long historical nature of those processes of migration, contact and mixing which produce uniqueness and hybridity in both place and culture. Holding together these two facets of the argument enables us both to situate the cultural and historical specificity of the questions which are posed by the current form of globalization, and to recognize that what those questions have thrown up are issues of principle about how we conceptualize both place and culture.

> **Summary of section 6.1**
>
> o   Globalization has not resulted in places all becoming the same but rather in greater permeability, openness and hybridity in terms of place and culture.
>
> o   Globalization is not new but is part of ongoing processes of social change which are *uneven* over space and time.
>
> o   The present distinctive phase of globalization has stimulated major conceptual questions.

6.2   Space–place relations

6.2.1   Places in space

Throughout this series we have been interpreting social space in terms of the geography of social relations (see, especially, **Allen, 1995**). This view of space emphasizes both its social construction and its necessarily power-filled nature. There are geographies of power. For example, we began this volume by exploring one aspect of the formation and re-formation of social space: the process of international migration. As Chapter 1 pointed out, what migration involves (thought of in this way) is the stretching out of two particular forms of power-filled social relations: the social relations of production (for instance, between the owners of capital, and workers and their families) and the personal social networks of migrants and their communities. Migration is thus an element of a globalization which is reorganizing space-as-social-relations.

Now, it is – as we have stressed many times in this volume – within this current phase of globalization that have been posed, in the first world at least, many of our current questions about the notion of place. What we have tried to do is to address those questions by drawing on our already developed concept of space as stretched-out social relations. In that view, globalization is a massive re-shaping (including a further stretching out) of those social relations which form social space. The question is: how can we think about places (a) using this approach to space and (b) taking account of all the effects of the current phase of globalization? Our answer has been to propose a re-thinking of the concept of place. In this volume we have argued against older, static representations of places as coherent, settled and bounded and for their definition as constructed out of the myriad social relations, from intimate local relations of neighbourhood or village to those social relations which are stretched out around the globe. Thought of in this way, places are essentially 'meeting-places', intersections of 'particular bundles of activity spaces, of connections and interrelations, of influences and movements' (Chapter 2, section 2.2.1) set within a wider space.

This way of thinking about places has a number of implications. It implies that boundaries are seen more clearly as temporary social constructs (even if important and useful) and as more porous. It implies that places are linked together by the social relations which construct the wider space. It underscores the inevitable hybridity of places: their character is always influenced by relations and contacts with other places. Thought of in this way, then, 'place' is a concept which can address very directly the contemporary tension between the local and the global (Chapter 3, section 3.1).

Activity 1   Take a few moments to run through those last paragraphs again. But this time read them with a particular place in mind – maybe the place you thought of in the context of Chapter 3, Activity 1.

Try to:

o   identify elements of its historical hybridity

o   identify some intersections of activity spaces

o   understand this place (if only in a sketchy way, without doing further research) as set within, and linked into, a wider space of social relations.

Keep a note of your responses, as you will be asked to think about this place later in your study of this chapter.

Now, while you keep that example in your mind, let us develop some further issues.

First, you may be objecting that there is more to your place than social relations: that it also has a very definite, and maybe very distinctive, physical character. There is no attempt in our argument to deny the physical, either its existence or its importance. It is there to be seen. But *what* we see is socially interpreted. It is imbued with meaning and the way in which we describe it represents feelings and experience. A building or landscape is not seen in the same way by everyone who looks at it: indeed, even individuals may vary in their reactions, over time or depending on circumstance. As soon as we use landscape or buildings in our definition and conceptualization of place, we are giving meaning to the physical in terms of the social. For example, speaking of a river as being the heart of a city indicates that it means more than just a moving body of water. The old saying that 'the Clyde made Glasgow and Glasgow made the Clyde' is a case in point. It is also a case where a river has acted as a focus rather than a barrier; yet rivers are often used to divide or bound territory. 'Heart' and boundary – these are two different interpretations of part of a physical environment.

Moreover, as Chapter 3 stressed, these interpretations of the physical environment (and of place more generally) are not the product of individual feelings and experiences alone. For these feelings, too, are caught up in the wider power relations which structure our lives (Chapter 3, section 3.1). They are neither uniquely individual nor a product only of that place itself in isolation. Thus in Chapter 3 we examined the way in which images of the natural environment of the West of Ireland were constructed within a context of the wider relations between Ireland and England and how they came to have a particular resonance within that context. A number of times, too, the chapters in the book have pointed to the important symbolic function of a particular landscape which has come, in many contexts, to stand for 'the heart of England'.

Activity 2   Put together the different references to this English landscape which have occurred in the book and examine its complexity. Think, for instance, of:

o   Mansfield Park, the Home Counties, and their dependence on income from abroad

o   Mr and Mrs Andrews

o   Steve Bell's appropriation of the same image for more subversive purposes, and its disruption and questioning by Ingrid Pollard

o   Cricket, lovely cricket – from village green to the Caribbean.

At a more local level, the 1980s saw the reinterpretation of the physical environment of the docklands of the East End of London as 'the Venice of the North'. The physical environment is an essential part of a place, but it is always an *interpreted* element. Moreover, that interpretation is both socially structured in a context of (unequal) power and set within a context wider than that of the particular place itself.

Second, our definitions of place and of space–place relations are essentially dynamic and differentiated, and both of these aspects are important. In Chapter 1 we used the context of international migration (the moving and mixing of people) to link ideas of globalization to ideas about space and place. Migration involves the movement of people over space and time: it has been going on since the dawn of human activity and probably no part of the globe has been unaffected by it. It has resulted in a juxtapositioning and mixing of social groups which in turn has produced unique outcomes in terms of both culture and place. It therefore – again – runs quite contrary to those old notions of place as settled and coherent. The effects of migration on place are multifarious: they may differ, for instance, between the leaving-end and the receiving-end. The places to which people go are generally economically more prosperous and often politically advantageous (though not necessarily, when migrants are also refugees). In-migration may lead to social mixing and hybridity or it may lead to ghettoization, exclusion and conflict. The places people leave may become depopulated and further marginalized in social and economic terms. They will probably also become endowed with a whole range of meanings around the term 'home'. Thus migration involves both the reorganization of space as social relations and a re-moulding of places within that space.

These different experiences of processes of social change highlight the importance of uneven development. Different places have very different experiences of globalization; they are differently incorporated into wider social relations. The same is true of social groups. The London Docklands Development Corporation emphasized the locational position of the place in terms of financial and communications linkages and the glamorous lifestyle they hoped would become associated with living there. But the existing local residents had very different experiences of social space and very different images and representations of the place.

Finally, there is a thread of argument emerging here which has been developing through the book and which will be picked up at a number of points through the rest of this chapter. It concerns the numerous parallels which can be drawn between 'place' on the one hand and 'culture' on the other. Real places and real cultures are both being challenged by the processes of globalization and the real or imagined threats to their current identity which these have thrown up. Moreover, in Chapter 5, section 5.2.1, Stuart Hall proposed a reconceptualization of culture in a way which parallels in spirit the reconceptualization of place proposed by Doreen Massey in Chapter 2.

Activity 3 Go back now to read that short section in Chapter 5, 'Making culture a "contested concept"' (section 5.2.1), and the Summary of section 5.2 which follows it.

What Stuart Hall is suggesting is a way of looking at cultures which sees them as 'not settled, enclosed or internally coherent' (just as have been so many previous concepts of place) but as meeting-places, as formed out of the intersection of different traditions, as not fixed at all but constantly changing, and as having no simple, single origin. Bear these parallels in mind as the argument continues, for they make even more complex the question of what the relationship is between place and culture.

Summary of section 6.2.1

o Space is socially constructed and can be imagined as formed out of stretched-out social relations.

o In this context places can be interpreted as particular sets of intersections of social relations.

o The physical environment is also an important element in the character of a place, but it too is always socially interpreted.

o Space–place relations are essentially dynamic.

o Migration has an important role in space–place relations and as a component of globalization.

o Different places, and different social groups within them, have different experiences of globalization.

o Cultures, too, may be thought of as meeting-places and as open, formed out of the juxtaposition of different cultural forces and discourses and their effects.

6.2.2 The uniqueness of place

The importance of movement and mixing in the construction and
reconstruction of both place and culture has been stressed throughout this
volume. Chapter 1 set the scene by demonstrating the long historical process
of movement and mixing of people across the globe, establishing cultural
and social linkages which have crosscut land masses, oceans and political
states – links of kinship and other personal and cultural relationships,
economic and communications links between people and places. These ideas
of moving and mixing were further developed in Chapter 2 using concepts
of activity space and meeting-place and challenging issues of boundaries and
boundedness with ideas of permeability and openness. But we also
challenged any notion that, because of all this moving and mixing and
openness, places would all become the same and cultures lose their
distinctiveness. In the case of the Cambridgeshire villages (Chapter 2, section
2.2.2), for example, the influx of new residents who work in multinational
high-technology industries has changed the character of those villages by
constructing, not bland similarity with other places, but a new uniqueness.
This example raises three interrelated and fundamental points about 'the
uniqueness of place' which we shall explore in some more detail. First, it
makes the point that people make places (the influx of new residents is part
of the construction of a new uniqueness); secondly, it indicates that those
people are bound into wider sets of social relations (as part of social space)
and that, consequently, places are interdependent (in this case, the people
work in multinational industry and their activity spaces are wide-ranging);
and, thirdly, it demonstrates that the character of places changes over time –
in other words, that the process of social change produces and reproduces
new uniquenesses.

The idea that people make places was developed in Chapter 3, in terms of 'a
sense of place'. How people feel about place is important. People identify
with (or against) aspects of place and contest local and even national
distinctiveness. But identifying with place always involves selectivity, and
contestation involves differences in interpretation and representation of
place. For example, in the case of the Wye Valley (in Chapter 4, section 4.2),
incomers were trying to preserve their idea of the character – the
distinctiveness – of the place, reflecting in their campaign the ideas and
images of 'quintessential rural England' which were discussed in Chapter 3,
section 3.4. They were identifying with certain, selective, local characteristics
and contesting how the place should be. In 'contests' like this, each 'side'
sees their particular image as the 'real' one. Moreover these images may be
exclusive, and rejecting of newcomers, or they may be more open. Different
senses of place, different geographical imaginations, contribute to the
distinctiveness and uniqueness of place.

Another way in which 'people make places', almost literally, is by the
deliberate construction of images. The question of who or what constructs
places, raises issues of power which we discuss in section 6.4 below, but it is
relevant here in the context of local uniqueness. In Britain in the 1980s and
1990s many local government authorities played an important role in this
process. In cities, towns and regions they have constructed, reconstructed
and declared their uniqueness through slogans and logos which highlight
distinctiveness (and superiority) or, as in the case of Liverpool, have done so

by declaring that they are too good to require such representations (**Meegan, 1995**)! In many cases such messages were concerned to overcome negative images which were often bestowed from outside the place. It was said that when, in the late 1960s and early 1970s, the London-based media wanted to illustrate urban violence and deprivation, the cameras and reporters headed for Glasgow. Hence, Glasgow became synonymous with the images constructed and portrayed – by outsiders. Gang fights, poverty, bad housing meant 'Glasgow'. Image-building from within the city (albeit, part of the city) began with the 'Glasgow's miles better' campaign in the late 1970s – a campaign deliberately aimed at counteracting the negative image, said to be aimed at making Glasgow people feel better about their own city as well as at promoting a better image to the outside world of potential investors and tourists. Both of these images – 'Shock City' and a smiling 'Mister Happy' – are representations of Glasgow and part of Glasgow's uniqueness. In each case the image is partial and selective, yet it was used to represent the whole place as though it were uniformly 'bad' or 'smiling'. Selecting particular aspects of place and presenting them as the 'real' embodiment of that place is therefore part of what we term 'the construction and reconstruction of place'.

This brings us to the second of our basic points: that places are constructed out of wider sets of social relations and, consequently, that we cannot understand the character, the uniqueness, of place by looking at that place alone. The case of Elveden (Chapter 4, section 4.4) might seem too obvious! We could hardly expect to explain the former residence of Duleep Singh by looking only at Elveden or even Suffolk. Clearly this aspect of local uniqueness has much wider connotations – in this case with Empire. Somewhat similarly, the fortunes of Mansfield Park were tied into the slave trade (Chapter 2, section 2.2.2) and the character of Liverpool is bound in with its wider historical connections – a point we will come to shortly. The point here is that the uniqueness of Elveden or Liverpool or anywhere else is not only internally constructed. Place is constructed out of the meeting and mixing of social relations. This is not to say that 'the local' is irrelevant: uniqueness is constructed (and reconstructed) by *combinations* of local characteristics with those wider social relations. Place is an 'articulation' of that specific mix in social space–time. Nowhere else can have precisely the same characteristics, the same combination of social processes.

Going back to our earlier example, the 'new' uniqueness of the Cambridgeshire villages was constructed from a merging of the existing uniqueness with the new sets of social relations which were, in themselves, constructed, at least in part, out of high-technology industry. The villages had existing, local, characteristics which made them attractive to the new residents as places to live in the 1980s and 1990s.

This, and our reference to Liverpool's 'historical connections', raises our third point about the construction of the uniqueness of place: that it is part of a process of social change – something which happens over time. One way to understand this is to visualize 'layers' of social relations accumulating over time. Each new layer interacts with and 'merges' with previous layers in a process which adds new characteristics and changes existing ones, or may even suppress and obliterate aspects of the 'old'.

Activity 4 It might be useful here to pause again and think further about the place you considered in Activity 1. This time, can you identify 'old' and 'new' characteristics? Are there relics of previous 'layers' which can only be explained by historical reference? Think, for example, of derelict industrial buildings, old property boundaries interrupted by new roads, buildings whose use has changed over time, street names which speak of an older world.

In a very general way we can recognize 'layers' in the Wye Valley (Chapter 4, section 4.2). The incomers have formed a new layer which has interacted, not necessarily very easily or 'neatly', with the set of social relations which was already there. The incomers changed local social relations by introducing their own attitudes and values which led, in turn, to conflict over how the place should be. Their ideas of tranquillity and seclusion have conflicted with local people's ideas about local economic development. If these ideas hold sway, a new layer may be characterized by tourism, linking the Wye Valley with new sets of social relations through visitors, marketing, finance. Looking further back in time, we can identify previous layers such as the period of industrialization prior to the more immediately pre-existing layer of farms and local agriculture.

Activity 5 If you have read **Meegan (1995)**, consider the development of Liverpool in terms of our notion of 'layers'. You could start by looking at the Contents page for that chapter.

Our understanding of past layers in part depends, as does our understanding of places as they are now, upon identifying links between that particular place and the wider context of interdependencies. These complex webs of social relations bind places together in global networks: Chapter 1 raised this point in terms of global migration where cities in the USA are linked to villages in Europe by ties of kinship and culture and the sending 'home' of money; people in Honduras are challenging their interdependencies with foreign-owned logging companies (Chapter 4, section 4.3); the Cambridgeshire villages now have links of interdependence with places which would previously have been 'far away'.

It is possible to see here, once again, parallels between the formation of places on the one hand and of cultures on the other. The notion of 'routes', as opposed to 'roots' (see Chapter 5, section 5.5), emphasizes the way in which, just as with places, the *uniqueness* of cultures is in part constructed out of their *interrelations*. Moreover, as that section stressed, these interrelations, or interdependencies, do not work to dilute an original uniqueness; on the contrary, they constantly produce new reworkings, combinations and transformations – new uniquenesses. It is to this conceptualization of the constant reproduction of uniqueness through interconnection which Paul Gilroy (1994) is partly referring in his notion of 'the changing same' (Chapter 5, section 5.5). While at any moment cultural identity is formed through interlinkages and routes to elsewhere, over time the process of the *combination* of the layers of those interconnections lends an element of continuity in the process of historical change. What we are beginning to see, then, is not a world all becoming the same, but the persistence of differences in both places and cultures, and with the ideas of each of them, and their relation to each other, having changed.

Summary of section 6.2.2

o   The uniqueness of place is constructed and reconstructed out of specific sets of social relations: each place is unique.

o   People make places: identity, representation and sense of place are important in the construction and reconstruction of uniqueness and may be actively promoted and deliberately constructed.

o   We cannot understand the uniqueness of place by looking only at that place: uniqueness of place is constructed and reconstructed out of systems of interdependencies.

o   The uniqueness of place is constructed and reconstructed over time.

o   The construction and reconstruction of place can be visualized through thinking in terms of the combination of successive 'layers'.

o   There are parallels between the formation of places and of cultures: the uniqueness of cultures is in part constructed out of their interrelations.

o   Places and cultures are retaining their differences but ideas about each and about their interrelationships have changed.

6.2.3   Uniqueness and uneven development

It is also important to remember that these interconnections, within which the uniqueness of places and of cultures are set, are unequal. Once again it is necessary to remember the geography of power.

Moreover, it is by thinking in terms of this unequal geography of intersecting social relations and influences that we may best approach the term *uneven development* and the role of individual places and cultures within it. It *is* possible to think of uneven development simply in terms of inequalities – for instance, inequalities in income levels, in unemployment, in cultural resources – between different regions or communities. And such measures of the geographical inequalities within and between countries are certainly important. But it is also possible to push the concept of uneven development a bit further, and to do so by building upon our already developed notions of space, place and culture. In this interpretation, what leaps to the mind's eye when thinking of uneven development is not so much inequalities on a set of indices such as employment/unemployment, as interconnected differences produced by the inequality of social relations over space. Take the example of north–south uneven development, whether it be in the form of that persistent inequality between the north of Britain and the south, or at a world scale in the far more glaring form of the gap between the industrialized first world countries of the North and the poorest countries of the South. One way of reading these gross geographical disparities is in terms of the evident inequalities which they register. But if we think in terms of space as social relations, both within and between these regions/parts of the world, then other things come to light.

First, looking at uneven development in this way can enable some approach to be made to its causes, for those causes are to be found in the social relations which structure it. Thus, if we take the example of the north and south in the UK, an understanding of the power-geography of social relations will immediately lead us to pick out, not just the evident inequalities, but also the *power relations* which exist between the two parts of the country. In the south lie the seats of political power, which radiate out in a relation of domination over the rest of the country. Here, too, are the vast majority of the headquarters of the country's companies (whether national or foreign-owned), and the base of the finance sector, so powerful in the rest of the economy. Here is the bulk of the media industry, from where what are taken to be 'normal' British attitudes and accents are broadcast, and where some of the dominant images of the country and of its regions are concocted. In many ways it is these geographically organized social relations of power which lie at the root of much of the uneven development between north and south in the United Kingdom.

Second, this way of looking at uneven development highlights the fact that not only the uniqueness of individual places, but also the uneven development which exists between them is in part founded on their interdependence. That is to say, the economic problems so frequently experienced by 'the north' are in some ways at least interconnected with the comparative economic success of 'the south'. Interdependence (as was argued in **Allen, 1995**) means that the fate of different places is bound together, sometimes in contradictory ways such as the relative health of one area being predicated upon the depression of another. The 'gap' between the 'first' world and the 'third' is not just a gap; it is also a connection. The uniquenesses of place, then, set within this concept of uneven development, are also interrelated, structured inequalities.

This notion of unevenness, moreover, applies to cultural relations as well as economic and to cultures as well as places. The flows of cultural influence, connection and borrowing and adapting, which go on around the world are multifold and complex, but they are not all equal in their power or in their effect. We may not after all, for instance, have been witness to a westernization/homogenization of the whole globe, but neither can the far greater complexity of what has happened be interpreted as anything other than unequal and uneven (see section 6.1).

Finally, the uniquenesses constructed within this framework of uneven development themselves play a role in the reproduction of uneven development over time. Multinational corporations roam the world looking for just the right combination of characteristics for a proposed new development; places already on the downside of uneven development, desperate for jobs 'at any price' may accept investment which brings only low wages and conditions, or which risks environmental damage (see **Sarre and Blunden, eds, 1995**); the very images of places, as we shall see in a later section, may be crucial in influencing their future in a world where uniqueness is constantly reproduced in a context of unequal development.

> **Summary of section 6.2.3**
>
> o   The geography of intersecting social relations is both unequal and uneven.
>
> o   Uneven development is not just the geography of inequalities; it also reflects the interconnections produced by the inequality of social relations over space
>
> o   Many of the causes of uneven development lie in the social relations which structure it: the power-geography of social relations.

6.3   Global–local relations

This discussion of the nature and relationship of space and place allows us to reflect also upon the meaning of, and the interplay between, the terms local and global. Throughout the book, these terms have been used in a manner which is flexible in relation to scale. There is no need for the local to be small: as pointed out in Chapter 3, section 3.2.1, just as there may be (or may be developing among some groups) a sense of 'place' at planetary level, so too the term 'local' in its usage here refers only to a scale which is smaller than the global to which it is opposed. It may be a village, it may be a continent. The global, likewise, may be defined in principle at any scale: it is the wider setting for the local.

But to speak, as we just did, of the local and global as being 'opposed' is in fact incorrect, or at least inadequate. All the discussions in this book point, not to their opposition, but to their interrelatedness. The most obvious way in which this has been stressed in previous chapters is through the message that 'the local and the global constitute each other', most particularly through the examples of the global constitution of the local. These examples have been numerous and varied, from the historic mixtures of the Honduran Mosquitia, to international contacts and influences in the culture of black music in Britain. In Chapter 4 we saw links of Empire in the apparently local village of Elveden, where an Indian maharajah, deposed by British Imperial power, brought his ideas of interior design from the palaces of his childhood to a country mansion in Suffolk, and paid for the silver in the local Anglican church. In such ways, 'the global' is part of what makes 'the local' what it is. This is true of place and it is true of culture: the very notion of hybridity emphasizes the fact. In a direct parallel with the discussion in Chapter 3, section 3.3.3, of the presence of 'the Other' within, in more general discussions of identity and the politics of identity we can say that the 'the global' is not just 'out there', it is part of the character of 'in here'.

This approach can inform the way in which we interpret contests over the meaning of place and the local. Thus, when the people of the Mosquitia line up against 'incomers', this is not *simply* a battle of local versus global, with the two sides sharply demarcated from each other, but an opposition between different constellations of local and global. The locals are not purely local, the 'global' invaders hail from other local places. (And remember how Sony, in Reading A in Chapter 3, described its strategy as 'global localization'.) What are confronting each other are highly differential relations of power in relation to space and place (Chapter 4, section 4.2). Moreover, one of the ways in which the indigenous people set about strengthening their case is precisely by 'de-localizing' it – by pointing out that behind their apparently local struggle over their area lie more general (more global?) issues, in particular the question of the land rights of indigenous groups. Already they have made contacts with other groups in Latin America; and the issue is one potentially with resonance on every continent. Few social groups, then, are simply local or global. Each is locked in – in complex and different ways – to the multiplicities of global–local relations.

We can see this same phenomenon of the global constitution of the local in another example which has been encountered a number of times in this book. When 'Europeans' discuss the nature of European identity, and who should have the right to live within the boundaries of the European Union (itself by no means the whole of 'Europe'), they are involved in an exercise of trying to define the continent's local character in the context of a wider global setting. Yet, as we have seen, those Europeans and that European identity are themselves already a product of contact with the world beyond. This 'Europe' is a product of defining itself against others, whether that be Islam or Japan. It is a product of the influences and importations and inheritances of trade and imperial connections. Moreover, and likewise, those against whom it would now define its identity or protect its borders have within their own culture, economies and societies strong elements of European influence. That does not mean that there is no uniqueness, no local character of place or culture remaining within the global context: there certainly is; but, as the last section showed and as the next will elaborate again in relation to identity, that uniqueness is constructed out of interconnection. From the point of view of *this* section, what should be emphasized is that the local and the global are not terms existing in counterposed opposition: in a very real way the global and the local constitute each other.

Yet, so far, we have concentrated on only one aspect of this mutual constitution: the global constitution of the local, the presence of the global within the local. What of the other way around – the local constitution of the global? At first sight this may seem to be obvious: the global is simply the locals added together. In a sense this is true. Yet if we consider seriously how we have conceptualized local/global (and place/space) in this book in terms of social relations, then a very particular meaning is lent to the term 'global'. For the global in this formulation is no more than the wider set of social relations and interactions. The global is simply all those uniquenesses and interdependencies through which the various local elements are constituted and interconnected. It is the immense complexity of social interactions within which all our activity spaces, our 'local' lives, the places where we live and those where we work or go on holiday, are set. And it is held together by no more than all those tenuous connections, those trading patterns, investment flows, cultural influences, thoughts of home – those millions of spatially-organized social practices which go on every day throughout the world.

One immediate implication of this way of thinking is that it is not just the global which influences the local but also vice versa; or, to put it another way, causality is not all 'top-down'. We have seen this in a multitude of ways. On the one hand it is certainly true that global reach and mobility can both lend and reflect power. (This point was also made in Volume 2 (**Allen and Hamnett, eds, 1995**) in relation to globalization.) Thus the strength of multinationals is integrally bound up with their international span and their ability to move around, which puts local areas, groups and organizations in many ways at the mercy of their global power. Yet we have also seen in this book many cases of local power in the face of global mobility: once again the notion of Fortress Europe comes to mind as it battens down its local hatches against a mobile population of international migrants, or potential migrants, the vast majority of whom, in spite of their global mobility, are anything but powerful in the face of first world localism. Or again, movements or phenomena which begin locally may spread to become more widespread (the example of Christianity has cropped up a number of times). And we have seen how, in the spread and development of black music, the issue has been the links between places and, even more, that they are not even simple linear links, spreading outwards from original roots but complex, circular and constantly accumulating interconnections. As was exemplified in Chapter 4 and in the discussion in section 6.2.2 above, 'the local' is not merely in passive receipt of global forces. The whole book has been full of examples of people actively *making* their local areas, out of recipes which each involve mixing and moulding both local and wider influences.

These ways in which place and space, local and global can be conceptualized have three further implications which are important to our enquiry.

First, it is evident that the pattern of social relations and interactions which construct global space is immensely complicated and multifaceted. If you think for a moment of all the social connections which exist even within one very small area – the economic relations, the cultural, the relations of affection, the political connections and so on – and recognize the complexities there, then the astonishing complexity of social space at any larger scale becomes immediately apparent. It is possible, of course, to pick out patterns. And this is essentially what we do when we analyse the form of international economic space in terms of an international division of labour. Although there is great complexity of detail, it is also possible to identify broad lines – most particularly the broad lines of, in this case, economic power. It is also important to recognize, however, that different kinds of social interaction have different geographies. The geography of the new international division of labour does not map directly on to the geography of religion, nor on to the geography of the women's movement, say, nor on to the geography of the black diaspora (Paul Gilroy's *The Black Atlantic*). As Chapter 3, section 3.2.1, pointed out, even senses of place may draw upon a whole range of different geographical scales. The important point here is that it is all too easy to think of global space as divided up into nested hierarchies of consistently smaller spaces. Thus we typically have: the world, the continents, trading blocs, nation-states, regions, cities and towns, and so on. The fact that you probably have objections to that list is an immediate indication that things are not so simple. In fact, there is no single set of spatial scales into which all social relations are organized.

Secondly, the existence of this overlapping and intersecting geography of different kinds of social relations also means that there are no 'all-purpose places'. That is to say, that defining a place in terms of its economic coherence, for instance, may give a different notion of it from defining it in terms of cultural characteristics. The nineteenth-century region of 'King

Cotton' in Lancashire, for instance, shared an economic focus on the production of and trade in that commodity, but the cultural characteristics and links of the different parts of the region were highly varied. Or again, in political terms Harlem is in the eastern part of the USA, but in cultural terms it could be seen as being in the western part of the Black Atlantic. This reinforces still further the point already made: that there can be no single definition of any place for all experiences.

Thirdly, and finally, this view further elaborates the understanding of uneven development spelled out in the last section. There, it was stressed that uneven development is best understood as the product of intersecting social relationships, rather than as an undulating surface. Here, we can point to the complexity of the patterns of those relations. Economic relations and uneven development may not map directly on to cultural relations and inequalities. Although there will evidently be connections between, say, economics, culture and politics, we cannot *assume* that they will have the same geographies.

Summary of section 6.3

o   The terms 'local' and 'global' are used flexibly in relation to scale: the local is smaller than the global which is the wider setting for the local.

o   The local and the global constitute one another.

o   The pattern of social relations and interactions which construct global space is immensely complicated and multifaceted: there is no single set of spatial scales into which all social relations are organized.

6.4   Place, power, identity

6.4.1   Identities past and future

Within this complexity of space, place and culture, one thing which has become increasingly evident in the course of this book is that intimate and intricate relationships exist between place, power and identity. Even at the very broadest level, the issues which have been addressed indicate the importance of these relationships. We have seen how the power and coherence of the identities of both place (Chapter 2) and culture (Chapter 5) can so easily be disrupted by spatial movement; and we have explored the shifts and reconstitutions of personal and cultural identity that result from migration (Chapters 1 and 5). We have examined the identities of place and the importance of place in identity (Chapter 3), and the mobilization of affective relations around the meanings of place and culture. We have examined the classification as 'other' of those who hail from elsewhere (Chapter 3, section 3.3.3) and the importance of that process in the construction of the identities of those who claim they do 'belong'. Such processes can lead to fragmentation into mutually antagonistic place-loyalties, or battles over the meaning of places and what should be their future, and who should have a right to be there (Chapter 4).

Place-identity, cultural identity and personal identity may, then, in various and complicated ways be related to each other. An identification with place may in certain circumstances be an important component in the formation of personal identity and of cultural identity. We have touched upon the latter a number of times: in the case of England and Englishness in Chapter 3, for instance, or the importance of 'Africa' to Jamaican cultural identity (Chapter 5). As we have seen, place is a key term in the systems of meaning we call culture (Chapter 5, sections 5.1.1 and 5.2.1). Yet these interconnections are not simple. As we have argued in Chapters 2 and 5, the notion of a single, simple 'place called home' – though often important in attempts to maintain cultural coherence – is highly questionable. In Chapter 2 some of the theoretical criticisms of this way of thinking, particularly from a feminist perspective, were explored; and Chapter 5 argues that, 'the effort – against the complex and tortured background of modern history – to actually *make* "culture" and "place" correspond with one another turns out to be a hopeless, expensive and sometimes violent and dangerous illusion' (section 5.2). By the end of Chapter 5 the arguments of the book had converged around the position that the identity of place, the identity of culture and the relation between the two need to be re-thought. This does not mean that their geographical connections are less strong, they are simply re-worked. Thus, in the case of place, as we saw in section 6.2.2, identity can be re-thought as a uniqueness which is a product of layers of interconnections, of the articulations of wider, and spatialized, social relations. And cultural identity, as was argued in Chapter 5, can be re-thought, not in terms of a simple long association with one place, but in terms of the constant mixing, the multiplicities which have come together through the complex geography of historical – and geographical – routes. Cultures still evolve, change and retain their uniqueness, in geographical places, but in this way of thinking about them their identity has not one but many imagined 'homes'.

The same complexity may also hold for the relationship between place identity and personal identity. We have seen that people may feel that their relation to a particular place is a significant aspect of their identity – the indigenous people in Honduras maybe, or the old Greek woman dancing in a bare hall in Sydney, Australia, and catching, as she dances the old dances, the scent of the pine trees of her girlhood village. Yet here, too, the challenge to the notion of a place called home is an important one. On the one hand, so many of those who think of home in this way are those who have had the opportunity (or have been forced) to leave: it is, in other words, their mobility rather than their stability in place which is the condition for their thinking of place in this way. And anyway, and on the other hand, as we have seen again and again in these chapters (especially Chapters 1, 2 and 5), the places they left so many years ago have changed: they are indeed imagined places. Or there may be yet other relations between place and personal identity (Chapter 3, section 3.3.3): people may feel excluded from the place in which they are forced to live; they may have contradictory relations to it; for some people migration might engender feelings of *dis*-location, *dis*-placement, of 'losing their place in the world' (Chapter 1, section 1.4.2); and there are people who, for one reason or another are constrained by the close, communal ties and prohibitions of the place where they were born, who feel a need to strike out – either to the big city or on wider travels – to escape one place for another, or others, in order to gain the freedom to assert the identities they want to create.

In the rest of this section we shall recapitulate some of these debates of the previous chapters, and reconstruct the argument step by step, about the connections between place, power and identity.

Before we turn to this argument, however, one further point needs to be made. The discussion so far in this section has been couched as though person, culture and place could each be understood as having only one intrinsic identity. As we have seen in earlier chapters, this is not so. Chapters 3 and 5 have shown in detail how cultural identities are formed historically, how they are subject to change over time, and how they may be actively disputed. The developing idea of black Jamaican identity is a case in point. The meanings of culture are social creations. Even more evidently, perhaps, the identity of any particular location is likely to be, if not actively disputed, then at least differently interpreted by distinct cultural and social groups. As we have seen in Chapters 3 and 4, the contest over the nature of place, and over the future of any particular place, involves as a key stake the question of which interpretation of the meaning of that place is, at least for the moment, to be hegemonic. It is this which we have referred to as 'the battles over the claiming and naming of particular envelopes of space–time' (Chapter 4, section 4.5).

Let us examine this term a little further. We have been working with a notion of space as social relations 'stretched out' (Chapter 2) and working towards a concept of places within that space, as particular articulations of those social relations as they have come together, over time, in that particular location. Thus we could interpret the Cambridgeshire village, for example, as in part formed out of the intersection of activity spaces, and could see, in the case of Liverpool for instance, how different sets of those intersections can be embedded into and upon one another over time. This making and re-making of places is a persistent and continuous process. But the way that it happens and how it should be understood is frequently the subject of controversy. There will be rival claims over the interpretation and meaning of places which may result in power struggles over their future. The views of some local groups in London's Docklands contesting the image held by the London Docklands Development Corporation is a classic case in point (Chapter 3). There are, then, rival claims to the meaning of places. But as we have also seen, these claims are frequently based on particular interpretations of what has been the past of this place and arguments about what should be its future. In London's Docklands the local groups conjured up a history of a collective community which put 'people before profit'. The LDDC, by contrast, used another romanticized version of that past in its project to reconstruct the place through property development. In the Wye Valley the different interpretations of the past were again a crucial element in the arguments about what should be the future. In other words, what is being contested is not just the identity of a *place*, but the identity of a place as it has existed and will exist for a period of history – an envelope of *space–time*.

Moreover, there is once again a parallel between place and culture. For the imagining of cultures, too, is over and over again based upon particular interpretations of their past. Chapter 5 analysed the ways in which the 'imagined communities' of a nation may be built upon those 'mythical landscapes, invented traditions, stories and ceremonies … which span time and space and "make up the threads that bind us invisibly to the past"

(Schwarz, 1986, p. 155).' Once again, as with 'place', the interpretation of the past is crucial to the geographical imagination of the present – and to the possibilities and realities of the future. As Chapter 5, section 5.2, argued in relation to ideas of national cultures, 'Nationalism often invokes a return to past glories or virtues... But its aim is really to produce something – a unified culture – in the future.' Or again – and once more drawing on Chapter 5 (in this case, section 5.4.2) – it was learning for the first time to tell the story of their past that helped to change the self-image of black Jamaicans and enabled them to try to force a new future.

The question is, of course, in the case of both place and of culture: which story of past and present will be told? For, as we have seen, the concept of 'tradition' is not a simple one. In Chapter 2, in Reading A, Harvey argued that senses of place necessarily entailed drawing on a notion of 'tradition', and that such a notion was often romanticized or commodified. In Reading B in the same chapter, Robins questioned whether we can any longer rely on such 'comforts of Tradition' and argues that we should face up to 'the responsibilities of Translation'. Chapter 5, section 5.5, takes up this line of argument in relation to culture, and in slightly different terms, by arguing that tradition itself can be thought about in different ways: 'In the "closed" version of culture, tradition is thought of as a one-way transmission belt; an umbilical cord, which connects us to our culture of origin.' Exactly the same kind of notion of tradition is often in play in 'closed' versions of place, with their internalized histories going back to 'time immemorial'. But there is an alternative version of the past which sees it as a process of constant mixing and accumulating: a tradition which is not 'lost' as you move further from some (anyway mythical) origin, but rather *built* as new developments, contacts and innovations are introduced.

The identities of both places and cultures, then, have to be made. And they may be made in different, even conflicting, ways. And in all this, *power* will be central: the power to win the contest over how the place should be seen, what meaning to give it; the power, in other words, to construct the dominant imaginative geography, the identities of place and culture.

Activity 6 As a way of making sure you have grasped this point, return now to one element of it that we have examined in this volume – the ways in which even something as intangible as 'a sense of place' is constructed in the context of relations of social power.

Re-read sections 3.3.2 and 3.3.3 of Chapter 3 and note down the different ways in which a sense of place may be analysed in relation to structures of power. (Hint: you may find it useful to begin by recapping the Summary!)

Summary of section 6.4.1

- Intricate and intimate relationships exist between place, power and identity.

- Relations between place, culture, person and identity have been re-thought using concepts of: envelopes of space–time, tradition, the making of identities, power.

6.4.2   Conceptualizing identities

What is it we mean by identity? In Chapter 2, section 2.3.2, it was argued that identity necessarily involves a process of differentiation from Others. But there are, as Chapters 2, 3 and 5 pointed out, various ways in which this process of differentiation can occur. Chapter 3 discussed in detail the process of differentiation through 'Othering', the nature of the power relations through which this occurs, and the problematical results and implications it may entail. However, there may be other means of differentiation. Thus Chapter 3, section 3.5, spoke of 'senses of place and identity … which do not involve Others [in the sense used above], but instead handle difference in more respectful kinds of ways.' And Chapter 2, section 2.3.2, spoke of identities of places as more 'open, porous and the products of links with other places, rather than as exclusive enclosures bound off from the outside world.' Chapter 5, again, argued for a similar approach to the construction of identity, but this time the identity of cultures … for the recognition of their hybrid nature. The construction of places through the specificity of their interconnections with elsewhere is precisely paralleled by the understanding of cultures through the multiplicity of their (geographically dispersed) roots/routes. Both emphasize interrelation rather than counterposition as a potentially important way of thinking about identity.

And yet, as Chapters 3, 4 and 5 have pointed out and illustrated, that is not how identities, whether of culture or of place, are most commonly thought of in today's world of time–space compression and globalization. And this is in spite of the fact that those very phenomena are currently emphasizing geographical interconnectedness as a central fact of all our lives. For the old notions of identity are very powerful. The indigenous peoples of the world often have a strong identification with particular places; cultural and place-identity may be utterly bound up with each other. In Chapters 3, 4 and 5 we have seen how specific constructions of the identities of place and culture, in terms of boundedness and through counterposition, can seem to be of signal importance – to individual people, to social groups, to the governments of nations. Thus, for example, Chapter 5 points out how investment in such closed and exclusivist notions of national culture and national identity is both very powerful in their potential hold on people and critical to the process of national identification: 'The nationalist passion for "belongingness" and the security which such closed conceptions of culture provide are not easily shifted by rational reflection' (Summary of section 5.2).

Moreover, the attachment to 'closed' identities can be as important to the struggles of oppressed peoples as to the machinations of the already powerful. As Chapter 5, section 5.4.1, pointed out, the metaphors of home and homeland, as well as having provoked damage and aggression, have also been important bases for resistance and liberation.

And yet we have argued that different ways of thinking are possible. Robins, at the end of Reading B in Chapter 2, asks 'Is it, then, possible to break this logic of identity?', and goes on: 'How do we begin to confront the challenge of post-modern geographies and the urgent question of cultural Translation?' The response which he suggests is one which resonates strongly with the arguments that have been emerging through the chapters of this volume. Against the ideal of a closed cultural home he suggests the experience of *diaspora*: 'In the experience of migration, difference is confronted: boundaries are crossed; cultures are mingled; identities become blurred.' The experience of diaspora '… allows us to understand relations between cultures [and, we would add, relations between culture and place] in new ways. The crossing of boundaries brings about a complexity of vision and also a sense of the permeability and contingency of cultures' (Robins, 1991, pp. 42, 43). Such views chime well also with the arguments of Sennett and of Sibley against the construction of geographies of rejection via the purification of spaces. Moreover, thought of like this, globalization is not just a threat to some existing notions of place and culture, but a stimulus to a positive new response.

Activity 7 In an article in the magazine *Granta*, the influential German author Günter Grass has written of the persecution which 'gypsies' have so often suffered in Europe:

They [the Romanies and the Sinti, the gypsies] have no allies. No politician represents their case, whether in the European Parliament or the Bundestag. No state they can appeal to would support their demands for compensation – pathetic, isn't it? – for Auschwitz, or make them a national priority.

The Romanies and Sinti are the lowest of the low. "Expel them!" says Herr Seiters and gets on the line to Romania. "Smoke them out!" shout the skinheads. But in Romania and everywhere else, gypsies are bottom of the heap as well. Why?

Because they are different. Because they steal, are restless, roam, have the Evil Eye and that stunning beauty that makes us ugly to ourselves. Because their mere existence puts our values into question …

Let half a million and more Sinti and Romanies live among us. We need them. They could help us by irritating our rigid order a little. Something of their way of life could rub off on us. They could teach us how meaningless frontiers are: careless of boundaries, Romanies and Sinti are at home all over Europe. They are what we claim to be: born Europeans!

(Grass, 1992, pp. 107–8)

What do you think of this argument?

In many ways it is very different from that of Iris Marion Young in Reading C of Chapter 2. Can you spell out how?

Summary of section 6.4.2

o It is possible to re-think ideas about identity in terms of interconnectedness rather than counterposition, inclusion rather than exclusion.

o The crossing of cultural, geographical and personal boundaries brings about complexity of vision, and a sense of permeability and contingency.

6.4.3   Place, culture and uneven development

Such a revised way of thinking about place and culture is intended to enable *both* the recognition of difference (between places and between cultures) and of the fact that such differences are continually reproduced, made anew in ever-changing forms, *and* at the same time the recognition of our essential interconnectedness.

However, it must also be recognized that all this 'mixing' – these diasporas and invasions and migrations – take place in the context of both social and geographical uneven development. This is the context of social power within which the staking of claims to envelopes of space–time, the defining and defending of cultures and places, actually takes place. Some cultures, and some places, are more vulnerable than others. We have already seen, most particularly in Chapter 4, that there is no logic which says that *either* the local people *or* the global relations of mixing and interpenetration are always to be preferred. *Rather, what is always in play is the specific form of the spatiality of power.* (We return, therefore, to the idea of the 'geography of power', as mentioned in Chapter 2.)

There are many ways in which the identities of places and cultures (the social meanings attached to them) interact with the production and reproduction of uneven development. Firstly, and most evidently, uneven development is not merely the context in which emerge many of these questions of place and culture; it is also the propulsive force which has produced them as real issues. Thus, it is the uneven development of imperialism, colonialism and economic growth which has formed not just the backcloth but an active cause of the geography of contact zones, transculturation and diaspora. Chapter 1 traced through in some detail the historical relation between uneven development in its widest sense and international migration, pointing to its different forms: in slavery, systems of indentured labour, imperialist expansion and the great outward migration of Europeans, to guestworkers, and the current polarized flows of (mainly male) professional employees and (more often female) seekers after any work at all. The relation between each of these flows and uneven development has been distinct. Slavery and imperialist expansion powered the establishment of a world economic system focused on Europe. The out-migration of Europeans allowed the spectacular economic growth of the Industrial Revolution without such severe problems of 'overpopulation' as might otherwise have taken place. Migrations the other way, whether guestworkers to Germany or people from the 'new Commonwealth' to the UK, expanded the available labour force in those countries when it was needed in mid-century. On the other hand, much such international migration must also be seen as perpetuating, and even worsening, the levels of uneven development (see, for instance, Reading A by Potts and Reading D by Castles and Kosack, and section 1.3 in the opening chapter). Chapter 5 picks up from Chapter 1 on many of the same historical moments, for it is in part out of the migrations propelled by uneven development that have emerged as issues the hybridity of places and cultures. As Chapter 3, section 3.3.2, puts it, 'senses of place… can be seen as a result of underlying structures of power such as colonialism and imperialism'.

The second way in which uneven development and the identities of place and culture are interrelated lies in the fact that the power relations implicit in uneven development (see section 6.2) are important determinants of which meaning becomes the dominant one. Already-powerful places and cultures have a head-start in constructing the imaginative geographies which will become the most widely diffused. In the preceding chapters, we have seen a number of instances of this, from coastal Honduras to the Docklands of the East End of London. But we can see it in a more general way, too. The casual way in which Honduras is so often referred to by people in the first world as a 'Banana Republic' (because its main function *in the international division of labour* – but in no other way – was once that of a location for fruit production) can only reinforce its underprivileged position in the distribution of world income. Or again, in the first chapter of Volume 1 (**Massey, 1995**), we saw how first-world images of the 'third world' are argued by aid agencies to have important effects on first–third world relations. In other words, the power of the dominant within uneven development can underpin its ability to mould the geographical imagination.

Thirdly, moreover, and as both the latter two examples show, that power to endow places and cultures with dominant meanings can also have effects *on* uneven development. Our images of the 'third world' will influence economic (including aid) relations with the people of those countries. Meanings and identities may be significant in the reproduction of uneven development. It is in part for this reason that policies designed actively to *change* the popular meaning of places have become so important. The efforts of the LDDC to shift the identity of London's Docklands was documented in Chapter 3. Glasgow's image campaign built around the slogan 'Glasgow's miles better' has already been mentioned a number of times. In both cases the particular meaning selected by the bodies trying to attract people and investment to the places in fact reflected the meanings of those places held by only certain groups of people. For other groups in both places, other identities were more meaningful. Indeed it was partly those other identities (working-class, militant, 'old-fashioned') which the newly dominant identities were designed to silence. And in both cases the campaigns did indeed relegate to a position of marginality those who held such views. A first effect was thus further to deplete the confidence of those already non-dominant groups.

Activity 8 Think again of the place you have been analysing in Activities 1 and 4. Does your own image of that place exclude certain groups?

There may also on occasions be a deep irony in this relation between identity and uneven development. Campaigns such as that in Glasgow (and many others of the same kind could be enumerated) set out to *create* and then to *celebrate* the particular character of the place they are advertising. They are making a claim to its particularity of identity in a world where globalization has been one of the forces undermining its economy. Globalization is one of the most important causes of the campaign's need to claim and advertise this identity, to bring in more investment to remedy the decline. And yet this advertisement is precisely directed towards bringing in *more* of those forces of globalization (whether it be manufacturing investment, or tourism, or whatever). It is, in other words, a desperate feeding on the very forces which have contributed to undermining that 'coherent sense of place' which is imagined to have existed in the past.

These points are important to take on board because they underline how issues of cultural and place-identity and meaning have real, material effects even back on economic uneven development itself. Glasgow, the LDDC and many another authority would not have spent so many millions of pounds on image repair and reconstruction had they not believed this to be the case.

Moreover, as the Glasgow example begins to hint, the mobilization of images can be used to *challenge* (that is, not only to reinforce) the currently dominant state of uneven development. Thus, as we saw in Chapter 5, the imagined geography of Africa ('as much a metaphor for "freedom" as a literal place') was the means by which Jamaican people began, after formal political independence had already been won, to imagine 'themselves ... into cultural independence from white, colonial Jamaica'.

In very many ways, then, the 'production of place' is bound up with the production of meaning – with the construction of our geographical imaginations – and both of these processes are part and parcel of uneven development, both as its precondition and as agents in its reproduction and, maybe one day, its amelioration.

Summary of section 6.4.3

o   Geographical interconnection takes place in the context of uneven development which is the context of social power.

o   Identities of places and cultures interact with the production and reproduction of uneven development: (a) uneven development may be the stimulus to raising questions of identity; (b) the power relations of uneven development may influence which meaning/identity becomes the dominant one; and (c) the power to endow dominant meanings can have *effects on* the future form of uneven development.

o   Uneven development and geographies of power: the mobilization of images can be used to challenge the currently dominant state of uneven development.

6.5   Conclusion

We began this book by setting it in the geographical and historical context in which it has been written – the first world at the end of the twentieth century. We argued that this is a context in which major challenges are being thrown down which question the geographical organization of global society.

New questions now increasingly hover on the horizon. Uneven development between countries has in many ways been growing worse in recent years. As Chapter 1 argued, the flows of international migration in the past have in some cases ameliorated uneven development and in other cases perpetuated and/or exacerbated it. What is without doubt is that there is a relation between the two. The dimensions of inequality in the world today look set, among other factors, to increase once again pressures for international movement, most particularly amongst the world's poor.

In this context, the way in which we think about place and culture and the relation between them is of central importance. The assumptions which we make about the identities and meanings of places and cultures and about the relations between the two will be, implicitly or explicitly, of fundamental significance in the debates which lie ahead. In this volume we have tried to address all three issues. If it ever was valid to think of cultures as being uniquely set in individual places from where they drew their roots, that view is certainly now open to challenge. And if it ever was at least a reasonable generalization to think of places as coherent cultural products, that view too is now no longer tenable. The relation between place and culture, and the way we conceptualize both of them in relation to geography, has to be re-thought, and we have tried here to suggest some ways in which this might be approached.

It should also be clear from everything that has gone before that geographical meaning and definition and social meaning and definition are closely related to each other. Our senses of place, for instance, not only reflect but also influence the power relations in the world around us. Thus we have seen, in Chapter 3 particularly, how claiming an identity for a particular place may involve setting that place against others – what might be termed 'spatial othering'. We have also seen, for instance in Chapter 2, how spatial organization, and in particular the ordering of space along the lines of social categories or groups, may be an important element in what we might call 'social othering'. Thus Sibley's arguments about purified spaces point clearly to the potential influence of spatial organization on social forces. In Chapter 3 we read of the process of 'establishing social difference by establishing spatial boundaries' (Chapter 3, section 3.3.2). In such instances 'closed' definitions of place and culture may reinforce each other; self-defined coherent cultures may wall themselves in in their homelands. By contrast, definitions of place and of culture which recognize the fact of openness and interdependence might have the opposite, mutually reinforcing effect.

This is not to argue, necessarily, for unconditional openness. For, as has been stressed, all these interdependences are in reality power relations, many of them unequal. The arguments about rights of international migration from poor countries to rich will not be the same as those about the penetration of indigenous cultures by multinational corporations. The balance of social power is completely different in each case. Once again, the spatial and the social must be considered together. Our social and our geographical imaginations are intimately related. And our geographical imaginations, and how they are acted out in our lives, are a key component in the forging of our social futures.

References

ALLEN, J. (1995) 'Crossing borders: footloose multinationals?' in Allen, J. and Hamnett, C. (eds).

ALLEN, J. and HAMNETT, C. (eds)(1995) *A Shrinking World? Global Unevenness and Inequality*, Oxford, Oxford University Press/The Open University (Volume 2 in this series).

ALLEN, J. and MASSEY, D. (eds)(1995) *Geographical Worlds*, Oxford, Oxford University Press/The Open University (Volume 1 in this series).

GRASS, G. (1992) 'Losses', *Granta*, No. 42, pp. 97–108.

GILROY, P. (1994) *The Black Atlantic*, London, Verso.

HARVEY, D. (1989) *The Condition of Postmodernity: An Enquiry into the Origins of Cultural Change*, Oxford, Blackwell.

MASSEY, D. (1995) 'Imagining the world' in Allen, J. and Massey, D. (eds).

MEEGAN, R. (1995) 'Local worlds' in Allen, J. and Massey, D. (eds).

SARRE, P. and BLUNDEN, J. (eds) (1995) *An Overcrowded World? Population, Resources and the Environment*, Oxford, Oxford University Press/The Open University (Volume 3 in this series).

ROBINS, K. (1991) 'Tradition and translation: national culture in its global context' in Corner, J. and Harvey, S. (eds) *Enterprise and Heritage: Crosscurrents of National Culture*, London, Routledge.

SCHWARZ, B. (1986) 'Conservatism, nationalism and imperialism' in Donald, J. and Hall, S. (eds) *Politics and Ideology*, Milton Keynes, Open University Press/The Open University.

SENNETT, R. (1971) *The Uses of Disorder*, Harmondsworth, Penguin.

SIBLEY, D. (1988) 'Purification of space', *Environment and Planning D: Society and Space*, Vol. 6, No. 4.

Acknowledgements

Grateful acknowledgement is made to the following sources for permission to reproduce material in this volume:

Text

Chapter 1: *Reading A*: Potts, L. (1990) *The World Labour Market*, Copyright © Lydia Potts 1990, Translation Copyright © Zed Books Ltd 1990, Zed Books Limited, London; *Reading B*: Foerster, R. F. (1924) *The Italian Emigration of our Times*, Cambridge, Harvard University Press, London, Humphrey Milford, Oxford University Press 1924, Copyright © 1969 by Arno Press, Inc.; *Reading C*: Zorbaugh, H. W. (1929) *The Gold Coast and the Slum: A Sociological Study of Chicago's Near North Side*, Copyright 1929 by The University of Chicago; *Reading D*: © Institute of Race Relations 1973, 1985. Reprinted from *Immigrant Workers and Class Structure in Western Europe* by Stephen Castles and Godula Kosack (2nd edn, 1985) by permission of Oxford University Press; *Reading E*: Sassen, S. (1988) *The Mobility of Labor and Capital*, © Cambridge University Press 1988; *Reading F*: Berger, J. and Mohr, J. (1975) *A Seventh Man*, Copyright © John Berger, text; Jean Mohr, pictures; 1975, Reproduced by permission of Penguin Books Ltd.; **Chapter 2:** *Reading A*: Harvey, D. (1989) *The Condition of Postmodernity: An Enquiry into the Origins of Cultural Change*, Basil Blackwell Ltd, Copyright © David Harvey 1989; *Reading C*: Young, I. M. (1986) 'The ideal of community and the politics of difference' in *Social Theory and Practice*, Vol. 12, No. 1, Spring 1986, pp. 1–26, Florida State University; **Chapter 3:** *Reading A*: Morley, D. and Robins, K. (1992) 'Techno-Orientalism: futures, phobias and foreigners' in *New Formations*, 16, pp. 139–56, © David Morley and Kevin Robins, Lawrence and Wishart Ltd; *Reading B*: Zonabend, F. (1989) *The Nuclear Peninsula*, © Editions Odile Jacob, Novembre 1989, English translation © Maison des Sciences and Cambridge University Press, 1993; **Chapter 4:** Dunn, P. (1994) 'Valley folk divided over "farm for tourists"', *The Independent*, 7 August 1994; Schwimmer, E. (1992) 'Land use map presented in congress seeks to affirm Indian rights in the Mosquitia', *Honduras This Week*, Vol. 5, No. 37, 26 September 1992; Zoba, W. M. (1992) '500 years later, Indian groups claim their place on map', *Honduras This Week*, Vol. 5, No. 37, 26 September 1992; Schwimmer, E. (1992) 'Miskito musician gives congress 'upbeat note'', *Honduras This Week*, Vol. 5, No. 37, 26 September 1992; Bunting, M. (1993) 'In pursuit of the Suffolk maharajah', *The Guardian*, 3 March 1993; 'Sikhs make Norfolk Pilgrimage', *The Eastern Daily Press*, 31 July 1993, Eastern Counties Newspapers Limited; 'Prince who bridges years, and cultures', *The Eastern Daily Press*, 23 October 1993, Eastern Counties Newspapers Limited; Tomforde, A. (1993) 'Where the law of blood still rules', *The Guardian*, 2 March 1993; Carvel, J. (1994) 'Europe to force visa laws on UK', *The Guardian*, 8 January 1994; Smith, H. (1993) 'Greece taxed by refugee influx', *The Guardian*, 27 January 1993; Lowry, S. (1994) 'French get tough on illegal immigrants', *The Daily Telegraph*, © The Telegraph plc, London, 1994; **Chapter 5:** *Reading A*: Hugill, B. (1994) 'Patten forces schools to play team games', *The Observer*, 8 May 1994; *Reading B*: Cohen, N. (1993) 'Accept African identity, Grant tells blacks', *The Independent*, 12 December 1993.

Table

Table 1.1: Adapted from Potts, L. (1990), *The World Labour Market*, Copyright © Lydia Potts 1990, Translation Copyright © Zed Books Ltd 1990, Zed Books Limited, London.

Figures

Figure 1.1: Fagan, B. M. (1990) *The Journey from Eden*, © 1990 Thames and Hudson Ltd, London; *Figure 1.2*: Potts, L. (1990) *The World Labour Market*, Copyright © Lydia Potts 1990, Translation Copyright © Zed Books Ltd 1990, Zed Books Limited, London; *Figure 1.3*: Segal, A. (1993) *An Atlas of International Migration*, © Aaron Segal 1993, Hans Zell Publishers; *p. 143*: Indigenous lands of the Honduran Mosquitia – 1992: zones of subsistence. A map made for and presented at the First Congress on Indigenous Lands of the Mosquitia, 22–23 September 1992, in Tegucigalpa, Honduras. A project administered by Mosquitia Pawisa (MOPAWI) and Mosquitia Asla Takanka (MASTA). Project design and management by Peter H. Herlihy PhD, Southeastern Louisiana University and Andrew P. Leake MA, MOPAWI. Information on land use compiled through the administration of questionnaires in community meetings by native Indian surveyors: Moisés Alemán, Paulino Bossen, Daniel Castellón, Quintín Castro, Máximo Chow, Dionisio Cruz, Simón Greham P., Duval Haylock, Daniel Kiath, Olegario López, Gilberto Maibeth, Hernán Martínez, Manuel Martínez, Eduardo Padilla, Electerio Pineda K., Ricardo Ramírez, Javier Rimundo G., Tomás Rivas, Cecilio Tatallón, Elmer Waldemar, Sinito Waylan and Edimor Wood M. Project sponsored by Cultural Survival, Inc., with the collaboration of Comisión Nacional del Medio Ambiente y Desarrollo (CONAMA), Federación Indígena Tawahka de Honduras (FITH), Inter American Foundation (IAF), Interamerican Geodetic Survey (IAGS), Instituto Geográfico Nacional (IGN), Caribbean Conservation Corporation, Pew Charitable Trusts, Wildlife Conservation International and Instituto Hondureño de Antropología e Historia ((IHAH). Technical field assistants: José Ramiro Andino (IGN), Prof. Cirilo Felman (MASTA), Nathan Pravia Lacayo (MOPAWI), Lic. Adalberto Padilla (MOPAWI), Héctor Ramírez (IGN) and Lic. Aurelio Ramos (MOPAWI).

Photographs

p. 13: Hulton-Deutsch Collection; *p. 21:* Gilles Peress/Magnum; *p. 26:* Stuart Franklin/Magnum; *p. 28*: Russell King; *p. 30:* Barbara Smith; *p. 47*: Tim Bishop/Times Newspapers Limited; *pp. 49, 56, 57, 59, 67, 68, 75*: Heather Clarke; *p. 62*: © National Trust Photographic Library/Photo: David Noton; *p. 94*: Léon Belly, *Pilgrims going to Mecca*, 1861, 1.61 x 2.42m Oil on Canvas. Paris, Musée du Louvre/Lauros-Giraudon; *p. 94*: David Roberts, *Portico of the Temple of Bacchus, Baalbeck*, Walker Art Gallery, National Museums and Galleries on Merseyside; *p. 101 (top)*: LDDC Press Office; *p. 101 (bottom)*: Peter Dunne and Lorraine Leeson, Docklands Community Poster Project (part of 'The Changing Picture of Docklands' series of billboards produced 1981–86); *p. 108*: John Linnell, *The Last Glean Before the Storm*, Walker Art Gallery, National Museums and Galleries on Merseyside; *p. 108*: Edwin Landseer, *Man Proposes, God Disposes*, The Holloway Collection, Victorian Studies Centre, Royal Holloway College, University of London; *p. 109*: Thomas Gainsborough, *Mr and Mrs Andrews*, Reproduced by courtesy of the Trustees, The National Gallery, London; *p. 110*: Mr and Mrs Andrews/Reagan and Thatcher postcard, Leeds Postcards and Steve Bell; *pp. 112–13*: Renault UK Limited, Publicis Limited, Rick Hawkes; *pp. 114, 115*: Copyright © Ingrid Pollard; *p. 137*: © The Independent/Nicholas Turpin; *p. 141*: © Eric Schwimmer/Honduras This Week; *p. 148*: © Suyapa Carias/Honduras This Week; *p. 154*: © Hulton-Deutsch Collection; *p. 155*: © Graham Turner/The Guardian; *p. 156*: © Hulton-Deutsch Collection; *p. 157*: Norfolk County Library and Information Service; *p. 161*: Photo copyright The Eastern Daily Press, Eastern County Newspapers Ltd; *p. 192*: Mansell Collection; *p. 194*: © Peter Till/The Guardian; *p. 198* (both): © Philip Wolmuth/Hutchinson Library.

Index

activity spaces 54–8, 59, 63, 218, 221, 231
  increasing complexity of 59, 60, 61, 62, 69
Africa
  North African immigrants 170–1
  slave trade 11–12
African identity 201–5, 211–13, 230, 231, 237
alienation: and mediation 81–2
asylum-seekers 20, 23, 26
baptism: and African identity 204–5
Black Environment Network 111, 116
black music: and diaspora 207–8
black people
  and African identity 201–5
  and rural England 116
boundaries
  construction in space 162
  culture and place 181
  drawing in space 61
  and the geography of rejection 67
  of Germany 165–6
  and the interdependence of places 67–9, 71
  permeability of 216
  and physical environment 219
  redrawing 168
  and sense of place 99, 103
  socially constructed 162, 218
  in the unoppressed city 74–5
boundedness of place 136, 162, 233
brain drains 24, 31, 33, 34
Britain (United Kingdom)
  black people and African identity 201–2, 205, 211–13
  and national identity 184
  visas and European Union 167–8
Cambridgeshire villages 59–61, 64, 65, 221, 223, 231
capital
  free movement of 162, 173
  mobility of 49, 54
  power of 102
carnivals 198–9
chain migration 17
Charlemagne 188–9
China: coolie labour from 12–13
Christianity: and European

cultural development 189
cities
  effects of immigration on 29–30
  and the English countryside 107
  global 199, 206
  informational 54
  and the politics of difference 73–5, 83–6
  public spaces of 84, 85
  and re-imagining places 72
  unoppressive 73, 74–5, 85
class: international class of the wealthy 111
colonial centre: and colonized periphery 52–3, 177
colonial migration 6, 10–15, 18, 31, 33, 34
colonization
  and cricket 193–6
  and culture 190–1
Commonwealth countries: and European Union 167–8
communities
  and face-to-face interaction 73, 80–1, 82–3, 84–5
  imagined 182–3, 189, 207
  purified 73
consumerism: global 176–7
contact zones 191–2, 193, 194
contract migration 24
coolie migration 12–13, 14, 31, 33, 34
creolization 199, 200
cricket: and British colonization 193–6, 219
cultural differences see differences, cultural
cultural diversity: and globalization 188–98
cultural fundamentalism 199–203
cultural hybridity 134, 159, 173, 186, 226
  and migration 18
cultural identity 2, 134, 176, 223, 230
  African 201–5
  and contestation of place 135, 136, 172
  in Elveden 153, 158
  and ethnicity 181
  and European nation-states 184–6
  and globalization 177

landscaping 181–3
  and place 51
  and sense of place 151
cultural influences: inequality of 70
cultural strategy: transculturation as 196
culture 175–213
  closed version of 206, 207, 238
  as a 'contested concept' 186–7, 220
  and globalization 176–7, 180
  and home 182
  and identity 176, 177, 178–81, 233
  and language 177, 178–80
  local 1, 2, 177
  and local–global relations 228–9
  and meeting-places 220
  and migration 8
  and place 1–2, 3–4, 177, 180–1, 186–7, 216–17, 220, 231–2, 237–8
  reconceptualizing 191–3
  and religion 180
  and 'return to roots' 199–205
  and uneven development 225, 235–7
  uniqueness of cultures 223, 224
  see also national cultures
definitions: and German citizenship laws 164
diasporas 193, 206–8, 209
  African 202, 203
  and identity 233–4
difference
  cultural 176, 177, 185, 206
  identities built on 162, 171
  and sense of place 99, 103, 104, 116
displacement: and migration 7
Eastern Europe: immigrants from 25, 169–70
economic activity
  decentralization of 41
  and linked fortunes 69
economic development: global economy and sense of place 92
economic growth: and international migration 16, 38, 39
economic migrants 170
economic restructuring: and a sense of place 100–2